Pillsbury

30-Minute

meals

Pillsbury 30-Minute *meals*

230 Simple and Flavorful Recipes for Everyday Cooking

The Pillsbury Company

Clarkson Potter / Publishers
New York

ALSO BY PILLSBURY®

Pillsbury: Best Chicken Cookbook

Pillsbury: Best Cookies Cookbook

*Pillsbury: Best Muffins
& Quick Breads Cookbook*

Pillsbury: Best of the Bake-Off® Cookbook

Pillsbury: Fast and Healthy® Cookbook

Pillsbury: Best Desserts

Pillsbury: The Best of Classic Cookbooks

Pillsbury: One-Dish Meals Cookbook

Pillsbury Complete Cookbook

**Cover photo: Light Chicken Parmesan, page 147
Page 2: Rigatoni with Sausage and Vegetables, page 173**

Copyright © 2001 by The Pillsbury Company

Published by Clarkson Potter/Publishers, New York, New York.
Member of the Crown Publishing Group.

Random House, Inc. New York, Toronto, London, Sydney, Auckland
www.randomhouse.com

CLARKSON N. POTTER is a trademark and POTTER and colophon are registered trademarks of Random House, Inc.

Pillsbury, the Pillsbury logo, Bake-Off, Classic Cookbooks and Fast and Healthy are registered trademarks of The Pillsbury Company
www.pillsbury.com

Some recipes have been previously published in slightly different form.

Printed in Japan

Library of Congress Cataloging-in-Publication Data
Pillsbury 30-minute meals: 230 simple and flavorful recipes for everyday cooking / The Pillsbury Company.
    Includes index.
    1. Quick and easy cookery.   I. Pillsbury Company.
TX833.5 .P557 2001
641.5′55—dc21
        00-066887

ISBN 0-609-60859-2

10 9 8 7 6 5 4 3 2 1

First Edition

CREDITS

THE PILLSBURY COMPANY

Publisher: Diane B. Anderson

Senior Food Editor: Andrea Bidwell, C.C.P.

Recipe Editors: Nancy A. Lilleberg, Grace R. Wells

Contributing Writer: Mary Caldwell

Copy Editors: Dawn Carlson, Ginger Hope

Contributing Editors: Jackie Sheehan, Kitty Shea

Photography: Knitting Design, Graham Brown Photography, Tad Ware Photography, The Studio Central

Food Stylists: Sue Brosious, Sue Brue, JoAnn Cherry, Sue Finley, Sharon Harding, Cindy Ojczyk, Lisa Golden Schroeder, Barb Standal

Recipe System: Amanda Bloomgren, Carrie Jacobson, Mary Prokott, Renee Schimel

Publication Secretary: Jackie Ranney

Nutrition Information: Karen Husu, R.D., Myrna Shaw, Gayle M. Smith

CLARKSON POTTER/PUBLISHERS
THE CROWN PUBLISHING GROUP

President and Publisher: Chip Gibson

Vice President-Editorial Director: Lauren Shakely

Senior Editor: Katie Workman

Editorial Assistant: Elaina Lin

Designer: Caitlin Daniels Israel

Executive Managing Editor: Amy Boorstein

Associate Managing Editor: Mark McCauslin

Senior Production Editor: Liana Faughnan

Senior Production Manager: Jane Searle

Publicist: Leigh Ann Ambrosi

contents

Welcome to
30-Minute Meals

Remember bubbling stew, hot-from-the-oven biscuits, clouds of whipped cream on a homemade pie? With today's schedules, a wholesome, homemade meal can seem like a rare luxury. We rush home, we're hungry, *"Where's supper?"*

Pizza delivery and fast-food takeout can be a great help, but there's nothing like home cooking. Most of us crave the nourishing flavors of meals prepared in our own kitchens, but we need them *fast*. This book offers 230 easy menus featuring delicious entrees that can be prepared, from start to finish, in less than half an hour.

If you think there's no substitute for the hours of kitchen time that yesterday's cooks put into their meals, consider this: They had no choice. Today's cook has the advantage of a whole range of convenient shortcuts and quick-cooking ingredients, not to mention the microwave.

Delicious meals can be on your table in 30 minutes or less. We'll show you how.

Kitchen Organization

Your workspace can either complicate your efforts in the kitchen or trim time, depending on how well it's organized. Invest some time upfront to put everything in its most purposeful place, then give your kitchen a quick once-over occasionally to ensure that it's still orderly.

- Time the running of your dishwasher so that dishes are clean and put away when it's time to prepare supper.
- Store utensils and cookware near where you usually use them—for instance, keep peelers, knives and cutting boards within reach of the sink. Store lids with their corresponding containers, casseroles and pots.
- Keep often-used ingredients conveniently at hand. Store flour and sugar canisters near the counter where you mix baked goods; keep a supply of staples—pasta, jarred spaghetti sauce, canned beans—near your work area; infrequently used ingredients, such as jarred artichoke hearts or canned chiles, can be kept on less convenient shelves.

- Purchase duplicates of your favorite tools (mixing and serving spoons, cutting boards, measuring cups/spoons) so there's always one handy when you need it. Keep a sugar bowl, salt shaker and pepper grinder in your work area as well as on the dining table.
- Keep on the counter often-used condiments and seasonings, such as olive oil and red wine vinegar. To reduce clutter, store less frequently used items, such as Worcestershire sauce or sesame oil, in the cupboard.
- If you have enough counter space, keep out the small appliances that you use most, such as a blender or food processor. Put away seldom-used items, such as a bread machine or standing mixer.

- Clean up as you go along, putting dirty mixing bowls and tools into the dishwasher or washing them by hand immediately. It's easier to work in a neat kitchen, and you won't face a mess after the meal.
- Keep plenty of aprons, kitchen towels and hotpads handy.
- Have on hand an ample supply of paper towels, scouring pads and so forth to keep cleanup running smoothly.
- Encourage the family to use some place other than the kitchen work area to deposit keys, homework, mail, newspapers and similar items
- Nobody's perfect! Keep a box of plastic strip bandages and a bottle of pain-reducing medicine (such as aspirin) handy in the kitchen.

Often-Used Utensils

Some cooks swear the only tool they need is a sharp knife, while others buy every gadget under the sun. Somewhere in between is a happy medium that keeps your kitchen clutter-free but stocked with useful tools that speed up meal preparation. Sharp tools help you work quicker and with less effort; dull tools are more likely to slip and cause injury. Sharpen or replace any tool that has a dull blade.

Kitchen Essentials

- Good-quality, sharp chef's knife
- Several small, sharp paring knives
- Knife sharpener
- Vegetable peeler
- Can opener

- Mixing spoons
- Spatulas (metal and plastic)
- Cutting boards
- Kitchen shears
- Basting brush
- Apple slicer/corer

- Sharp grater
- Scoop-shaped dry measuring cups
- Liquid measuring cup with spout
- Measuring spoons

Timesaving Tips

- Water boils faster if the lid is on the pot and if the water is unsalted.
- For quick cleanup of your food processor, spray the blades with nonstick spray before using.
- Use kitchen shears to cut pizza, fresh herbs and dried fruits.

- Chop some onions, green pepper and celery, and keep them refrigerated in separate, tightly covered containers.
- Don't peel unless you have to. With potatoes and zucchini, for instance, it's fine—and faster—to simply scrub the skins.

- Cook extra pasta and use it the next day with another sauce or as a cold salad. Leftover cooked vegetables can go into soup; extra grilled meat or chicken can be used in sandwiches or stir-fries.

The Well-Rounded Meal

When planning a meal, choose from a variety of food groups, and aim for a pleasing balance of flavors, textures and colors. A plate of poached fish, mashed potatoes and steamed parsnips, for example, looks bland and beige; likewise, an entree, salad and side dish that each features a creamy sauce make poor dinner companions.

If your meal is short on variety, a quick garnish can go a long way:

- Strips of roasted red bell pepper
- Cherry tomatoes
- A small cluster of grapes

- Finely chopped herbs, such as parsley or a fresh herb sprig
- Lemon wedges
- A few olives or pickles

- Orange slices
- A sprinkling of paprika or chili powder

Pantry Pointers

You don't always have time to stop at the market for fresh ingredients. One of the tricks of quick cooking is to keep your kitchen stocked with a good selection of nonperishables, long-lasting fresh foods and frozen items so you can quickly put together a good dinner. The lists below give you some ideas of items that speed preparation time:

Bread and Bakery Items

- Crackers
- Dessert baking mixes

- Flour (plain or flavored) and corn tortillas
- Prebaked pizza shells

- Prebaked pocket (pita) bread
- Refrigerated dough for bread or biscuits

Dairy Case

- Cheeses: shredded, sliced, blocks

- Eggs

- Sour cream or plain yogurt

Frozen Foods

- Berries (individually quick frozen or in syrup)
- Cooked meatballs, chicken patties, breaded chicken strips
- Fish fillets

- Potato preparations (hash browns, French fries and the like)
- Rice and pasta dishes, such as ravioli and tortellini

- Shrimp
- Individual and mixed vegetables
- Vegetable "meal starters"

Foods to Buy Fresh and Freeze at Home

- Boneless, skinless chicken breasts (wrap individually)
- Ground meat (wrap individual patties of about ¼ pound each)
- Hot dogs
- Boneless pork chops (wrap individually)
- Preseasoned, ready-to-cook meats
- Peeled or cooked shrimp

Cans, Jars and Mixes

- Alfredo sauce
- Artichoke hearts (marinated)
- Baby corn
- Corn niblets or kernels
- Dry beans
- Canned beans (black, kidney, chickpeas, cannelini and refried)
- Beef stew
- Bouillon cubes
- Bread crumbs
- Chicken and beef broth
- Chiles
- Couscous
- Fruit
- Minced garlic
- Gravy and sauces
- Jams and jellies
- Evaporated milk or long-life milk in cartons
- Mushrooms
- Olives
- Dried pasta
- Pickles
- Pimientos
- Pizza sauce
- Instant mashed potatoes
- Rice (quick-cooking and regular, plain and flavored)
- Roasted bell peppers (marinated)
- Salsa
- Soups (ready-to-serve, condensed, dry mixes, ramen noodles)
- Spaghetti sauce
- Tomatoes (whole, chopped, sauce, paste)
- Tuna, salmon, shrimp, clams, crab
- Water chestnuts

Fresh Produce That Keeps Well

- Cabbage
- Carrots (including baby-cut)
- Celery
- Citrus fruit
- Garlic
- Iceberg lettuce
- Onions
- Potatoes and sweet potatoes
- Shallots
- Winter squash

Seasonings and Sauces

- Assorted vinegars
- Assorted oils, especially olive oil and vegetable oil
- Barbecue sauce
- Cajun seasoning
- Caribbean or jerk seasoning
- Dried herbs such as oregano, basil, thyme, tarragon and other favorites
- Fresh ginger
- Hot sauce
- Italian seasoning
- Ketchup
- Lemon pepper, garlic pepper and similar blends
- Mayonnaise
- Mustard, especially Dijon
- Salad dressings
- Soy sauce
- Stir-fry sauce, such as sweet-and-sour sauce
- Taco seasoning
- Teriyaki sauce
- Worcestershire sauce

Shortcuts from the Supermarket

Look for time-saving supermarket ingredients that are already chopped, cut to size, mixed, seasoned or precooked:

- Chicken cuts
- Barbecued whole chickens
- Cold cuts and deli meats (such as cooked chicken)
- Coleslaw and salad blends
- Deli salads (macaroni, potato, pasta, coleslaw)

- Precut fruits and vegetables from salad bar
- Ham steaks
- Meat and vegetables cut and seasoned for stir-fry or kabobs
- Pepperoni slices
- Pickled vegetables from deli
- Seasoned pork tenderloins

- Precooked mashed potatoes
- Cooked sausage
- Prepared seafood patties and salads
- Cooked shrimp and lobster
- Prewashed spinach and salad greens
- Spreads and dips

Ready, Set, Shop

Making a List

To simplify grocery shopping, design your own shopping form. Make a list of all the foods and grocery items you usually buy. Arrange them in the order you find them in the store. Add space for unusual or special items.

Make copies of the list and keep it posted in your kitchen. As you use up items or plan menus, mark needed items on the list. When it's time to shop, you won't need to take inventory, and you'll be less likely to forget an item.

Heading to the Market

If your schedule permits, you'll save time if you can shop during the grocery store's low-traffic hours. Also, produce and fish may not be as fresh by Sunday afternoon, and shelves may need restocking.

Let Your Fingers Do the Shopping

Internet sites that allow you to shop for groceries online and have them delivered are becoming popular in some areas. You can create your shopping list online and add or subtract items each time you log on. Delivery charges range from minimal (or free, as an introductory offer) to moderate. Such services are favored by those who find shopping difficult (families with young children, senior citizens, people with vision or mobility impairments as well as working people who lack time.

Simple Glazes and Sauces

A simple mixture can add new zest to familiar favorites. Season according to your taste.

Blend Together	Use For
Honey and Dijon mustard	Spread for sandwiches; glaze for grilled chicken or salmon
Plain nonfat yogurt and horseradish	Topping for grilled beef and boiled or baked potatoes, or poached salmon
Melted butter with lemon juice and lemon zest	Topping for green beans, asparagus or zucchini; dip for artichokes
Melted apricot preserves (or currant jelly), splash of cider vinegar and tarragon	Glaze for poultry
Sour cream, chopped mint and chopped onion	Toss with cucumbers for salad; condiment for grilled meats
Ketchup, horseradish and lemon juice	Dip for cold shrimp
Mayonnaise, pickle relish and lemon juice	Condiment for grilled seafood
Melted butter with brown sugar	Glaze for carrots, sweet potatoes or acorn squash

Quick Vinaigrette

Bottled dressing is a quick way to turn plain greens into a delicious salad, but making vinaigrette from scratch actually isn't much harder.

¾ cup oil

¼ cup vinegar

salt and pepper or herbs to taste

Yield: 1 cup

For a classic vinaigrette, mix three parts oil and one part vinegar (season to taste with salt and pepper and/or herbs) in a blender, or shake them well in a tightly closed jar. To mix by hand, begin whisking the vinegar and add the oil a few drops at a time, then in a slow, steady stream while whisking vigorously.

Note: If a dressing separates after it stands a while, rewhisk or shake it before dressing the salad.

Variations

- Add more vinegar if you like a tangier dressing or want to reduce the fat content; fruit vinegars or flavored vinegars give a different nuance to the taste.
- Extra-virgin olive oil or walnut oil add more assertive flavor than canola or corn oil.
- Substitute orange or lemon juice for vinegar.
- For an Asian-flavored dressing, use rice wine vinegar, peanut oil, a few drops of sesame oil and a pinch of sugar.

Speedy and Sensational Salads

One of the quickest ways to round out a meal, a salad can be nearly instant (toss a bag of prewashed, mixed greens with bottled dressing) or more elaborate, and it can be easily varied every night. First, choose one or more greens from the chart (at right), then mix in "extras" you have on hand.

Vegetables

- Artichoke hearts
- Asparagus
- Canned beans (such as kidney, garbanzo or pinto)
- Cooked beets, julienne-cut (matchsticks)
- Fresh or roasted bell pepper, sliced
- Broccoli florets
- Carrots, shredded, thinly sliced or julienne-cut
- Cauliflower florets

- Sliced celery
- Corn kernels, canned or cooked
- Cucumber, chopped or sliced
- French-fried onions
- Green beans, cooked
- Chopped fresh herbs (such as basil, tarragon or parsley)
- Mushrooms, fresh or canned, sliced or quartered
- Olives, sliced or whole
- Onions, thinly sliced

- Pimientos
- Radishes, sliced
- Sprouts (such as alfalfa, bean, broccoli or radish)
- Fresh tomatoes, either cherry or cut into wedges or sliced
- Sun-dried tomatoes, packed in oil or reconstituted in hot water
- Water chestnuts, sliced
- Zucchini, sliced

Fruit

- Apples, sliced or cubed*
- Avocado, cut into slices or chunks*

- Dried fruit (such as raisins or apricots)
- Grapefruit segments
- Grapes (seedless green or red)

- Mandarin orange segments
- Pears, sliced or cubed
- Pomegranate seeds

  *toss with vinaigrette or citrus to prevent discoloration

Protein (to create a main-dish salad)

- Anchovy fillets
- Crumbled bacon
- Beef (such as leftover grilled steak) shredded, cubed or julienne-cut

- Cheese, cubed, shredded or crumbled
- Chicken or turkey, cooked, cubed or julienne-cut
- Ham or deli cold cuts, cubed or julienne-cut

- Hard-cooked eggs, sliced or cut into wedges
- Seafood, cooked, smoked or canned
- Tofu, cubed or crumbled

Extras

- Capers
- Croutons

- Toasted nuts (such as walnuts or pine nuts)
- Chopped pickles

- Sunflower seeds
- Tortellini or other cooked pasta

Guide to Salad Greens

TYPE	DESCRIPTION
Arugula (also called roquette or rocket)	Slender, toothed leaves with a peppery bite. Especially good as an accent with milder greens.
Belgian or French endive	Smooth, elongated, compact heads of slender, crisp leaves that shade from white to pale green; slightly bitter flavor. Shred and serve alone or with other greens; use leaves whole with dips.
Bibb lettuce	Small heads of tender, buttery-textured leaves with a slightly sweet, mild flavor.
Boston lettuce	Similar to Bibb lettuce, but with a looser head.
Chicory (also called curly endive)	Fringed, curly leaves with a sharp, bitter taste. Darker green, tougher outer leaves have a stronger flavor than the lighter, sometimes yellow inner leaves. Good with milder greens.
Chinese cabbage (also called celery cabbage or Napa cabbage)	Elongated heads that may be slender or fat; wide-ribbed, tender leaves and crisp stalks are equally good raw or cooked. Slightly spicy flavor. Mix with American- or Asian-style salads.
Escarole	Wide, crisp, flat leaves with curled edges. Slightly bitter flavor. The tender, pale inner leaves are milder. Use with other greens.
Green cabbage	Heavy, tightly packed heads that vary from medium green on the outside to white on the inside. Shred for coleslaw.
Iceberg lettuce	Crisp, watery leaves with slight mild to sweet flavor.
Leaf lettuce	Leaves are ruffled or curly, green or red-tipped. Sprout out loosely rather than being a compact head. Mild flavor and tender texture.
Mâche (also called lamb's lettuce)	Dark green leaves shaped like lambs' tongues with mild, sweet flavor and soft texture.
Radicchio	Small, compact heads of variegated red and white leaves with slightly bitter flavor. Generally costly, but a small amount is enough for color contrast and flavor accent.
Red cabbage	Similar in shape and flavor to green cabbage.
Romaine lettuce	Firm, crisp leaves with a mild, sweet flavor. Inner yellow leaves are sweeter and more tender than dark green exterior leaves.
Savoy cabbage	Like green cabbage, with slightly more delicate leaves. Can be used interchangeably with green cabbage.
Sorrel	Long, crisp, arrow-shaped leaves with a pungent, sour flavor.
Spinach	Crinkled or flat, crisp leaves with soft texture and mild flavor. Hearty enough for main-dish salads. Wash to remove grit.
Watercress	Delicate, spicy green. Good accent for salads and sandwiches.

Lettuce-less Salads

While the word "salad" brings to mind leafy greens, lettuce is not a requirement. Here are some easy side-dish salads:

- Drained, canned corn (or cooked corn, cut from the cob), chopped tomato, chopped fresh basil, balsamic vinaigrette
- Canned kidney beans (rinsed and drained), chopped red onion, fresh or dried thyme, red wine vinaigrette
- Chopped fresh pear tossed with lemon juice and olive oil, crumbled blue cheese, toasted walnuts
- Chopped apple, walnuts, celery, mayonnaise
- Canned black beans (rinsed and drained), corn kernels, salsa
- Bean sprouts, shredded carrot, rice wine vinaigrette and a touch of soy sauce and sesame oil
- Cooked pasta, chopped roasted bell pepper, sliced ripe olives, creamy dressing
- Chopped avocado, chopped tomato, chopped onion, lemon juice and olive oil
- Tortellini, cooked green beans, fresh parsley, creamy Italian dressing
- Canned or fresh pineapple chunks, drained mandarin orange segments, sliced fresh banana

Tempting Toppings for Refrigerated Rolls

Dress up refrigerated breads with these tempting toppings.

Before Baking		After Baking
BRUSH WITH	**SPRINKLE WITH**	**BRUSH WITH**
Beaten egg	Sesame seeds	Melted butter
Italian dressing	Caraway	Margarine mixed with fresh herbs
	Poppy seeds	
	Garlic salt	
	Grated Parmesan cheese	

Quick Desserts

Something sweet brings a meal to a satisfying conclusion, whether you opt for ripe fresh fruit or a scoop of ice cream. A quick dress-up can make a simple dessert even more special. Some ideas:

- Drizzle fresh fruit with honey, fruit-flavored yogurt or shredded fresh mint.
- Crown ice cream with chocolate syrup, chopped toasted nuts or a spoonful of a favorite liqueur.
- Use purchased pound cake, angel cake or sponge cake as shortcake, topping with fresh or frozen berries and whipped cream.

- Dress up almost any cake, pie, pudding, frozen confection or fruit with a dollop of whipped cream and some sprinkles or a maraschino cherry.
- Heat banana slices, peach slices or berries briefly in the microwave and serve with ice cream or sorbet.

- Heat cookies or brownies in the microwave for a warm-from-the-oven treat.
- Mix frozen berries, canned pineapple chunks and fresh banana slices for a fast fruit cup. Sprinkle with shredded coconut

Easy-As-Pie Pies

Prepare a one-crust baked shell as directed on a package of Pillsbury® Refrigerated Pie Crust, or use a prepared graham cracker crust. Spoon any of the following into the cooled, baked shell:

One-Crust Pies to Make in Minutes

PIE	INGREDIENTS	PREPARATION
Fruit and Cream Pie	2 cups whipping cream ¼ cup powdered sugar 3 cups fresh fruit (strawberry slices, blueberries, peach slices)	1. Combine whipping cream and powdered sugar. Beat until peaks form. Fold in fresh fruit. Spoon into baked shell. 2. Refrigerate 1 hour before serving. Store in refrigerator.
Fresh Strawberry Pie	1 quart fresh, cleaned strawberries 1 (12-oz.) container strawberry glaze ½ cup whipping cream, whipped	1. Combine strawberries with glaze. Spoon into baked shell. 2. Serve with whipped cream. Store in refrigerator.
Cookie and Caramel Ice Cream Pie	4 cups ice cream, softened ½ cup caramel ice cream topping 1 cup crushed cookies	1. Spread 2 cups ice cream into baked shell. Top with half of caramel topping and half of the cookies. Repeat layering. 2. Freeze 1 hour before serving. Store in freezer.
Easy Pudding Pie	1 (5.9-oz.) pkg. instant pudding mix (any flavor) ½ cup whipping cream, whipped	1. Prepare pudding according to package directions for pie. Pour into baked shell. 2. Refrigerate 3 hours or until set. Top with whipped cream before serving. Store in refrigerator.

beef

OPPOSITE PAGE:
Pizza Skillet Hot Dish, page 31

☺ Kid-Pleasing Recipe
🕐 20-Minutes-or-Less Recipe

menu

EASY TEX-MEX HASH

Buttered whole kernel corn

Hot fudge sundaes

Microwave the corn while the hash cooks on the stove.

Easy Tex-Mex Hash

To serve this hash for brunch, make four wells in the mixture. Break an egg into each well. Cover and cook until the eggs are done.

Yield: 4 (1-cup) servings

---

1 lb. lean ground beef

1 tablespoon oil

3 cups frozen potatoes O'Brien with onions and peppers (from 24-oz. pkg.)

1 cup chunky-style salsa

2 teaspoons chili powder, if desired

4 oz. (1 cup) shredded colby-Monterey Jack cheese blend

---

1. Brown ground beef in large nonstick skillet until thoroughly cooked, stirring frequently. Remove ground beef from skillet; cover to keep warm. Discard drippings.

2. In same skillet, heat oil over medium heat until hot. Add potatoes; cook and stir 8 to 10 minutes or until browned.

3. Stir in salsa, chili powder and cooked ground beef. Cook 5 to 8 minutes or until thoroughly heated, stirring occasionally.

4. Sprinkle with cheese. Cover; cook 2 to 4 minutes or until cheese is melted.

Nutrition Information Per Serving: Serving Size: 1 Cup • Calories 440 • Calories from Fat 240 • % Daily Value: Total Fat 27 g 42% • Saturated Fat 12 g 60% • Cholesterol 95 mg 32% • Sodium 730 mg 30% • Total Carbohydrate 20 g 7% • Dietary Fiber 2 g 8% • Sugars 3 g • Protein 28 g • Vitamin A 20% • Vitamin C 10% • Calcium 25% • Iron 15%
Dietary Exchanges: 1 1/2 Starch, 3 1/2 Medium-Fat Meat, 1 1/2 Fat OR 1 1/2 Carbohydrate, 3 1/2 Medium-Fat Meat, 1 1/2 Fat

Ramen Skillet Supper

Noodles, beef and vegetables mingle in a dish that might be a saucy stew or a thick soup. Stir-fry sauces can vary in flavor, so sample the dish while it cooks and adjust it to taste with a sprinkle of sugar or cayenne.

Yield: 4 (1½-cup) servings

1 lb. lean ground beef

2½ cups water

2 (3-oz.) pkg. oriental-flavor ramen noodle soup mix

½ cup purchased stir-fry sauce

3 cups frozen broccoli florets, carrots and cauliflower

1. Brown ground beef in large skillet over medium-high heat until thoroughly cooked, stirring frequently. Drain.

2. Add water, contents of 1 of the soup mix seasoning packets, stir-fry sauce and frozen vegetables; mix well. (Discard remaining seasoning packet or reserve for a later use.) Bring to a boil. Reduce heat to medium-low; cover and cook 5 minutes or until vegetables are tender, stirring occasionally.

3. Break up ramen noodles; add to skillet. Cover; cook 5 to 8 minutes or until sauce is of desired consistency, stirring occasionally and separating noodles as they soften.

Nutrition Information Per Serving: Serving Size: 1½ Cups • Calories 460 • Calories from Fat 210 • % Daily Value: Total Fat 23 g 35% • Saturated Fat 10 g 50% • Cholesterol 70 mg 23% • Sodium 2,000 mg 83% • Total Carbohydrate 35 g 12% • Dietary Fiber 3 g 12% • Sugars 5 g • Protein 27 g • Vitamin A 60% • Vitamin C 20% • Calcium 4% • Iron 20%
Dietary Exchanges: 2 Starch, 1 Vegetable, 2 Lean Meat, 3 Fat OR 2 Carbohydrate, 1 Vegetable, 2 Lean Meat, 3 Fat

menu

RAMEN SKILLET SUPPER

Egg rolls with sweet-and-sour sauce

Orange sherbet and sugar cookies

Warm the egg rolls in the oven or toaster oven while you prepare the entree. Don't microwave them, or they'll get soggy.

menu

**BARBECUE BEEF AND
VEGETABLE SKILLET**

Tossed salad with Parmesan salad
dressing

Refrigerated buttermilk biscuits

Fresh grapes

Assemble the salad in advance,
but wait to toss with the dressing
until just before serving. Preheat
the oven for the biscuits. Substitute refrigerated potatoes for the
frozen, if you like. Bake the biscuits while the main dish simmers.

Barbecue Beef and Vegetable Skillet

This dish provides full flavor and meat-and-potato satisfaction, and its speedy cooking time makes it ideal for supper on a busy night.

Yield: 5 (1½-cup) servings

1 lb. lean ground beef

3 cups frozen seasoned chunky-style hash-brown potatoes
(from 28-oz. pkg.)

3 cups frozen cut green beans

1 cup frozen bell pepper and onion stir-fry

1 cup barbecue sauce

½ cup water

1. Brown ground beef in large skillet over medium-high heat until thoroughly cooked, stirring frequently. Drain.

2. Add potatoes, green beans and bell pepper and onion stir-fry; mix well. Reduce heat to medium; cover and cook 8 to 12 minutes or until vegetables are tender, stirring occasionally.

3. Add barbecue sauce and water; mix well. Cover; simmer 3 to 5 minutes or until thoroughly heated.

Nutrition Information Per Serving: Serving Size: 1½ Cups • Calories 350 •
Calories from Fat 150 • % Daily Value: Total Fat 17 g 26% • Saturated Fat 5 g 25% •
Cholesterol 55 mg 18% • Sodium 920 mg 38% • Total Carbohydrate 29 g 10% •
Dietary Fiber 5 g 20% • Sugars 5 g • Protein 20 g • Vitamin A 20% • Vitamin C 25% •
Calcium 4% • Iron 15%
Dietary Exchanges: 1½ Starch, 1 Vegetable, 2 Medium-Fat Meat, 1 Fat OR
1½ Carbohydrate, 1 Vegetable, 2 Medium-Fat Meat, 1 Fat

menu

TEX-MEX TAMALE SKILLET

Lettuce wedge salad with ranch salad dressing

Chocolate chip cookies

Prepare the salad while the tamale skillet simmers, but wait to add the dressing until just before serving. Heat the oven while the tamale skillet cooks, and bake a batch of refrigerated cookies. Set the timer so that you remember they're in the oven during dinner.

Tex-Mex Tamale Skillet

Corn tortilla strips, softened in the salsa-beef mixture, are almost like noodles in this skillet supper. Choose mild, medium or hot salsa according to your family's "heat" preference.

Yield: 4 (1½-cup) servings

1 lb. lean ground beef

1 (16-oz.) jar salsa

1 (11-oz.) can vacuum-packed whole kernel corn with red and green peppers

4 (6-inch) soft corn tortillas, halved, cut crosswise into ½-inch strips

4 oz. (1 cup) shredded hot pepper Monterey Jack cheese

2 tablespoons chopped fresh cilantro, if desired

1. Brown ground beef in large skillet over medium-high heat until thoroughly cooked, stirring frequently. Drain.

2. Add salsa, corn and tortilla strips; mix well. Reduce heat to medium; cover and cook 10 to 15 minutes or until tortilla strips are tender, stirring occasionally. (If mixture seems dry, add 2 to 3 tablespoons water.)

3. Sprinkle with cheese. Cover; cook an additional 5 minutes or until cheese is melted. Sprinkle with cilantro.

Nutrition Information Per Serving: Serving Size: 1½ Cups • Calories 480 • Calories from Fat 230 • % Daily Value: Total Fat 25 g 38% • Saturated Fat 12 g 60% • Cholesterol 100 mg 33% • Sodium 1,600 mg 67% • Total Carbohydrate 34 g 11% • Dietary Fiber 3 g 12% • Sugars 8 g • Protein 29 g • Vitamin A 15% • Vitamin C 0% • Calcium 25% • Iron 15%
Dietary Exchanges: 2 Starch, 3 Medium-Fat Meat, 2 Fat OR 2 Carbohydrate, 3 Medium-Fat Meat, 2 Fat

Mexican Beef and Tomato Tortillas

Used widely in Southwestern, Mexican and Indian cuisine, cumin comes from a seed that resembles caraway. Its earthy flavor goes well with tomatoes and beans.

Yield: 4 servings

½ lb. lean ground beef

1 (15.5-oz.) can pinto beans, drained, rinsed

1 (10-oz.) can tomatoes with green chiles, undrained

4 teaspoons chili powder

½ teaspoon cumin

8 (6-inch) soft corn tortillas

3 oz. (¾ cup) shredded sharp Cheddar cheese

½ cup sour cream, if desired

1. Brown ground beef in medium nonstick skillet over medium-high heat for 2 to 4 minutes, stirring frequently. Remove beef from skillet; drain on paper towels.

2. Wipe skillet dry with paper towels. Return beef to skillet; stir in beans, tomatoes, chili powder and cumin. Bring to a boil. Reduce heat; cover and simmer 10 minutes.

3. Meanwhile, heat tortillas as directed on package.

4. To serve, sprinkle cheese evenly over tortillas. Top each with beef mixture and sour cream; fold tortillas in half.

Nutrition Information Per Serving: Serving Size: ¼ of Recipe • Calories 460 • Calories from Fat 210 • % Daily Value: Total Fat 23 g 35% • Saturated Fat 12 g 60% • Cholesterol 70 mg 23% • Sodium 690 mg 29% • Total Carbohydrate 39 g 13% • Dietary Fiber 7 g 28% • Sugars 4 g • Protein 24 g • Vitamin A 35% • Vitamin C 8% • Calcium 35% • Iron 15%
Dietary Exchanges: 2½ Starch, 2½ Medium-Fat Meat, 2 Fat OR 2½ Carbohydrate, 2½ Medium-Fat Meat, 2 Fat

MEXICAN BEEF AND TOMATO TORTILLAS

Ripe papaya slices drizzled with lime juice

Chocolate pudding topped with whipped cream and cinnamon

Prepare instant pudding and let it chill until dessert, if you haven't purchased it ready to serve. Cut the papayas while the tortilla mixture simmers. If you double this recipe, try a can of black beans or 2 cups of corn kernels in place of a second can of pinto beans. Cilantro makes a nice garnish for this dish.

Southwestern
Pasta Skillet

Cook a pound of pasta or two at a time. Serve it
with pasta sauce one night; the next night, use
the leftovers in a skillet supper such as this.

Yield: 5 (1½-cup) servings

8 oz. (2¾ cups) uncooked rotini (spiral pasta)

1 lb. lean ground beef

1 (15-oz.) can spicy chili beans, undrained

1 (11-oz.) can vacuum-packed whole kernel corn with red
      and green peppers, drained

12 oz. mild Mexican pasteurized prepared cheese product,
      cubed (3 cups)

1. Cook rotini to desired doneness as directed on
package. Drain; cover to keep warm.

2. Meanwhile, brown ground beef in 12-inch
nonstick skillet over medium-high heat until
thoroughly cooked, stirring frequently. Drain.

3. Stir in beans, corn and cheese. Cover; cook
over medium-low heat until cheese is melted
and mixture is thoroughly heated, stirring
occasionally.

4. Gently stir cooked rotini into ground beef
mixture until coated.

Nutrition Information Per Serving: Serving Size: 1½ Cups • Calories 730 •
Calories from Fat 320 • % Daily Value: Total Fat 36 g 55% • Saturated Fat 20 g 100% •
Cholesterol 115 mg 38% • Sodium 1,210 mg 50% • Total Carbohydrate 61 g 20% •
Dietary Fiber 6 g 24% • Sugars 6 g • Protein 41 g • Vitamin A 20% • Vitamin C 0% •
Calcium 50% • Iron 25%
Dietary Exchanges: 4 Starch, 4 Medium-Fat Meat, 3 Fat OR 4 Carbohydrate,
4 Medium-Fat Meat, 3 Fat

Tortilla Dip Supper

Made with ground beef, refried beans and cheese, a nacho-style appetizer becomes a casual dinner. To "lighten" this dish, make it with light sour cream, reduced-fat cheese and baked tortilla chips.

Yield: 5 servings

1 lb. lean ground beef

1 (16-oz.) can refried beans

1 (8-oz.) can tomato sauce

1 cup salsa

½ cup sour cream

4 oz. (1 cup) shredded Cheddar cheese

2 cups shredded lettuce

2 medium tomatoes, chopped

8 oz. (5 cups) tortilla chips

1. Brown ground beef in large skillet over medium-high heat until thoroughly cooked, stirring frequently. Drain.

2. Add refried beans, tomato sauce and salsa; mix well. Cook and stir 4 to 5 minutes or until thoroughly heated and bubbly.

3. In small bowl, combine sour cream and cheese; mix well. Spoon over beef mixture. Cover; cook over low heat for 3 to 4 minutes or until thoroughly heated. Remove from heat. To serve, top with lettuce and tomatoes. Serve with tortilla chips for dipping.

Nutrition Information Per Serving: Serving Size: ⅕ of Recipe • Calories 670 • Calories from Fat 330 • % Daily Value: Total Fat 37 g 57% • Saturated Fat 15 g 75% • Cholesterol 90 mg 30% • Sodium 1,520 mg 63% • Total Carbohydrate 52 g 17% • Dietary Fiber 9 g 36% • Sugars 8 g • Protein 31 g • Vitamin A 30% • Vitamin C 20% • Calcium 30% • Iron 25%
Dietary Exchanges: 3 Starch, 1 Vegetable, 3 Medium-Fat Meat, 4 Fat OR 3 Carbohydrate, 1 Vegetable, 3 Medium-Fat Meat, 4 Fat

menu

TORTILLA DIP SUPPER

Red and green grape clusters

Chocolate chip ice cream

Rinse the grapes and set them in a serving bowl. Shred the lettuce and chop the tomatoes while the dip mixture cooks.

menu

**SAUCY GROUND
BEEF-TOPPED POTATOES**

Tossed green salad with cucumber
and Italian salad dressing

Sugar cookies

This recipe is quick to prepare,
but you can make the ground
beef mixture ahead and refrigerate it until serving time. Reheat it
in the microwave while the potatoes are standing.

Saucy Ground Beef-Topped Potatoes

For dinners that are ready in a snap, freeze
ground beef in individual portions of about ¼
pound each. You'll be able to thaw the exact
amount you need quickly and easily.

Yield: 3 servings

3 medium baking potatoes

½ lb. lean ground beef

1 (14-oz.) jar (2 cups) spaghetti sauce

1 (7-oz.) can vacuum-packed whole kernel corn, drained

1 oz. (¼ cup) shredded mozzarella cheese

1. Pierce potatoes with fork. Place on microwave-safe paper towel in microwave oven. Microwave on HIGH for 10 to 13 minutes or until tender, turning potatoes over and rearranging halfway through cooking. Let stand 3 minutes.

2. Meanwhile, brown ground beef in medium nonstick skillet over medium heat for 8 to 10 minutes or until thoroughly cooked, stirring frequently. Drain. Stir in spaghetti sauce and corn. Cover; simmer 4 to 5 minutes or until thoroughly heated, stirring occasionally.

3. To serve, cut potatoes in half lengthwise; place on 3 individual plates. Mash potatoes slightly with fork. Top each potato with ⅔ cup beef mixture. Sprinkle with cheese.

Nutrition Information Per Serving: Serving Size: ⅓ of Recipe • Calories 440 • Calories from Fat 140 • % Daily Value: Total Fat 15 g 23% • Saturated Fat 5 g 25% • Cholesterol 50 mg 17% • Sodium 840 mg 35% • Total Carbohydrate 55 g 18% • Dietary Fiber 7 g 28% • Sugars 5 g • Protein 22 g • Vitamin A 10% • Vitamin C 35% • Calcium 10% • Iron 20%
Dietary Exchanges: 3½ Starch, 1½ Medium-Fat Meat, 1 Fat OR 3½ Carbohydrate, 1½ Medium-Fat Meat, 1 Fat

Sirloin and Mushrooms in Rich Beef-Dijon Sauce

For a richer sauce, substitute heavy cream for the milk. For a lighter version, use skim milk.

Yield: 4 servings

8 oz. uncooked angel hair pasta

1 lb. boneless beef top sirloin steak, cut into 1-inch pieces

2 garlic cloves, minced

1 (8-oz.) pkg. (3 cups) sliced fresh mushrooms

1 cup beef broth

¼ cup diagonally sliced green onions

2 tablespoons all-purpose flour

3 tablespoons milk

2 tablespoons Dijon mustard

Coarse ground black pepper

1. Cook pasta to desired doneness as directed on package.

2. Meanwhile, spray 12-inch nonstick skillet with nonstick cooking spray. Heat over medium-high heat until hot. Add beef and garlic; cook about 4 minutes, stirring frequently. Add mushrooms, broth and onions. Reduce heat; cover and cook 3 minutes. Uncover; cook an additional 2 to 3 minutes.

3. In small bowl, combine flour and milk; blend until smooth. Add to skillet; cook and stir 2 minutes or until slightly thickened. Stir in mustard until smooth.

4. Drain pasta; arrange on serving platter. Spoon beef-mushroom mixture and sauce over pasta. Sprinkle with pepper.

SIRLOIN AND MUSHROOMS IN RICH BEEF-DIJON SAUCE

Baby carrots with butter and chopped chives

Refrigerated crescent dinner rolls

Chocolate mousse

Early in the day, prepare the mousse from scratch or a mix. While you wait for the pasta water to boil and the oven to pre-heat, assemble and cut up the ingredients for the entree. While the beef cooks, microwave the carrots and bake the rolls.

menu

Nutrition Information Per Serving: Serving Size: ¼ of Recipe • Calories 400 • Calories from Fat 80 • % Daily Value: Total Fat 9 g 14% • Saturated Fat 3 g 15% • Cholesterol 50 mg 17% • Sodium 340 mg 14% • Total Carbohydrate 50 g 17% • Dietary Fiber 2 g 8% • Sugars 3 g • Protein 29 g • Vitamin A 0% • Vitamin C 4% • Calcium 4% • Iron 30%
Dietary Exchanges: 3 Starch, 1 Vegetable, 2½ Lean Meat OR 3 Carbohydrate, 1 Vegetable, 2½ Lean Meat

Beef Chow Mein

Studded with readily available Asian ingredients—ginger, bean sprouts, water chestnuts—this recipe is a nice addition to your ground-beef repertoire.

Yield: 4 servings

1 lb. lean ground beef

1 (14½-oz.) can ready-to-serve beef broth

2 tablespoons soy sauce

½ teaspoon ginger

1½ cups sliced celery

1 (16-oz.) can bean sprouts, drained

1 (8-oz.) can sliced water chestnuts, drained

1 (4-oz.) can mushroom pieces and stems, drained

2 tablespoons cornstarch

3 tablespoons water

4 cups chow mein noodles or hot cooked rice

1. Brown ground beef in large skillet over medium heat until thoroughly cooked, stirring frequently. Drain.

2. Add broth, soy sauce, ginger, celery, bean sprouts, water chestnuts and mushrooms; mix well. Cover; simmer 15 minutes, stirring occasionally.

3. Meanwhile, in small bowl, combine cornstarch and water; blend until smooth.

4. Stir cornstarch mixture into beef mixture. Cook until mixture boils and thickens. Serve over chow mein noodles or rice. If desired, serve with additional soy sauce.

Nutrition Information Per Serving: Serving Size: ¼ of Recipe • Calories 550 • Calories from Fat 260 • % Daily Value: Total Fat 29 g 45% • Saturated Fat 8 g 40% • Cholesterol 70 mg 23% • Sodium 1,320 mg 55% • Total Carbohydrate 43 g 14% • Dietary Fiber 5 g 20% • Sugars 3 g • Protein 28 g • Vitamin A 2% • Vitamin C 6% • Calcium 6% • Iron 25%
Dietary Exchanges: 2½ Starch, 1 Vegetable, 2½ Medium-Fat Meat, 3 Fat OR 2½ Carbohydrate, 1 Vegetable, 2½ Medium-Fat Meat, 3 Fat

BEEF CHOW MEIN

Cantaloupe and honeydew melon slices

Purchased almond cookies

If you opt for rice instead of crispy noodles, start the water for it before you begin to cook the chow mein. Assemble everything you need for the chow mein. Slice the melons while the chow mein cooks.

Taco Skillet Dinner

Think of this as macaroni and cheese for grownups. Taco seasoning and toppings perk up the familiar blend of cheese-sauce-with-noodles.

Yield: 4 (1½-cup) servings

1 lb. lean ground beef

1 (1.25-oz.) pkg. taco seasoning mix

2½ cups water

7 oz. (2 cups) uncooked elbow macaroni

4 oz. (1 cup) shredded Cheddar cheese

2 green onions, sliced

½ cup sour cream

1 medium tomato, chopped

1. Brown ground beef in large skillet over medium-high heat until thoroughly cooked, stirring frequently. Drain.

2. Add taco seasoning mix, water and macaroni; mix well. Bring to a boil. Stir; reduce heat to medium-low. Cover; cook 8 to 10 minutes or until macaroni is of desired doneness, stirring occasionally.

3. Sprinkle with cheese and onions. Top with sour cream. Sprinkle with tomato.

Nutrition Information Per Serving: Serving Size: 1½ Cups • Calories 610 • Calories from Fat 280 • % Daily Value: Total Fat 31 g 48% • Saturated Fat 16 g 80% • Cholesterol 115 mg 38% • Sodium 1,060 mg 44% • Total Carbohydrate 48 g 16% • Dietary Fiber 2 g 8% • Sugars 4 g • Protein 35 g • Vitamin A 20% • Vitamin C 8% • Calcium 25% • Iron 25%
Dietary Exchanges: 3 Starch, 3½ Medium-Fat Meat, 2½ Fat OR 3 Carbohydrate, 3½ Medium-Fat Meat, 2½ Fat

Pizza Skillet Hot Dish

Here's a clever technique: The spaghetti cooks right in the sauce. Refrigerated marinara sauce can be substituted for the spaghetti sauce.

Yield: 4 (1¼-cup) servings

½ lb. lean ground beef

2 oz. (½ cup) sliced pepperoni, chopped

1 (14-oz.) jar (2 cups) spaghetti sauce

¾ cup water

7 oz. (2 cups) uncooked ready-cut spaghetti (short curved pasta)

¼ cup sliced ripe olives

½ green bell pepper, cut into bite-sized strips

4 oz. (1 cup) shredded mozzarella cheese

1. Brown ground beef in large skillet over medium-high heat until thoroughly cooked, stirring frequently. Add pepperoni; cook 1 minute. Drain.

2. Stir in spaghetti sauce, water and uncooked spaghetti. Bring to a boil. Stir; reduce heat to medium-low. Cover; cook 10 to 15 minutes or until spaghetti is of desired doneness, stirring occasionally.

3. Add olives; stir gently to mix. Arrange pepper strips over top. Sprinkle with cheese. Remove from heat. Cover; let stand 3 to 5 minutes or until cheese is melted.

Nutrition Information Per Serving: Serving Size: 1¼ Cups • Calories 620 • Calories from Fat 270 • % Daily Value: Total Fat 30 g 46% • Saturated Fat 12 g 60% • Cholesterol 95 mg 32% • Sodium 990 mg 41% • Total Carbohydrate 48 g 16% • Dietary Fiber 3 g 12% • Sugars 2 g • Protein 39 g • Vitamin A 15% • Vitamin C 20% • Calcium 25% • Iron 25%
Dietary Exchanges: 3 Starch, 4½ Medium-Fat Meat, 1 Fat OR 3 Carbohydrate, 4½ Medium-Fat Meat, 1 Fat

PIZZA SKILLET HOT DISH

Garlic bread

Italian green beans

Frosted ginger cookies

While the entree cooks, wrap the garlic bread in foil and warm it in the oven. If you aren't using prepared garlic bread, butter slices of Italian bread or split rolls, sprinkle them with garlic powder, wrap in foil and warm in a 350°F. oven for 10 minutes or so. Cook the green beans in the microwave. Purchase the cookies at the bakery or make them ahead.

Mom's Skillet Goulash

Every country seems to have its own homey stew, the quintessential comfort food for a family supper. This skillet recipe is inspired by goulash, a Hungarian dish.

Yield: 6 (1½-cup) servings

8 oz. (2⅔ cups) uncooked rotini (spiral pasta)

1 lb. lean ground beef

1½ cups sliced celery

1 cup chopped onions

2 (14.5-oz.) cans diced tomatoes, undrained

1 (10¾-oz.) can condensed tomato soup

1 teaspoon dried basil leaves

½ teaspoon salt

¼ teaspoon pepper

1. Cook rotini to desired doneness as directed on package. Drain.

2. Meanwhile, in 12-inch skillet or Dutch oven, combine ground beef, celery and onions. Cook over medium heat until beef is thoroughly cooked, stirring frequently. Drain.

3. Add cooked rotini and all remaining ingredients; mix well. Bring to a boil. Reduce heat; simmer 10 minutes, stirring occasionally.

Nutrition Information Per Serving: Serving Size: 1½ Cups • Calories 370 • Calories from Fat 110 • % Daily Value: Total Fat 12 g 18% • Saturated Fat 4 g 20% • Cholesterol 45 mg 15% • Sodium 730 mg 30% • Total Carbohydrate 44 g 15% • Dietary Fiber 3 g 12% • Sugars 9 g • Protein 21 g • Vitamin A 25% • Vitamin C 60% • Calcium 8% • Iron 25%
Dietary Exchanges: 2½ Starch, 1 Vegetable, 1½ Medium-Fat Meat, ½ Fat OR 2½ Carbohydrate, 1 Vegetable, 1½ Medium-Fat Meat, ½ Fat

Peppered Cube Steaks with Mashed Potatoes and Gravy

For a touch of color, garnish this dish with a sprig of parsley or some chopped green onion.

Yield: 4 servings

4 beef cube steaks (about 1 lb.)

1 teaspoon garlic-pepper blend

1 ⅓ cups water

2 tablespoons margarine or butter

½ cup milk

1 ⅓ cups mashed potato flakes

1 cup beef broth

¼ cup water

1 tablespoon cornstarch

1. Sprinkle both sides of each cube steak with garlic-pepper blend. Spray 12-inch nonstick skillet with nonstick cooking spray. Heat over medium-high heat until hot. Add steaks; cook 6 to 8 minutes, turning once.

2. Meanwhile, in medium saucepan, combine 1⅓ cups water and margarine. Bring to a boil. Remove from heat. Stir in milk and potato flakes with fork until potatoes are of desired consistency.

3. Remove steaks from skillet; cover to keep warm. In same skillet, combine broth, ¼ cup water and cornstarch; cook until bubbly and thickened, stirring constantly. Serve gravy over steaks and potatoes.

Nutrition Information Per Serving: Serving Size: ¼ of Recipe • Calories 300 • Calories from Fat 100 • % Daily Value: Total Fat 11 g 17% • Saturated Fat 3 g 15% • Cholesterol 65 mg 22% • Sodium 440 mg 18% • Total Carbohydrate 22 g 7% • Dietary Fiber 2 g 8% • Sugars 2 g • Protein 28 g • Vitamin A 6% • Vitamin C 0% • Calcium 6% • Iron 15%
Dietary Exchanges: 1½ Starch, 3½ Very Lean Meat, 1½ Fat OR 1½ Carbohydrate, 3½ Very Lean Meat, 1½ Fat

menu

PEPPERED CUBE STEAKS WITH MASHED POTATOES AND GRAVY

French green beans with toasted almonds

Tomato slices sprinkled with chopped chives

Angel food cake with fresh or frozen berries

Slice the tomatoes and heat the beans just before preparing the steak. If you are using fresh berries instead of frozen, rinse, drain and chill them while the steaks cook.

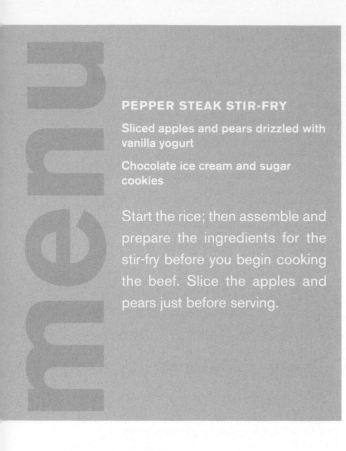

PEPPER STEAK STIR-FRY

Sliced apples and pears drizzled with vanilla yogurt

Chocolate ice cream and sugar cookies

Start the rice; then assemble and prepare the ingredients for the stir-fry before you begin cooking the beef. Slice the apples and pears just before serving.

Pepper Steak Stir-Fry

Purchased stir-fry sauce gives this vegetable-beef dish depth of flavor in an instant. Use your favorite flavor.

Yield: 4 servings

---

1 1/3 cups uncooked regular long-grain white rice

2 2/3 cups water

1/2 cup beef broth

1/2 cup purchased garlic and ginger stir-fry sauce

2 teaspoons cornstarch

1 tablespoon oil

3/4 lb. beef flank or boneless top sirloin steak, cut lengthwise into 2-inch-wide strips, thinly sliced

2 garlic cloves, minced

2 green bell peppers, cut into 1-inch pieces

1 medium onion, cut into 1/2-inch pieces

1 tomato, cut into 12 wedges

---

1. Cook rice in water as directed on package.

2. Meanwhile, in small bowl, combine broth, stir-fry sauce and cornstarch; blend well. Set aside.

3. Heat oil in large skillet or wok over medium-high heat until hot. Add beef and garlic; cook and stir 2 to 3 minutes or until beef is browned. Remove from skillet; cover to keep warm.

4. Reduce heat to medium. In same skillet, combine bell peppers and onion; cook and stir 5 to 7 minutes or until vegetables are crisp-tender.

5. Stir cornstarch mixture until smooth; add to skillet. Cook and stir 2 to 3 minutes or until sauce is thickened and bubbly. Stir in tomato and beef; cook until thoroughly heated. Serve over rice.

Nutrition Information Per Serving: Serving Size: 1/4 of Recipe • Calories 420 • Calories from Fat 110 • % Daily Value: Total Fat 12 g 18% • Saturated Fat 3 g 15% • Cholesterol 35 mg 12% • Sodium 760 mg 32% • Total Carbohydrate 58 g 19% • Dietary Fiber 2 g 8% • Sugars 9 g • Protein 19 g • Vitamin A 8% • Vitamin C 50% • Calcium 4% • Iron 20%
Dietary Exchanges: 3 1/2 Starch, 1 Vegetable, 1 Lean Meat, 1 Fat OR 3 1/2 Carbohydrate, 1 Vegetable, 1 Lean Meat, 1 Fat

Easy Beef Stroganoff

Stroganoff is a creamy stew traditionally made with chunks of beef. Brighten this quick version, if you wish, with a garnish of chopped parsley or thin strips of roasted red pepper.

Yield: 4 servings

---

8 oz. (4 cups) uncooked wide egg noodles

1 lb. lean ground beef

½ cup finely chopped onion

2 tablespoons all-purpose flour

½ cup water

1 (4-oz.) can mushroom pieces and stems, drained

1 cup light sour cream

---

1. Cook noodles to desired doneness as directed on package. Drain; cover to keep warm.

2. Meanwhile, in large skillet, brown ground beef and onion until beef is thoroughly cooked, stirring frequently. Drain. Stir in flour. Add water and mushrooms; cook, stirring constantly, until mixture thickens.

3. Reduce heat; stir in sour cream. If desired, add salt and pepper to taste. Serve over noodles.

Nutrition Information Per Serving: Serving Size: ¼ of Recipe • Calories 530 • Calories from Fat 190 • % Daily Value: Total Fat 21 g 32% • Saturated Fat 9 g 45% • Cholesterol 145 mg 48% • Sodium 310 mg 13% • Total Carbohydrate 54 g 18% • Dietary Fiber 3 g 12% • Sugars 7 g • Protein 31 g • Vitamin A 8% • Vitamin C 0% • Calcium 10% • Iron 25%
Dietary Exchanges: 3½ Starch, 3 Lean Meat, 2 Fat OR 3½ Carbohydrate, 3 Lean Meat, 2 Fat

EASY BEEF STROGANOFF
Buttered peas
Crusty French bread slices
Cherry pie with vanilla ice cream

While waiting for the pasta water to boil, preheat the oven to 350°F. Wrap the French bread slices in foil, and assemble everything you need for the stroganoff. Warm the bread in the preheated oven for about 10 minutes. and microwave the peas while the beef mixture cooks. Drain the cooking liquid off of the hot peas, and stir a little butter into them.

Spicy Beef and Vegetables

To save yourself prep time, purchase meat precut for stir-fries in your grocery store.

Yield: 4 servings

Pasta

4 oz. uncooked vermicelli

Sauce

2 tablespoons soy sauce

2 tablespoons hoisin sauce

1 tablespoon honey

1 teaspoon cornstarch

1/2 teaspoon crushed red pepper flakes

Stir-Fry

3/4 lb. boneless beef sirloin steak, cut into thin bite-sized strips

1 medium onion, cut into thin wedges

2 medium zucchini, cut into 2 × 1/4 × 1/4-inch strips

1 small red bell pepper, cut into thin strips

1 garlic clove, minced

1 (14-oz.) can baby corn nuggets, drained, rinsed, if desired

1. Cook vermicelli to desired doneness as directed on package. Drain; cover to keep warm.

2. Meanwhile, in small bowl, combine all sauce ingredients; blend well. Set aside.

3. Spray large nonstick skillet with nonstick cooking spray. Heat over medium-high heat until hot. Add beef and onion; cook and stir 3 to 5 minutes or until beef is no longer pink and onion is crisp-tender.

SPICY BEEF AND VEGETABLES

Deli Asian cabbage salad

Fresh orange slices

Vanilla pudding with almond flavor and fortune cookies

Served at Chinese New Year celebrations, fresh oranges are said to bring good luck. While you're waiting for the pasta water to boil, assemble and cut up the ingredients needed for the stir-fry; then slice the oranges.

menu

4. Add zucchini, bell pepper and garlic; cook and stir 2 to 4 minutes or until vegetables are crisp-tender. Stir sauce well. Add sauce and corn to skillet; cook 2 to 4 minutes or until sauce is bubbly and thickened, stirring frequently. Serve beef mixture over vermicelli.

Nutrition Information Per Serving: Serving Size: 1/4 of Recipe • Calories 290 • Calories from Fat 45 • % Daily Value: Total Fat 5 g 8% • Saturated Fat 2 g 10% • Cholesterol 45 mg 15% • Sodium 720 mg 30% • Total Carbohydrate 39 g 13% • Dietary Fiber 4 g 16% • Sugars 13 g • Protein 22 g • Vitamin A 20% • Vitamin C 40% • Calcium 6% • Iron 25%
Dietary Exchanges: 1 Starch, 1 Fruit, 1 Vegetable, 2 1/2 Lean Meat OR 2 Carbohydrate, 1 Vegetable, 2 1/2 Lean Meat

PAN-FRIED STEAKS WITH MUSTARD SAUCE

Buttered new potatoes with chopped chives

Deli broccoli salad

Whole-grain rolls

Butter pecan ice cream

Cook the potatoes in a pot of boiling water or on a plate in the microwave; then start the steaks. When the potatoes are tender, drain them, then toss them with butter and chives.

Pan-Fried Steaks with Mustard Sauce

The piquant, full-bodied mustard sauce cooks in the same pan as the steaks, saving on cleanup and making the most of every flavorful morsel left in the skillet.

Yield: 4 servings

4 (4-oz.) beef tenderloin steaks (1 inch thick)

2 teaspoons coarse ground black pepper

2 garlic cloves, minced

⅓ cup dry red wine

⅓ cup beef broth

1 tablespoon country-style Dijon mustard

1. Coat both sides of steaks with pepper. Spray medium nonstick skillet with nonstick cooking spray. Heat over medium-high heat until hot. Add steaks; cook 6 to 12 minutes or until of desired doneness, turning once.

2. Add garlic; cook and stir 1 minute or until golden brown. Add wine and broth; boil 1 minute. Remove steaks from skillet; cover to keep warm. With wire whisk, stir in mustard until sauce is well blended. Serve sauce over steaks.

Nutrition Information Per Serving: Serving Size: ¼ of Recipe • Calories 160 • Calories from Fat 70 • % Daily Value: Total Fat 8 g 12% • Saturated Fat 3 g 15% • Cholesterol 50 mg 17% • Sodium 200 mg 8% • Total Carbohydrate 2 g 1% • Dietary Fiber 0 g 0% • Sugars 0 g • Protein 18 g • Vitamin A 0% • Vitamin C 0% • Calcium 0% • Iron 15%
Dietary Exchanges: 2½ Lean Meat, ½ Fat

Teriyaki Beef and Mushrooms

Distinctive shiitake mushrooms, sold in the grocery store produce aisle as well as in Asian markets, can be pricey, but they give authentic flavor to this spicy beef-and-vegetable dish.

Yield: 4 servings

1⅓ cups uncooked regular long-grain white rice

2⅔ cups water

⅓ cup teriyaki sauce

2 tablespoons dry sherry

2 teaspoons cornstarch

1 teaspoon grated gingerroot

1 tablespoon oil

¾ lb. boneless beef top sirloin steak, cut into thin bite-sized strips

6 to 7 oz. fresh shiitake mushrooms, sliced

2 cups frozen sugar snap peas

4 oz. (1 cup) fresh bean sprouts

1. Cook rice in water as directed on package.

2. Meanwhile, in small bowl, combine teriyaki sauce, sherry, cornstarch and gingerroot; blend well. Set aside.

3. Heat oil in large skillet or wok over medium-high heat until hot. Add beef; cook and stir 3 to 4 minutes or until beef is browned and of desired doneness. Remove beef from skillet; cover to keep warm.

4. In same skillet, combine mushrooms and sugar snap peas. Cover; cook over medium-high heat for 4 to 5 minutes or until peas are crisp-tender, stirring once or twice.

5. Stir cornstarch mixture until smooth. Add cornstarch mixture, beef and sprouts to skillet; cook and stir until sauce is bubbly and thickened. Serve over rice.

Nutrition Information Per Serving: Serving Size: ¼ of Recipe • Calories 420 • Calories from Fat 70 • % Daily Value: Total Fat 8 g 12% • Saturated Fat 2 g 10% • Cholesterol 45 mg 15% • Sodium 1,000 mg 42% • Total Carbohydrate 64 g 21% • Dietary Fiber 4 g 16% • Sugars 7 g • Protein 24 g • Vitamin A 4% • Vitamin C 10% • Calcium 6% • Iron 35%
Dietary Exchanges: 3½ Starch, ½ Fruit, 1 Vegetable, 1½ Lean Meat OR 4 Carbohydrate, 1 Vegetable, 1½ Lean Meat

Favorite Salisbury Steak

A traditional favorite for dressing up ground beef, Salisbury steak gets ladled with mushroom sauce for exceptional flavor.

Yield: 6 servings

Patties

1 lb. extra-lean ground beef

½ cup unseasoned dry bread crumbs

½ cup milk

1 egg white

¼ cup finely chopped onion

1 teaspoon Worcestershire sauce

¼ teaspoon salt

¼ teaspoon pepper

Gravy

¾ cup beef broth

¼ cup dry red wine or beef broth

1 tablespoon cornstarch

¼ teaspoon dried thyme leaves

1 (2.5-oz.) jar sliced mushrooms, drained

1. In medium bowl, combine all patty ingredients; mix gently. (Mixture will be moist.) Shape into 6 oval patties, about ¾ inch thick.

2. Spray large nonstick skillet with nonstick cooking spray. Heat over medium heat until hot. Add patties; cook 3 minutes on each side or until browned. Remove patties from skillet; drain, if necessary.

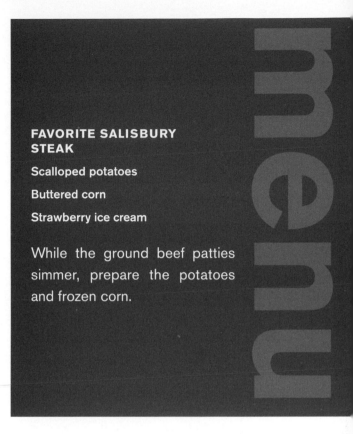

FAVORITE SALISBURY STEAK

Scalloped potatoes

Buttered corn

Strawberry ice cream

While the ground beef patties simmer, prepare the potatoes and frozen corn.

3. In small bowl, combine broth, wine, cornstarch and thyme; blend well. Pour into same skillet. Cook over low heat until mixture boils and thickens, stirring constantly. Stir in mushrooms. Return patties to skillet. Cover; simmer about 15 minutes or until patties are no longer pink in center.

Nutrition Information Per Serving: Serving Size: ⅙ of Recipe • Calories 200 • Calories from Fat 90 • % Daily Value: Total Fat 10 g 15% • Saturated Fat 4 g 20% • Cholesterol 50 mg 17% • Sodium 390 mg 16% • Total Carbohydrate 10 g 3% • Dietary Fiber 1 g 4% • Sugars 2 g • Protein 18 g • Vitamin A 0% • Vitamin C 0% • Calcium 4% • Iron 10%
Dietary Exchanges: ½ Starch, 2 Medium-Fat Meat OR ½ Carbohydrate, 2 Medium-Fat Meat

menu

GRILLED STEAK WITH TERIYAKI MUSHROOMS

Rice and vermicelli mixture

Grilled vegetable kabobs

Cheesecake wedges

Skewer favorite vegetables, such as zucchini chunks, tomato wedges and onions. Grill the vegetables, brushed with olive oil, alongside the steaks while the rice mixture cooks on the stove.

tip

To broil steak, place on broiler pan; broil 4 to 6 inches from heat using times in recipe as a guide, turning once.

Grilled Steak with Teriyaki Mushrooms

Fresh gingerroot brings an unmistakable zing to this beef dish. We call for red bell pepper in this recipe, but green or yellow could be substituted.

Yield: 3 servings

---

1 (1-lb.) boneless beef sirloin steak (1 inch thick)

3 tablespoons teriyaki sauce

1/2 teaspoon coarse ground black pepper

1/2 cup chopped red bell pepper

1 (3-oz.) can sliced mushrooms broiled in butter, undrained

---

1. Heat grill. Brush both sides of steak with 2 tablespoons of the teriyaki sauce; sprinkle both sides with black pepper.

2. When ready to grill, place steak on gas grill over medium-high heat or on charcoal grill 4 to 6 inches from medium-high coals. Cook 10 to 15 minutes or until steak is of desired doneness, turning once.

3. Meanwhile, spray medium nonstick skillet with nonstick cooking spray. Heat over medium-high heat until hot. Add bell pepper; cook and stir 2 minutes. Add mushrooms with liquid and remaining tablespoon teriyaki sauce. Cook 2 to 3 minutes or until thoroughly heated and bell pepper is tender, stirring occasionally. Serve sauce over steak.

Nutrition Information Per Serving: Serving Size: 1/3 of Recipe • Calories 200 • Calories from Fat 60 • % Daily Value: Total Fat 7 g 11% • Saturated Fat 3 g 15% • Cholesterol 80 mg 27% • Sodium 820 mg 34% • Total Carbohydrate 5 g 2% • Dietary Fiber 1 g 4% • Sugars 3 g • Protein 29 g • Vitamin A 20% • Vitamin C 35% • Calcium 0% • Iron 20%
Dietary Exchanges: 1/2 Starch, 4 Very Lean Meat, 1/2 Fat OR 1/2 Carbohydrate, 4 Very Lean Meat, 1/2 Fat

Rib-Eye Steaks with Avocado Salsa

Fresh avocado imparts a velvety texture and richness to purchased salsa; chopped red onion and fresh cilantro enhance the flavor. All together, it makes a fine, fast relish for grilled rib-eye steaks.

Yield: 4 servings

Salsa

½ cup salsa

1 medium avocado, peeled, pitted and coarsely chopped

2 tablespoons finely chopped red onion

2 tablespoons chopped fresh cilantro

Steaks

4 boneless beef rib-eye steaks (¾ inch thick)

1 teaspoon garlic salt

1. Heat grill. In medium bowl, combine all salsa ingredients; mix well.

2. When ready to grill, sprinkle both sides of each steak with garlic salt. Place steaks on gas grill over medium heat or on charcoal grill 4 to 6 inches from medium coals. Cook 8 to 12 minutes or until of desired doneness, turning once or twice. Serve steaks with salsa.

Nutrition Information Per Serving: Serving Size: ¼ of Recipe • Calories 400 • Calories from Fat 200 • % Daily Value: Total Fat 22 g 34% • Saturated Fat 7 g 35% • Cholesterol 115 mg 38% • Sodium 800 mg 33% • Total Carbohydrate 6 g 2% • Dietary Fiber 3 g 12% • Sugars 2 g • Protein 44 g • Vitamin A 8% • Vitamin C 6% • Calcium 0% • Iron 25%
Dietary Exchanges: ½ Starch, 6 Lean Meat, 1 Fat OR ½ Carbohydrate, 6 Lean Meat, 1 Fat

menu

RIB-EYE STEAKS WITH AVOCADO SALSA

Warmed flour tortillas

Green salad

Chocolate ice cream cones

Prepare the greens for the salad ahead of time but wait to toss with dressing until just before serving. Wrap the flour tortillas in foil and warm them on the grill alongside the steaks. Serve a warmed tortilla, folded into quarters or rolled, on each plate. Keep extra tortillas warm in a cloth-lined bread basket on the table.

tip

To broil steaks, place on broiler pan; broil 4 to 6 inches from heat using times in recipe as a guide, turning once or twice.

menu

**ZESTY BEEF AND NOODLE
VEGETABLE SOUP**

Grilled cheese sandwiches

Grape clusters

Grill the cheese sandwiches
while the soup simmers.

Zesty Beef and Noodle Vegetable Soup

If you don't have the tomatoes with green chiles,
use one can of each.

Yield: 4 (1¾-cup) servings

½ lb. extra-lean ground beef

3½ cups water

1 (14½-oz.) can diced tomatoes with green chiles,
    undrained

1 cup frozen mixed vegetables

1 beef bouillon cube or 1 teaspoon beef-flavor instant
    bouillon

1 (2.8-oz.) pkg. beef-flavor baked ramen noodle soup mix

4 tablespoons sour cream, if desired

1. Brown ground beef in Dutch oven or large
saucepan over medium-high heat until thoroughly cooked, stirring frequently. Drain.

2. Add water, tomatoes, vegetables, bouillon and
contents of seasoning packet from soup mix; mix
well. Bring to a boil. Break up ramen noodles;
add to soup. Simmer 3 to 5 minutes or until
noodles are tender, stirring occasionally to separate noodles.

3. Top individual servings with 1 tablespoon
sour cream.

Nutrition Information Per Serving: Serving Size: 1¾ Cups • Calories 210 •
Calories from Fat 90 • % Daily Value: Total Fat 10 g 15% • Saturated Fat 4 g 20% •
Cholesterol 40 mg 13% • Sodium 880 mg 37% • Total Carbohydrate 16 g 5% •
Dietary Fiber 2 g 8% • Sugars 4 g • Protein 14 g • Vitamin A 20% • Vitamin C 10% •
Calcium 6% • Iron 10%
Dietary Exchanges: 1 Starch, 1½ Medium-Fat Meat, ½ Fat OR 1 Carbohydrate,
1½ Medium-Fat Meat, ½ Fat

menu

EASY BEEF STROGANOFF SOUP

Refrigerated soft breadsticks

Fresh strawberries with whipped topping

Start the water for the noodles, and preheat the oven for the breadsticks. Put the breadsticks in the oven. Rinse, hull and slice the strawberries while the soup simmers. Toss the berries with a little sugar, and chill them until dessert.

Easy Beef Stroganoff Soup

In this clever variation of a favorite stew, the water in which the pasta cooked becomes the base for a creamy soup. If you wish, substitute mushroom gravy for the beef gravy.

Yield: 4 (1¼-cup) servings

2 cups water

3 oz. (1¾ cups) uncooked medium egg noodles

1 lb. lean ground beef

½ teaspoon garlic-pepper blend

1 (12-oz.) jar beef gravy

1 (2.5-oz.) jar sliced mushrooms, drained

½ cup sour cream

1. Bring water to a boil in medium saucepan. Add noodles; cook 6 to 8 minutes or until tender. Do not drain.

2. Meanwhile, in medium skillet, cook ground beef and garlic-pepper blend over medium heat for 8 to 10 minutes or until beef is browned and thoroughly cooked, stirring frequently. Drain.

3. To noodles in saucepan, add cooked ground beef, gravy, mushrooms and sour cream; cook until thoroughly heated. If desired, sprinkle individual servings with chopped fresh parsley.

Nutrition Information Per Serving: Serving Size: 1¼ Cups • Calories 420 • Calories from Fat 230 • % Daily Value: Total Fat 25 g 38% • Saturated Fat 11 g 55% • Cholesterol 105 mg 35% • Sodium 660 mg 28% • Total Carbohydrate 22 g 7% • Dietary Fiber 1 g 4% • Sugars 2 g • Protein 26 g • Vitamin A 4% • Vitamin C 0% • Calcium 6% • Iron 20%
Dietary Exchanges: 1½ Starch, 3 Medium-Fat Meat, 1½ Fat OR 1½ Carbohydrate, 3 Medium-Fat Meat, 1½ Fat

Easy Minestrone with Meatballs

Ingredients from the freezer and the pantry combine in an ingenious recipe that turns traditional minestrone soup into a robust meatball-and-potato stew.

Yield: 4 (1½-cup) servings

2 (19-oz.) cans ready-to-serve minestrone soup

12 frozen cooked Italian meatballs, slightly thawed

½ cup frozen southern-style hash-brown potatoes (from 32-oz. pkg.)

1 oz. (¼ cup) shredded fresh Parmesan cheese

1. In medium saucepan, combine all ingredients except cheese. Bring to a boil.

2. Reduce heat; simmer 10 minutes or until slightly thickened and meatballs are hot. Sprinkle individual servings with cheese.

Nutrition Information Per Serving: Serving Size: 1½ Cups • Calories 420 • Calories from Fat 210 • % Daily Value: Total Fat 23 g 35% • Saturated Fat 10 g 50% • Cholesterol 60 mg 20% • Sodium 1,820 mg 76% • Total Carbohydrate 32 g 11% • Dietary Fiber 9 g 36% • Sugars 6 g • Protein 22 g • Vitamin A 25% • Vitamin C 0% • Calcium 15% • Iron 20%
Dietary Exchanges: 2 Starch, 2 High-Fat Meat, 1½ Fat OR 2 Carbohydrate, 2 High-Fat Meat, 1½ Fat

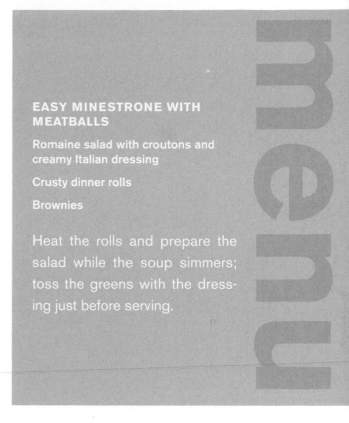

menu

EASY MINESTRONE WITH MEATBALLS

Romaine salad with croutons and creamy Italian dressing

Crusty dinner rolls

Brownies

Heat the rolls and prepare the salad while the soup simmers; toss the greens with the dressing just before serving.

menu

SPAGHETTI AND MEATBALL SOUP

Breadsticks

Italian biscotti cookies with spumoni ice cream

Bake the breadsticks (or set out purchased breadsticks) while the soup is cooking. You can make a double batch of this soup and freeze some for an ultra-speedy dinner later.

Spaghetti and Meatball Soup

Those who consider the sauce the best part of a pasta meal will love this bowl-style spaghetti soup. Sprinkle the soup with chopped fresh parsley or Parmesan cheese.

Yield: 5 (1½-cup) servings

4 cups water

4 oz. (1 cup) uncooked ready-cut spaghetti (short curved pasta)

20 frozen cooked meatballs

1 (27- to 30-oz.) jar spaghetti sauce

1. Bring water to a boil in large saucepan. Add spaghetti and meatballs; cook about 10 minutes or until spaghetti is tender. Do not drain.

2. Stir in spaghetti sauce. Cook until thoroughly heated. If desired, sprinkle individual servings with grated Parmesan cheese.

Nutrition Information Per Serving: Serving Size: 1½ Cups • Calories 510 • Calories from Fat 260 • % Daily Value: Total Fat 29 g 45% • Saturated Fat 13 g 65% • Cholesterol 75 mg 25% • Sodium 1,530 mg 64% • Total Carbohydrate 38 g 13% • Dietary Fiber 7 g 28% • Sugars 2 g • Protein 24 g • Vitamin A 15% • Vitamin C 15% • Calcium 10% • Iron 25%
Dietary Exchanges: 2½ Starch, 2½ High-Fat Meat, 1½ Fat OR 2½ Carbohydrate, 2½ High-Fat Meat, 1½ Fat

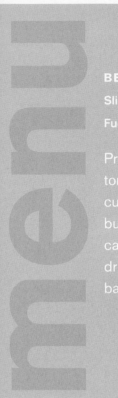

menu

BEEF AND BISCUITS

Sliced fresh tomatoes

Fudgesicles or ice cream sandwiches

Preheat the oven; then slice the tomatoes. Before baking the biscuits, brush the tops with melted butter and sprinkle them with caraway seed, sesame seed or dried thyme. While the biscuits bake, warm the stew.

Beef and Biscuits

This homestyle dish is perfect for a chilly evening. Ladle the stew into shallow soup bowls so the biscuits can soak up the gravy.

Yield: 5 servings

1 (10.2-oz.) can (5 biscuits) large refrigerated buttermilk biscuits

1 (40-oz.) can beef stew

1 cup frozen sweet peas

½ teaspoon dried thyme leaves

1 tablespoon Worcestershire sauce

1. Heat oven to 375°F. Bake biscuits as directed on can; keep warm.

2. Meanwhile, in large saucepan, combine stew, peas, thyme and Worcestershire sauce; mix well. Bring to a boil over medium-high heat. Reduce heat to medium-low; simmer 10 to 15 minutes or until thoroughly heated, stirring frequently.

3. To serve, split warm biscuits; place 2 halves on each serving plate. Spoon stew mixture over biscuit halves.

Nutrition Information Per Serving: Serving Size: ⅕ of Recipe • Calories 430 • Calories from Fat 190 • % Daily Value: Total Fat 21 g 32% • Saturated Fat 7 g 35% • Cholesterol 35 mg 12% • Sodium 1,590 mg 66% • Total Carbohydrate 44 g 15% • Dietary Fiber 5 g 20% • Sugars 7 g • Protein 16 g • Vitamin A 80% • Vitamin C 15% • Calcium 6% • Iron 20%
Dietary Exchanges: 3 Starch, 1 Medium-Fat Meat, 2½ Fat OR 3 Carbohydrate, 1 Medium-Fat Meat, 2½ Fat

Hamburger Stew
with Garlic
Mashed Potatoes

Meat and potatoes come together in a creative, hearty main course. If you like, substitute thyme for the marjoram.

Yield: 4 servings

Stew

½ lb. lean ground beef

¼ cup chopped onion

1 cup frozen mixed vegetables

1 (14.5-oz.) can diced tomatoes, drained

1 (12-oz.) jar home-style beef gravy

¼ teaspoon dried marjoram leaves

¼ teaspoon pepper

Potatoes

1 cup water

2 tablespoons margarine or butter

½ teaspoon garlic salt

½ cup milk

1⅓ cups mashed potato flakes

1 tablespoon chopped fresh parsley

1. In large nonstick skillet, brown ground beef and onion over medium-high heat until beef is thoroughly cooked, stirring occasionally. Add all remaining stew ingredients. Bring to a boil. Reduce heat to low; simmer 8 to 10 minutes or until vegetables are tender, stirring occasionally.

2. Meanwhile, in medium saucepan, bring water, margarine and garlic salt to a boil. Remove from heat; add milk. Stir in potato flakes and parsley. Cover to keep warm.

HAMBURGER STEW
WITH GARLIC
MASHED POTATOES

Sliced oranges drizzled with honey

Chocolate sandwich cookies

Before browning the ground beef, chop the onion and drain the tomatoes. While the stew simmers, slice the oranges; drizzle them with honey just before serving.

3. To serve, fluff potatoes with fork. Serve stew over potatoes.

Nutrition Information Per Serving: Serving Size: ¼ of Recipe • Calories 360 • Calories from Fat 140 • % Daily Value: Total Fat 16 g 25% • Saturated Fat 6 g 30% • Cholesterol 40 mg 13% • Sodium 1,110 mg 46% • Total Carbohydrate 36 g 12% • Dietary Fiber 4 g 16% • Sugars 5 g • Protein 18 g • Vitamin A 30% • Vitamin C 20% • Calcium 10% • Iron 15%
Dietary Exchanges: 2 Starch, 1 Vegetable, 1½ Medium-Fat Meat, 1½ Fat OR 2 Carbohydrate, 1 Vegetable, 1½ Medium-Fat Meat, 1½ Fat

menu

BEEF STEW

Refrigerated buttermilk biscuits

Lemon meringue pie

While waiting for the oven to preheat, chop and assemble the ingredients for the stew. Put the biscuits in the oven while the stew simmers. Thaw a frozen pie while you eat dinner, or serve one from the bakery.

Beef Stew

Beef-mushroom soup mix flavors and enriches this thick stew. Substitute beer, red wine or beef broth for some or all of the water called for in the recipe.

Yield: 5 (1⅓-cup) servings

¾ lb. boneless beef top sirloin steak, cut into ½-inch cubes

1 small onion, chopped

3 cups frozen southern-style hash-brown potatoes (from 32-oz. pkg.)

1½ cups thinly sliced carrots

1 cup thinly sliced celery

1 (4.5-oz.) jar sliced mushrooms, drained

1 envelope dry beef-mushroom soup mix

¼ teaspoon dried thyme leaves, crushed

¼ teaspoon pepper

3½ cups water

1. Heat nonstick Dutch oven or large saucepan over medium-high heat until hot. Add beef and onion; cook and stir 5 minutes or until beef is browned.

2. Stir in potatoes, carrots, celery and mushrooms; cook and stir 2 minutes. Add soup mix, thyme, pepper and water; mix well. Bring to a boil. Reduce heat; simmer 15 minutes or until vegetables are tender. If desired, sprinkle individual servings with chopped fresh parsley.

Nutrition Information Per Serving: Serving Size: 1⅓ Cups • Calories 200 • Calories from Fat 35 • % Daily Value: Total Fat 4 g 6% • Saturated Fat 1 g 5% • Cholesterol 35 mg 12% • Sodium 540 mg 23% • Total Carbohydrate 24 g 8% • Dietary Fiber 3 g 12% • Sugars 4 g • Protein 16 g • Vitamin A 210% • Vitamin C 15% • Calcium 4% • Iron 15%
Dietary Exchanges: 1½ Starch, 1½ Lean Meat OR 1½ Carbohydrate, 1½ Lean Meat

Beef 'n Bean Tostadas

Some time ago, salsa surpassed ketchup as the most widely purchased condiment in the United States. It's also a quick way to spice up the ground meat for this Mexican-inspired dish.

Yield: 12 tostadas; 6 servings

1 (16-oz.) can refried beans

1 (4.5-oz.) can chopped green chiles, drained

12 tostada shells

1 lb. lean ground beef

1 (16-oz.) jar salsa

1½ cups shredded lettuce

3 oz. (¾ cup) shredded Cheddar cheese

¾ cup diced tomato

1. Heat oven to 375°F. In medium bowl, combine beans and chiles; mix well. Spread 2 to 3 tablespoons bean mixture on each tostada shell; place on ungreased large cookie sheet. Bake at 375°F. for 5 to 7 minutes or until hot.

2. Meanwhile, brown ground beef in large skillet over medium heat until thoroughly cooked, stirring frequently. Drain. Stir in 1½ cups of the salsa. Cook for 2 to 3 minutes or until thoroughly heated.

3. Serve tostada shells topped with hot beef mixture, shredded lettuce, cheese, tomato and remaining salsa.

Nutrition Information Per Serving: Serving Size: ⅙ of Recipe • Calories 410 • Calories from Fat 180 • % Daily Value: Total Fat 20 g 31% • Saturated Fat 8 g 40% • Cholesterol 60 mg 20% • Sodium 1,240 mg 52% • Total Carbohydrate 33 g 11% • Dietary Fiber 7 g 28% • Sugars 5 g • Protein 24 g • Vitamin A 20% • Vitamin C 15% • Calcium 20% • Iron 20%
Dietary Exchanges: 2 Starch, 2 Medium-Fat Meat, 2 Fat OR 2 Carbohydrate, 2 Medium-Fat Meat, 2 Fat

BEEF 'N BEAN TOSTADAS

Spanish rice

Sliced fresh peaches and cream

Grate the cheese earlier in the day and refrigerate it, tightly covered, until needed. When it's time to fix supper, preheat the oven and start the rice, then prepare the tostadas. Shred the lettuce and dice the tomatoes while the tostadas bake. Slice the peaches just before serving and toss them with a little orange juice (spiked with a splash of liqueur, if desired).

Kids-Love-It Chili

This spicy tomato dish makes a good dinner as well as a warm, satisfying alternative to sugary after-school snacks.

Yield: 4 (1½-cup) servings

1 lb. lean ground beef

1 (15.5- or 15-oz.) can kidney beans, drained

1 (15.25-oz.) can whole kernel corn, drained

1 (10¾-oz.) can condensed tomato soup

2 cups water

1 tablespoon instant minced onion

2 teaspoons chili powder

2 oz. (½ cup) shredded Cheddar cheese

1. Brown ground beef in large saucepan over medium-high heat until thoroughly cooked, stirring frequently. Drain.

2. Add all remaining ingredients except cheese; mix well. Simmer 10 minutes or until thoroughly heated. Sprinkle individual servings with cheese.

Nutrition Information Per Serving: Serving Size: 1½ Cups • Calories 500 • Calories from Fat 200 • % Daily Value: Total Fat 22 g 34% • Saturated Fat 9 g 45% • Cholesterol 85 mg 28% • Sodium 1,160 mg 48% • Total Carbohydrate 43 g 14% • Dietary Fiber 7 g 28% • Sugars 11 g • Protein 32 g • Vitamin A 35% • Vitamin C 50% • Calcium 20% • Iron 25%
Dietary Exchanges: 3 Starch, 3 Lean Meat, 2 Fat OR 3 Carbohydrate, 3 Lean Meat, 2 Fat

Philly Cheese Steak Crescent Pizza

Deli roast beef and shredded mozzarella give a new twist to Philadelphia's signature sandwich.

Yield: 8 servings

---

1 (8-oz.) can refrigerated crescent dinner rolls

8 oz. thinly sliced cooked roast beef (from deli)

1 tablespoon purchased Italian salad dressing

4 to 6 oz. (1 to 1½ cups) shredded mozzarella cheese

2 tablespoons olive or vegetable oil

1 cup coarsely chopped or thinly sliced green bell pepper

1 cup coarsely chopped or thinly sliced onions

½ teaspoon beef-flavor instant bouillon

---

1. Heat oven to 375°F. Unroll dough in ungreased 13x9-inch pan. Press over bottom and ½ inch up sides. Firmly press perforations to seal. Wrap beef tightly in foil. Place both crescent dough and beef in oven. Bake at 375°F. for 10 minutes or until crust is light golden brown.

2. Arrange warm beef over partially baked crust. Brush with salad dressing. Sprinkle with cheese. Return to oven; bake an additional 8 to 10 minutes or until edges of crust are golden brown and cheese is melted.

3. Meanwhile, heat oil in medium skillet over medium heat until hot. Add bell pepper, onions and bouillon; cook and stir 3 to 5 minutes or until vegetables are tender, stirring frequently. Spoon cooked vegetables over melted cheese.

Nutrition Information Per Serving: Serving Size: ⅛ of Recipe • Calories 230 • Calories from Fat 120 • % Daily Value: Total Fat 13 g 20% • Saturated Fat 4 g 20% • Cholesterol 20 mg 7% • Sodium 650 mg 27% • Total Carbohydrate 15 g 5% • Dietary Fiber 1 g 4% • Sugars 3 g • Protein 12 g • Vitamin A 4% • Vitamin C 15% • Calcium 10% • Iron 8%
Dietary Exchanges: 1 Starch, 1½ Lean Meat, 1½ Fat OR 1 Carbohydrate, 1½ Lean Meat, 1½ Fat

menu

PHILLY CHEESE STEAK CRESCENT PIZZA

Spinach salad

Chocolate pudding

Prepare instant pudding if you haven't purchased it ready to serve. While waiting for the oven to preheat for the rolls, cut up ingredients needed for the pizza. While the pizza bakes, assemble the spinach salad, but wait to dress it until serving time.

Sassy Southwestern Burgers

Burgers may be super-easy to prepare, but that doesn't mean they have to be predictable. Blending the ground meat with salsa and taco spices results in a moist, nicely seasoned patty.

Yield: 4 sandwiches

1 lb. lean ground beef

6 tablespoons salsa

2 tablespoons taco seasoning mix (from 1.25-oz. pkg.)

4 burger buns, split

4 (1-oz.) slices hot pepper Monterey Jack cheese

1. Heat grill. In medium bowl, combine ground beef, 2 tablespoons of the salsa and the taco seasoning mix; mix well. Shape mixture into 4 patties, ½ inch thick.

2. When ready to grill, place patties on gas grill over medium heat or on charcoal grill 4 to 6 inches from medium coals. Cook 11 to 13 minutes or until patties are thoroughly cooked, turning once.

3. Meanwhile, place buns, cut side down, on grill. Cook 1 to 2 minutes or until buns are lightly toasted. Place 1 slice of cheese on each patty; cook an additional 1 minute or until cheese is melted.

4. Place patties on bottom halves of buns. Top each with 1 tablespoon salsa and top half of bun.

Nutrition Information Per Serving: Serving Size: 1 Sandwich • Calories 460 • Calories from Fat 230 • % Daily Value: Total Fat 26 g 40% • Saturated Fat 12 g 60% • Cholesterol 100 mg 33% • Sodium 910 mg 38% • Total Carbohydrate 26 g 9% • Dietary Fiber 1 g 4% • Sugars 6 g • Protein 30 g • Vitamin A 10% • Vitamin C 0% • Calcium 30% • Iron 15%
Dietary Exchanges: 1½ Starch, 3½ Medium-Fat Meat, 1½ Fat OR 1½ Carbohydrate, 3½ Medium-Fat Meat, 1½ Fat

menu

SASSY SOUTHWESTERN BURGERS

Chopped fresh vegetable salad with ranch salad dressing

Tortilla chips

Watermelon wedges

Ice cream bars

While waiting for the grill to heat, chop favorite vegetables—such as bell pepper, cucumber, tomato, carrot and onion—for the salad, and slice the watermelon. Grill the burgers last.

tip

To broil patties, place on broiler pan; broil 4 to 6 inches from heat using times in recipe as a guide, turning once. Place buns, cut side up, on broiler pan; broil 1 to 2 minutes.

**SUPER-SIMPLE
SLOPPY JOES**

Carrot and celery sticks

Deli cole slaw or potato salad

Brownies topped with vanilla ice cream

While waiting for the oven to pre-heat for the biscuits, start the sloppy Joe mixture. Prepare the carrot and celery sticks in advance or while the mixture simmers.

Super-Simple
Sloppy Joes

We're not certain who Joe was, but a couple of generations of cooks have sure enjoyed his saucy tomato-beef sandwiches.

Yield: 8 sandwiches

---

1 (1 lb. 0.3-oz.) can large refrigerated buttermilk biscuits

1 lb. lean ground beef

½ cup chopped green bell pepper

1 small onion, chopped

1 (10¾-oz.) can condensed tomato soup

¼ cup water

1¼ teaspoons chili powder

⅛ to ¼ teaspoon hot pepper sauce

---

1. Bake biscuits as directed on can.

2. Meanwhile, cook ground beef, bell pepper and onion in large skillet until beef is thoroughly cooked, stirring frequently. Drain. Stir in all remaining ingredients. Cover; simmer 10 minutes or until thoroughly heated.

3. Split warm biscuits. Spoon beef mixture onto biscuits.

Nutrition Information Per Serving: Serving Size: 1 Sandwich • Calories 350 • Calories from Fat 160 • % Daily Value: Total Fat 18 g 28% • Saturated Fat 6 g 30% • Cholesterol 35 mg 12% • Sodium 870 mg 36% • Total Carbohydrate 31 g 10% • Dietary Fiber 1 g 4% • Sugars 7 g • Protein 15 g • Vitamin A 8% • Vitamin C 30% • Calcium 4% • Iron 15%
Dietary Exchanges: 2 Starch, 1 Medium-Fat Meat, 2½ Fat OR 2 Carbohydrate, 1 Medium-Fat Meat, 2½ Fat

Italian Patty Melts

Thanks to Italian seasoning and melted mozzarella, the cheeseburger goes Continental.

Yield: 4 sandwiches

---

1 lb. lean ground beef

2 tablespoons grated Parmesan cheese

1 teaspoon dried Italian seasoning

2 teaspoons oil

1 medium green bell pepper, cut into 8 rings

4 (3/4-oz.) slices mozzarella cheese

4 sandwich buns, split

---

1. In medium bowl, combine ground beef, Parmesan cheese and Italian seasoning; mix well. Shape mixture into four 4-inch patties.

2. Heat oil in large skillet over medium-high heat until hot. Add bell pepper rings; cook 2 to 3 minutes or until crisp-tender. Remove from skillet.

3. Place patties in same skillet. Reduce heat to medium; cook 10 to 12 minutes or until thoroughly cooked, turning once. Top each patty with 2 bell pepper rings and 1 slice of the cheese. Cover; cook 1 to 2 minutes or until cheese is melted. Serve in buns.

Nutrition Information Per Serving: Serving Size: 1 Sandwich • Calories 440 • Calories from Fat 220 • % Daily Value: Total Fat 24 g 37% • Saturated Fat 9 g 45% • Cholesterol 85 mg 28% • Sodium 460 mg 19% • Total Carbohydrate 24 g 8% • Dietary Fiber 2 g 8% • Sugars 6 g • Protein 31 g • Vitamin A 6% • Vitamin C 20% • Calcium 25% • Iron 20%
Dietary Exchanges: 1 1/2 Starch, 4 Medium-Fat Meat, 1/2 Fat OR 1 1/2 Carbohydrate, 4 Medium-Fat Meat, 1/2 Fat

menu

ITALIAN PATTY MELTS

Deli Italian pasta salad

Selection of olives

Tapioca pudding and fresh blueberry parfaits

Layer the tapioca pudding and blueberries in parfait glasses and refrigerate them. Cut up the bell pepper; then prepare the patty melts.

menu

PHILADELPHIA MEATBALL HEROES

Onion rings

Strawberry gelatin with whipped topping

Make or purchase the gelatin ahead of time, or prepare it using the quick-set method and let it firm up in the refrigerator while you fix and eat dinner. Heat the oven for the onion rings, slice the peppers and onions for the entree and put the onion rings into the oven as you begin the sauce.

Philadelphia Meatball Heroes

Sautéed bell peppers and onions jazz up a hearty meatball sandwich. On another night, use the same combo to garnish chicken breasts or pork chops.

Yield: 6 sandwiches

1 (18-oz.) pkg. frozen cooked meatballs, thawed

1 (14-oz.) jar (2 cups) spaghetti sauce

1 cup sliced green bell peppers

1 cup sliced red bell peppers

1 onion, sliced

6 unsliced hot dog or hoagie buns

4 oz. (1 cup) shredded Cheddar cheese

1. In large saucepan, combine meatballs and spaghetti sauce; cook over medium heat for 10 to 12 minutes or until meatballs are hot, stirring occasionally.

2. Meanwhile, spray medium skillet with non-stick cooking spray. Add bell peppers and onion; cook over medium-high heat for 5 to 6 minutes or until peppers are crisp-tender, stirring frequently.

3. Split each bun lengthwise, cutting to but not through bottom; place on ungreased cookie sheet. Place meatballs in buns. Top each with pepper mixture and cheese. Broil 4 to 6 inches from heat for 2 to 3 minutes or until cheese is melted.

Nutrition Information Per Serving: Serving Size: 1 Sandwich • Calories 580 • Calories from Fat 320 • % Daily Value: Total Fat 35 g 54% • Saturated Fat 15 g 75% • Cholesterol 70 mg 23% • Sodium 1,490 mg 62% • Total Carbohydrate 43 g 14% • Dietary Fiber 6 g 24% • Sugars 11 g • Protein 24 g • Vitamin A 45% • Vitamin C 60% • Calcium 25% • Iron 20%
Dietary Exchanges: 2 Starch, 1 Fruit, 2½ High-Fat Meat, 2½ Fat OR 3 Carbohydrate, 2½ High-Fat Meat, 2½ Fat

Easy Steak Sandwiches

Crusty rolls are best for this moist steak drizzled with the pan juices, but don't despair if all you have is soft bread: Simply serve the sandwich with a knife and fork.

Yield: 4 sandwiches

⅓ cup beef broth

½ teaspoon garlic powder

1 teaspoon Worcestershire sauce

Dash pepper

¾ lb. beef round sandwich tip steaks (⅛ inch thick)

1 small onion, thinly sliced

4 (4- to 6-inch) French rolls, split

4 leaves romaine lettuce, if desired

1. In large nonstick skillet, combine broth, garlic powder, Worcestershire sauce and pepper. Bring to a boil. Add steaks and onion; cook over medium-high heat for 2 to 4 minutes or until beef is of desired doneness, turning once.

2. To serve, drizzle cooking liquid over cut surfaces of rolls. Layer lettuce, steak and onion in rolls.

Nutrition Information Per Serving: Serving Size: 1 Sandwich • Calories 300 • Calories from Fat 50 • % Daily Value: Total Fat 6 g 9% • Saturated Fat 2 g 10% • Cholesterol 45 mg 15% • Sodium 540 mg 23% • Total Carbohydrate 38 g 13% • Dietary Fiber 2 g 8% • Sugars 4 g • Protein 23 g • Vitamin A 6% • Vitamin C 4% • Calcium 6% • Iron 20%
Dietary Exchanges: 2½ Starch, 2 Lean Meat OR 2½ Carbohydrate, 2 Lean Meat

menu

EASY STEAK SANDWICHES

Deli three-bean salad

Cherry tomatoes

Vanilla pudding with banana slices

Prepare instant pudding if you haven't purchased it ready to serve; wait to slice the bananas until you're ready for dessert. Slice the onion and shred the lettuce, and set them aside until the sandwiches are done. While the steak mixture cooks, scoop the bean salad into a serving dish, and rinse the cherry tomatoes.

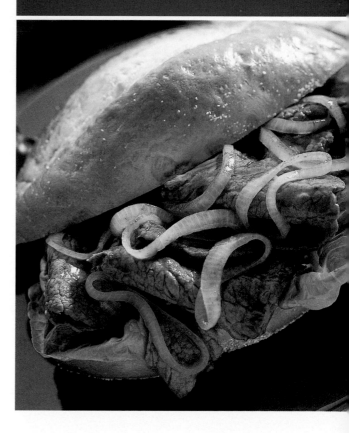

French Dip Burgers

Rather than cutting the French bread in straight slices, cut slices at an angle to afford more room for the burgers.

Yield: 4 sandwiches

1 cup water

1 (1-oz.) pkg. dry onion soup mix

2 tablespoons water

1 lb. lean ground beef

8 (½-inch-thick) diagonal slices French bread

1. Heat grill. In small saucepan, combine 1 cup water and 2 tablespoons of the soup mix. Bring to a boil. Reduce heat to low; simmer while preparing burgers.

2. In medium bowl, combine 2 tablespoons water and the remaining soup mix; mix well. Add ground beef; mix well. Shape mixture into 4 oval-shaped patties, ½ inch thick.

3. When ready to grill, place patties on gas grill over medium heat or on charcoal grill 4 to 6 inches from medium coals. Cook 11 to 13 minutes or until patties are thoroughly cooked, turning once.

4. Meanwhile, place bread slices on grill. Cook 1 to 2 minutes or until lightly toasted, turning once. Place each patty between 2 slices French bread. Serve with hot broth for dipping.

Nutrition Information Per Serving: Serving Size: 1 Sandwich • Calories 370 • Calories from Fat 150 • % Daily Value: Total Fat 17 g 26% • Saturated Fat 6 g 30% • Cholesterol 70 mg 23% • Sodium 1,000 mg 42% • Total Carbohydrate 30 g 10% • Dietary Fiber 2 g 8% • Sugars 4 g • Protein 25 g • Vitamin A 0% • Vitamin C 0% • Calcium 6% • Iron 15%
Dietary Exchanges: 2 Starch, 3 Medium-Fat Meat OR 2 Carbohydrate, 3 Medium-Fat Meat

Beefy Greek Pita Folds

The cucumber/yogurt mixture spooned over this sandwich is a variation of *tzatziki*, a classic Greek sauce that's also good with chicken.

Yield: 4 sandwiches

1 lb. lean ground beef

1 small onion, cut in half lengthwise, sliced

3 garlic cloves, minced

1 teaspoon dried oregano leaves

½ teaspoon salt

¼ cup sliced ripe olives

½ cup finely chopped peeled cucumber

½ cup chopped seeded tomato

1 (8-oz.) container low-fat plain yogurt

1 teaspoon dried dill weed

4 (6- or 7-inch) soft Greek-style pita breads, warmed

1. In medium skillet, combine ground beef, onion, garlic, oregano and ¼ teaspoon of the salt; cook over medium-high heat for 8 to 10 minutes or until beef is thoroughly cooked, stirring frequently. Drain. Stir in olives.

2. Meanwhile, in medium bowl, combine cucumber, tomato, yogurt, dill and remaining ¼ teaspoon salt; mix well.

3. Spoon ¼ of beef mixture onto half of each pita. Top each with yogurt mixture; fold other half of pita over filling. Serve with remaining yogurt mixture.

Nutrition Information Per Serving: Serving Size: 1 Sandwich • Calories 450 • Calories from Fat 160 • % Daily Value: Total Fat 18 g 28% • Saturated Fat 7 g 35% • Cholesterol 75 mg 25% • Sodium 770 mg 32% • Total Carbohydrate 42 g 14% • Dietary Fiber 2 g 8% • Sugars 5 g • Protein 29 g • Vitamin A 6% • Vitamin C 8% • Calcium 20% • Iron 20%
Dietary Exchanges: 3 Starch, 3 Medium-Fat Meat OR 3 Carbohydrate, 3 Medium-Fat Meat

menu

BEEFY GREEK PITA FOLDS

Green salad

Greek olives or ripe olives

Sliced apples and pears drizzled with maple syrup

Assemble the salad, but wait to toss it with dressing until just before serving. Chop the onion and garlic, and begin cooking them with the ground beef. Prepare the sauce and warm the pitas while the beef cooks. Cut the apples and pears just before serving, using a segmented apple cutter to core and section them with one motion.

Bistro Beef

A French restaurant of humble origins, the bistro has been widely romanticized. To make this week-night meal special, put on soft music and light candles.

Yield: 4 servings

8 slices French bread, diagonally sliced ½ inch thick

Nonstick cooking spray

2 tablespoons grated Parmesan cheese

1 tablespoon olive or vegetable oil

¾ lb. beef sirloin or flank steak, cut into thin bite-sized strips

1 small onion, sliced

1 teaspoon minced garlic (1 to 2 cloves)

1½ cups frozen bell pepper and onion stir-fry

2 tablespoons water

2 teaspoons cornstarch

1 teaspoon Worcestershire sauce

1. Place bread slices on ungreased cookie sheet. Spray bread with nonstick cooking spray; sprinkle with Parmesan cheese. Broil 4 to 6 inches from heat for 1 to 2 minutes or until lightly browned. Set aside.

2. Heat oil in large skillet over medium-high heat until hot. Add beef, onion and garlic; cook 3 to 4 minutes or until beef is browned, stirring occasionally. Add bell pepper and onion stir-fry; cook 2 to 3 minutes or until crisp-tender.

3. In small bowl, combine water, cornstarch and Worcestershire sauce; blend well. Add to beef mixture; cook and stir until slightly thickened.

4. Place 2 toasted bread slices on each of 4 individual serving plates. Top each with beef mixture.

menu

BISTRO BEEF

Broccoli spears sprinkled with Parmesan cheese

Fresh mixed berries and cream

Rinse and chill the berries until you are ready for dessert. Cut the French bread, steak, onion and garlic before you begin to cook. Steam or microwave the broccoli just before you begin to cook the beef.

Nutrition Information Per Serving: Serving Size: ¼ of Recipe • Calories 300 • Calories from Fat 90 • % Daily Value: Total Fat 10 g 15% • Saturated Fat 3 g 15% • Cholesterol 45 mg 15% • Sodium 400 mg 17% • Total Carbohydrate 31 g 10% • Dietary Fiber 3 g 12% • Sugars 4 g • Protein 21 g • Vitamin A 4% • Vitamin C 8% • Calcium 8% • Iron 15%
Dietary Exchanges: 2 Starch, 2 Lean Meat, ½ Fat OR 2 Carbohydrate, 2 Lean Meat, ½ Fat

menu

CHILI DOGS

Carrot sticks

Potato chips

Apple wedges

While the grill heats, prepare the carrot sticks. Cut the apples just before serving.

tip

To broil hot dogs, place on broiler pan; broil 4 to 6 inches from heat using times in recipe as a guide, turning frequently. Place buns, cut side up, on broiler pan; broil 30 to 60 seconds.

Chili Dogs

Supper doesn't get more homey—or more popular with kids—than this. For those who like their chili fiery, set out a bottle of hot-pepper sauce.

Yield: 6 sandwiches

6 hot dogs

1 (15-oz.) can spicy chili beans, undrained

6 hot dog buns, split

¼ cup chopped onion, if desired

3 (¾-oz.) slices American cheese, each cut into 4 strips

1. Heat grill. When ready to grill, place hot dogs on gas grill over medium heat or on charcoal grill 4 to 6 inches from medium-high coals. Cook 5 to 6 minutes or until thoroughly heated, turning frequently.

2. Meanwhile, heat beans in small saucepan over medium heat until hot.

3. Place buns, cut side down, on grill; cook 30 to 60 seconds or until lightly toasted.

4. Place hot dogs in buns. Top each with about ¼ cup beans, onion and 2 cheese strips. If desired, place sandwiches on grill; cover grill and heat until cheese is melted.

Nutrition Information Per Serving: Serving Size: 1 Sandwich • Calories 370 • Calories from Fat 170 • % Daily Value: Total Fat 19 g 29% • Saturated Fat 8 g 40% • Cholesterol 35 mg 12% • Sodium 1,170 mg 49% • Total Carbohydrate 35 g 12% • Dietary Fiber 4 g 16% • Sugars 7 g • Protein 14 g • Vitamin A 4% • Vitamin C 0% • Calcium 15% • Iron 15%
Dietary Exchanges: 2½ Starch, 1 High-Fat Meat, 2 Fat OR 2½ Carbohydrate, 1 High-Fat Meat, 2 Fat

Crescent Dogs

Here's a variation on the beloved "pig in a blanket," with melted cheese added to make the combo even more tasty.

Yield: 8 sandwiches

---

8 hot dogs

4 (¾-oz.) slices American cheese, each cut into 6 strips

1 (8-oz.) can refrigerated crescent dinner rolls

---

1. Heat oven to 375°F. Slit hot dogs to within ½ inch of ends. Insert 3 strips of cheese into each slit.

2. Separate dough into triangles. Wrap dough triangle around each hot dog. Place on ungreased cookie sheet, cheese side up.

3. Bake at 375°F. for 12 to 15 minutes or until golden brown.

Nutrition Information Per Serving: Serving Size: 1 Sandwich • Calories 330 • Calories from Fat 230 • % Daily Value: Total Fat 26 g 40% • Saturated Fat 10 g 50% • Cholesterol 40 mg 13% • Sodium 1,010 mg 42% • Total Carbohydrate 13 g 4% • Dietary Fiber 0 g 0% • Sugars 3 g • Protein 11 g • Vitamin A 2% • Vitamin C 0% • Calcium 8% • Iron 8%
Dietary Exchanges: 1 Starch, 1 High-Fat Meat, 3½ Fat OR 1 Carbohydrate, 1 High-Fat Meat, 3½ Fat

CRESCENT DOGS

Vegetable soup

Chocolate chip cookies

Simmer the soup while the crescent dogs bake. Garnish the soup, if you like, with chopped fresh herbs, grated Parmesan cheese, oyster crackers or salad croutons.

menu

pork & lamb

OPPOSITE PAGE:
Chili-Charred Fajita Kabobs, page 98

☺ **Kid-Pleasing Recipe**
🕐 **20-Minutes-or-Less Recipe**

menu

**PORK, BROCCOLI AND
NOODLE SKILLET**

Carrot and celery sticks

Dinner rolls

Vanilla pudding and fruit cocktail

Prepare instant pudding if you haven't purchased it ready to serve. Start the water for the noodles and preheat the oven, then cut up the pork, mushrooms and garlic. Warm the rolls while the pork cooks. For a pretty touch, layer the pudding and fruit cocktail in a sundae glass.

Pork, Broccoli and Noodle Skillet

Broccoli florets bring flavor and color contrast to this soothing pork dish in mushroom gravy.

Yield: 5 (1½-cup) servings

6 oz. (4 cups) uncooked dumpling egg noodles

1 (14-oz.) pkg. frozen broccoli florets

1 tablespoon margarine or butter

1 lb. pork tenderloin, cut crosswise into ¼-inch slices

1 cup sliced fresh mushrooms

1 garlic clove, minced

1 (12-oz.) jar mushroom gravy

1 tablespoon Worcestershire sauce

1. In Dutch oven or large saucepan, cook noodles as directed on package, adding broccoli during last 3 to 5 minutes of cooking time. Cook until noodles and broccoli are tender. Drain. Return to saucepan; cover to keep warm.

2. Meanwhile, melt margarine in 12-inch nonstick skillet over medium-high heat. Add pork; cook and stir 3 to 5 minutes or until browned. Add mushrooms and garlic; cook and stir 2 to 4 minutes or until mushrooms are tender.

3. Add gravy and Worcestershire sauce; mix well. Cook and stir over medium-high heat until mixture is bubbly and thickened.

4. Add pork mixture to cooked noodles and broccoli; toss gently to coat.

Nutrition Information Per Serving: Serving Size: 1½ Cups • Calories 320; Calories from Fat 80 • % Daily Value: Total Fat 9 g 14% • Saturated Fat 2 g 10% • Cholesterol 85 mg 28% • Sodium 510 mg 21% • Total Carbohydrate 33 g 11% • Dietary Fiber 3 g 12% • Sugars 3 g • Protein 27 g • Vitamin A 10% • Vitamin C 40% • Calcium 4% • Iron 20%
Dietary Exchanges: 2 Starch, 1 Vegetable, 2½ Lean Meat OR 2 Carbohydrate, 1 Vegetable, 2½ Lean Meat

Spicy Thai Pork Lo Mein

While Americans are most used to peanut butter as a sandwich spread, cooks in Thailand, Indonesia and Africa use it to add richness, texture and nuttiness to sauces. In this recipe, peanut butter is a perfect base for a pork-and-noodle sauce enlivened with lime juice and pureed chili peppers.

Yield: 4 (1½-cup) servings

3 boneless pork loin chops, cut into ¾-inch pieces

2 (1 lb. 5-oz.) pkg. frozen lo mein stir-fry meal starter

3 tablespoons peanut butter

2 tablespoons lime juice

2 to 4 teaspoons chili puree with garlic

1. Spray 12-inch nonstick skillet or wok with nonstick cooking spray. Heat over medium-high heat until hot. Add pork; cook and stir 5 minutes. Add frozen vegetables with noodles and sauce from packets. Reduce heat to medium; cover and cook 7 to 10 minutes or until vegetables are crisp-tender and pork is no longer pink in center, stirring frequently.

2. Meanwhile, in small bowl, combine peanut butter, lime juice and chili puree; blend well.

3. Add peanut butter mixture to skillet; cook and stir until thoroughly heated.

Nutrition Information Per Serving: Serving Size: 1½ Cups • Calories 430 • Calories from Fat 120 • % Daily Value: Total Fat 13 g 20% • Saturated Fat 3 g 15% • Cholesterol 50 mg 17% • Sodium 1,540 mg 64% • Total Carbohydrate 46 g 15% • Dietary Fiber 7 g 28% • Sugars 14 g • Protein 29 g • Vitamin A 90% • Vitamin C 45% • Calcium 8% • Iron 20%
Dietary Exchanges: 2 Starch, 1 Fruit, 1 Vegetable, 3 Lean Meat, ½ Fat OR 3 Carbohydrate, 1 Vegetable, 3 Lean Meat, ½ Fat

SPICY THAI PORK LO MEIN

Watermelon and honeydew melon wedges

Lemon pudding in sponge cake cups

Cut up the pork first. Cut the melons and arrange on salad plates. For quick lemon tarts, spoon prepared pudding into purchased sponge cake cups.

Garlic and Basil Pork and Pasta

Fresh basil is one of summer's pleasures. Its natural affinity for fresh tomatoes comes out in this garlicky pasta dish.

Yield: 4 (1-cup) servings

4 oz. uncooked linguine, broken in half

2 medium zucchini (6 to 8 inches long)

½ lb. ground pork

2 garlic cloves, minced

1 tablespoon oil

2 medium tomatoes, seeded, coarsely chopped

3 tablespoons chopped fresh basil

½ teaspoon salt

⅛ teaspoon pepper

¼ cup grated Parmesan cheese

1. Cook linguine to desired doneness as directed on package.

2. Meanwhile, cut zucchini lengthwise into ¼-inch-thick slices. Cut each slice lengthwise into long ¼-inch-thick strips. Set aside.

3. Heat large skillet or wok over medium-high heat until hot. Add pork and 1 of the minced garlic cloves; cook and stir until pork is no longer pink, gently breaking pork into large bite-sized pieces. Remove from skillet; drain.

4. In same skillet, heat oil until hot. Add zucchini and remaining minced garlic clove; cook and stir 5 to 7 minutes or until zucchini is tender.

5. Drain linguine; cover to keep warm.

GARLIC AND BASIL PORK AND PASTA

Brown-and-serve dinner rolls

Kiwi fruit

Put the water on to boil for the pasta, and preheat the oven for the rolls. While the water is heating, prepare the zucchini, garlic, tomatoes and basil. When the linguine goes into the boiling water, put the rolls into the oven. Slice the kiwi when you are ready for dessert.

menu

6. To zucchini in skillet, add tomatoes, basil, salt and pepper; cook and stir until tomatoes are thoroughly heated. Add cooked linguine and pork; cook and stir until thoroughly heated. Sprinkle with cheese.

Nutrition Information Per Serving: Serving Size: 1 Cup • Calories 310 • Calories from Fat 130 • % Daily Value: Total Fat 14 g 22% • Saturated Fat 5 g 25% • Cholesterol 40 mg 13% • Sodium 420 mg 18% • Total Carbohydrate 28 g 9% • Dietary Fiber 3 g 12% • Sugars 4 g • Protein 18 g • Vitamin A 15% • Vitamin C 25% • Calcium 10% • Iron 15%
Dietary Exchanges: 1½ Starch, 1 Vegetable, 2 Lean Meat, 1½ Fat OR 1½ Carbohydrate, 1 Vegetable, 2 Lean Meat, 1½ Fat

Nutrition Information Per Serving: Serving Size: ¼ of Recipe • Calories 440 • Calories from Fat 120 • % Daily Value: Total Fat 13 g 20% • Saturated Fat 4 g 20% • Cholesterol 70 mg 23% • Sodium 510 mg 21% • Total Carbohydrate 52 g 17% • Dietary Fiber 2 g 8% • Sugars 11 g • Protein 29 g • Vitamin A 10% • Vitamin C 15% • Calcium 8% • Iron 20%
Dietary Exchanges: 2 Starch, 1½ Fruit, 3 Lean Meat, ½ Fat OR 3½ Carbohydrate, 3 Lean Meat, ½ Fat

Tex-Mex Pineapple Pork Chops

Rice absorbs flavor from cooking it with the pineapple. Since the center-cut pork chops cook in the same pot, cleanup is simple.

Yield: 4 servings

1 tablespoon oil

4 (4- to 6-oz.) center-cut pork chops (¾ inch thick)

5 garlic cloves, minced

1½ cups water

1 (8-oz.) can crushed pineapple in unsweetened juice, undrained

1 cup uncooked regular long-grain white rice

1 cup salsa

2 tablespoons sour cream

2 tablespoons chopped fresh cilantro or parsley

1. Heat oil in large nonstick skillet or Dutch oven over medium-high heat until hot. Add pork chops; cook 1 to 2 minutes or just until they begin to brown, turning once. Add garlic; cook and stir 30 to 45 seconds.

2. Add water, pineapple with liquid and rice; mix well. Bring to a boil. Reduce heat to medium-low; cover and simmer 20 minutes or until pork is no longer pink in center, rice is tender and liquid is absorbed.

3. To serve, arrange pork chops on serving platter. Add salsa and sour cream to rice mixture; mix well. Cook 1 minute or until thoroughly heated. Spoon rice mixture around pork chops. Sprinkle with cilantro. If desired, serve with additional salsa or sour cream.

Polynesian Pork
on Rice

This quick pork dish contrasts sweet and tangy, tender and crunchy.

Yield: 4 servings

1 ⅓ cups uncooked regular long-grain white rice

2 ⅔ cups water

2 tablespoons soy sauce

2 tablespoons dry sherry or apple juice

1 tablespoon cornstarch

4 boneless pork loin chops (⅜ to ½ inch thick)

1 tablespoon oil

1 garlic clove, minced

1 (1-lb.) pkg. frozen broccoli florets, carrots and water chestnuts

1 (8¼-oz.) can pineapple chunks in syrup, undrained

1. Cook rice in water as directed on package.

2. Meanwhile, in shallow dish, combine soy sauce, sherry and cornstarch; blend well. Add pork chops; turn to coat. Let stand at room temperature for 5 minutes to marinate.

3. Heat oil in large skillet over medium-high heat until hot. Remove pork chops from marinade; reserve marinade. Place pork chops in skillet. Reduce heat to medium; cover and cook 8 to 10 minutes or until pork is no longer pink in center, turning once. Remove pork chops from skillet; cover to keep warm.

4. Add garlic and frozen vegetables to skillet. Cover; cook over medium-high heat for 4 to 6 minutes or until vegetables are tender.

5. Stir in pineapple with syrup and reserved marinade. Cook and stir until bubbly and thickened. Serve pork chops and vegetables over rice.

menu

POLYNESIAN PORK ON RICE

Cherry tomatoes

Pound cake slices with whipped cream

This all-in-one-meal needs little else to make it complete; just rinse some cherry tomatoes and add a few to each plate.

Nutrition Information Per Serving: Serving Size: ¼ of Recipe • Calories 470 • Calories from Fat 90 • % Daily Value: Total Fat 10 g 15% • Saturated Fat 3 g 15% • Cholesterol 50 mg 17% • Sodium 220 mg 9% • Total Carbohydrate 69 g 23% • Dietary Fiber 4 g 16% • Sugars 14 g • Protein 25 g • Vitamin A 60% • Vitamin C 30% • Calcium 6% • Iron 20%
Dietary Exchanges: 3½ Starch, 1 Fruit, 1 Vegetable, 2 Lean Meat OR 4½ Carbohydrate, 1 Vegetable, 2 Lean Meat

SKILLET HAM AND PENNE PASTA

Dinner rolls

Orange sorbet and vanilla ice cream

Put the water on for the pasta; then slice the green onions, ham, zucchini and tomatoes. While the skillet mixture cooks, heat the rolls in the oven. Purchase orange sorbet and vanilla ice cream swirled together in a single container, or simply put a scoop of each into individual dishes.

Skillet Ham and Penne Pasta

This colorful supper combines yellow corn, red tomato and green zucchini in a creamy sauce flavored with shredded fresh Parmesan cheese.

Yield: 4 (1½-cup) servings

8 oz. (about 2½ cups) uncooked penne (tube-shaped pasta)

1 tablespoon margarine or butter

1 cup frozen whole kernel corn

½ cup sliced green onions

6 oz. cooked ham, cut into 1½ × ¼ × ¼-inch julienne strips (1 cup)

1 medium zucchini, cut into 1½ × ¼ × ¼-inch julienne strips

4 Italian plum tomatoes, quartered, sliced (2 cups)

¼ teaspoon salt

⅛ teaspoon freshly ground black pepper

½ cup half-and-half

1 oz. (¼ cup) shredded fresh Parmesan cheese

1. Cook penne to desired doneness as directed on package. Drain; cover to keep warm.

2. Meanwhile, melt margarine in 12-inch non-stick skillet over medium-high heat. Add corn, onions, ham and zucchini; cook and stir 4 to 6 minutes or until vegetables are crisp-tender.

3. Add cooked penne and all remaining ingredients except cheese. Reduce heat to medium; cook and stir 3 to 5 minutes or until thoroughly heated. Stir in cheese.

Nutrition Information Per Serving: Serving Size: 1½ Cups • Calories 420 • Calories from Fat 110 • % Daily Value: Total Fat 12 g 18% • Saturated Fat 5 g 25% • Cholesterol 35 mg 12% • Sodium 920 mg 38% • Total Carbohydrate 56 g 19% • Dietary Fiber 4 g 16% • Sugars 8 g • Protein 21 g • Vitamin A 20% • Vitamin C 25% • Calcium 15% • Iron 20%
Dietary Exchanges: 3½ Starch, 1 Vegetable, 1½ Very Lean Meat, 1½ Fat OR 3½ Carbohydrate, 1 Vegetable, 1½ Very Lean Meat, 1½ Fat

Skillet Canadian Bacon and Potatoes

Potatoes are classic comfort food, especially when they're blanketed in a warm, creamy sauce.

Yield: 4 servings

3½ cups water

2 teaspoons margarine or butter

1 (7.8-oz.) pkg. creamy scalloped potato mix

1¼ cups milk

½ lb. Canadian bacon or cooked ham slices, cut into strips

1 (9-oz.) pkg. frozen sugar snap peas in a pouch, thawed, drained

1. In large nonstick skillet, combine water and margarine. Bring to a boil over medium-high heat. Stir in potato slices, reserving sauce mix packet; return to a boil. Boil 15 minutes.

2. Do not drain potatoes. Stir in contents of sauce mix packet from potatoes, milk, Canadian bacon and peas. Reduce heat to medium; cook an additional 4 to 5 minutes or until sauce is slightly thickened, stirring occasionally. If desired, add pepper to taste.

Nutrition Information Per Serving: Serving Size: ¼ of Recipe • Calories 390 • Calories from Fat 90 • % Daily Value: Total Fat 10 g 15% • Saturated Fat 3 g 15% • Cholesterol 35 mg 12% • Sodium 1,720 mg 72% • Total Carbohydrate 54 g 18% • Dietary Fiber 5 g 20% • Sugars 11 g • Protein 20 g • Vitamin A 6% • Vitamin C 8% • Calcium 15% • Iron 8%
Dietary Exchanges: 2½ Starch, 1 Fruit, 1 Vegetable, 1½ Very Lean Meat, 1½ Fat OR 3½ Carbohydrate, 1 Vegetable, 1½ Very Lean Meat, 1½ Fat

menu

SKILLET CANADIAN BACON AND POTATOES

Watercress tossed with balsamic vinaigrette

Brownies

Applesauce sprinkled with cinnamon

Make the brownies ahead of time or purchase them at the bakery. While the potato mix boils, rinse and drain the greens, substituting baby spinach if watercress isn't available. Toss greens with dressing just before serving. Sprinkle the applesauce with cinnamon just before serving.

Creamy Scalloped Potatoes and Ham Supper

With the addition of ham and vegetables, a favorite potato dish becomes an all-in-one meal.

Yield: 4 (1¼-cup) servings

3½ cups water

1 (7.8-oz.) pkg. sour cream and chives potato mix

1 cup milk

2 cups cubed cooked ham

2 cups frozen mixed vegetables, thawed

1 teaspoon prepared mustard

1. Bring water to a boil in large saucepan over high heat. Stir in potato slices, reserving sauce mix packet. Boil 15 minutes.

2. Stir in milk, contents of sauce mix packet from potatoes, ham, vegetables and mustard. Reduce heat to medium; cook and stir 4 to 5 minutes or until mixture is thoroughly heated and sauce is of desired consistency, stirring frequently.

Nutrition Information Per Serving: Serving Size: 1¼ Cups • Calories 380 • Calories from Fat 80 • % Daily Value: Total Fat 9 g 14% • Saturated Fat 4 g 20% • Cholesterol 45 mg 15% • Sodium 1,950 mg 81% • Total Carbohydrate 53 g 18% • Dietary Fiber 4 g 16% • Sugars 6 g • Protein 21 g • Vitamin A 30% • Vitamin C 10% • Calcium 15% • Iron 10%
Dietary Exchanges: 3 Starch, 1 Vegetable, 1½ Lean Meat, ½ Fat OR 3 Carbohydrate, 1 Vegetable, 1½ Lean Meat, ½ Fat

Ham Dijon Pasta

If you have leftover ham, you can use it in this recipe. Otherwise, ask the deli staff to cut you a single chunk of ham rather than sandwich slices.

Yield: 3 (1²/₃-cup) servings

---

8 oz. (3½ cups) uncooked bow tie pasta (farfalle)

6 oz. lean cooked ham, cut into 1 × ¼ × ¼-inch strips (1½ cups)

¼ cup whipping cream

1 tablespoon Dijon mustard

2 tablespoons sliced green onions

---

1. Cook pasta to desired doneness as directed on package, adding ham during last minute of cooking time. Drain; place in serving bowl.

2. Meanwhile, in small bowl, combine whipping cream and mustard; blend well. Add cream mixture and onions to cooked pasta and ham; toss gently to coat.

Nutrition Information Per Serving: Serving Size: 1²/₃ Cups • Calories 420 • Calories from Fat 110 • % Daily Value: Total Fat 12 g 18% • Saturated Fat 6 g 30% • Cholesterol 55 mg 18% • Sodium 950 mg 40% • Total Carbohydrate 58 g 19% • Dietary Fiber 2 g 8% • Sugars 3 g • Protein 21 g • Vitamin A 6% • Vitamin C 0% • Calcium 4% • Iron 20%
Dietary Exchanges: 4 Starch, 1½ Lean Meat, 1 Fat OR 4 Carbohydrate, 1½ Lean Meat, 1 Fat

HAM DIJON PASTA

Buttered whole green beans

Raspberry gelatin with whipped topping

If you haven't purchased the gelatin ready to serve, prepare using the shortcut method with ice cubes, then refrigerate it while the pasta cooks. It will be quick-set and ready to eat in 30 minutes.

menu

menu

CREAMY BOW TIE PASTA WITH BROCCOLI AND HAM

Salad with garlicky dressing and croutons

Sliced strawberries

While the pasta water comes to a boil, wash and drain the greens and add any other salad ingredients to the bowl. Make quick croutons with toasted rye bread: Break or cut the toast into small pieces. Add dressing and croutons just before serving. Once the pasta has been drained and mixed with the Alfredo sauce, rinse and slice the berries and refrigerate them until dessert.

Creamy Bow Tie Pasta with Broccoli and Ham

Bow tie pasta, known in Italy as *farfalle* ("butterflies") or *farfallete* ("little butterflies"), is both visually appetizing and easy to eat. Chunks of ham give a pleasant burst of salty contrast to the creamy sauce.

Yield: 5 (1¼-cup) servings

---

6 oz. (2 cups) uncooked bow tie pasta (farfalle)

2 cups frozen broccoli florets

1 (10-oz.) container refrigerated Alfredo sauce

2 cups (about ¾ lb.) diced cooked ham

1 (4-oz.) can mushroom pieces and stems, drained

---

1. Cook pasta to desired doneness as directed on package, adding broccoli during last 3 minutes of cooking time. Drain; return to saucepan.

2. Add Alfredo sauce, ham and mushrooms; cook over medium-low heat until thoroughly heated, stirring occasionally.

Nutrition Information Per Serving: Serving Size: 1¼ Cups • Calories 410 • Calories from Fat 200 • % Daily Value: Total Fat 22 g 34% • Saturated Fat 11 g 55% • Cholesterol 65 mg 22% • Sodium 1,130 mg 47% • Total Carbohydrate 32 g 11% • Dietary Fiber 2 g 8% • Sugars 3 g • Protein 20 g • Vitamin A 2% • Vitamin C 10% • Calcium 10% • Iron 10%
Dietary Exchanges: 2 Starch, 1 Vegetable, 1½ Lean Meat, 3 Fat OR 2 Carbohydrate, 1 Vegetable, 1½ Lean Meat, 3 Fat

Cajun Black Beans with Sausage and Corn

This dish falls on the mild side of Cajun cuisine. If you like more fiery overtones, shake in a few drops of hot pepper sauce or a bit of cayenne.

Yield: 4 (1¼-cup) servings

2 tablespoons oil

2 garlic cloves, minced

1 cup frozen bell pepper and onion stir-fry

1½ cups frozen whole kernel corn

½ lb. cooked kielbasa or Polish sausage, coarsely chopped

½ teaspoon salt

¼ teaspoon black and red pepper blend

½ teaspoon dried thyme leaves

1½ cups chopped fresh tomatoes

1 (15-oz.) can black beans, drained, rinsed

1. Heat oil in large skillet over medium-high heat until hot. Add garlic; cook and stir 1 minute. Add bell pepper and onion stir-fry; cook and stir 2 to 3 minutes or until crisp-tender.

2. Add corn, kielbasa, salt, pepper blend and thyme; mix well. Cook 3 to 5 minutes or until corn is tender, stirring occasionally.

3. Add tomatoes and beans; cook 3 to 5 minutes or until thoroughly heated, stirring occasionally.

Nutrition Information Per Serving: Serving Size: 1¼ Cups • Calories 390 • Calories from Fat 210 • % Daily Value: Total Fat 23 g 35% • Saturated Fat 7 g 35% • Cholesterol 40 mg 13% • Sodium 1,110 mg 46% • Total Carbohydrate 30 g 10% • Dietary Fiber 7 g 28% • Sugars 5 g • Protein 15 g • Vitamin A 10% • Vitamin C 20% • Calcium 6% • Iron 15%
Dietary Exchanges: 2 Starch, 1½ High-Fat Meat, 2 Fat OR 2 Carbohydrate, 1½ High-Fat Meat, 2 Fat

menu

CAJUN BLACK BEANS WITH SAUSAGE AND CORN

Rice

Fudge swirl ice cream

Put the water on to boil for the rice before you begin preparing the bean mixture, For extra flavor, cook the rice in chicken or beef broth instead of water.

PEPPERONI-RAVIOLI SUPPER

Antipasto of marinated mushrooms, ripe olives and pickled peppers

Garlic breadsticks

Lemon sorbet

Arrange the antipasto items on a serving plate. Add rolled cold cut slices or cubes of cheese if you wish. While the ravioli cooks, bake the garlic breadsticks in the oven. If you don't have bread-sticks, butter slices of Italian bread or split rolls, sprinkle with garlic powder, wrap in foil and warm in a 350°F oven for 10 minutes or so.

Pepperoni-Ravioli Supper

For greater color contrast, look for green ravioli (pasta colored with spinach).

Yield: 5 (1⅓-cup) servings

---

2 (9-oz.) pkg. refrigerated cheese-filled ravioli

1 (28-oz.) jar spaghetti sauce

1 (4.5-oz.) jar sliced mushrooms, drained

1 (3.5-oz.) pkg. pepperoni slices, halved (about 1 cup)

4 oz. (1 cup) shredded mozzarella cheese

---

1. Cook ravioli to desired doneness as directed on package. Drain; cover to keep warm.

2. Meanwhile, in large saucepan, combine spaghetti sauce, mushrooms and pepperoni; mix well. Bring to a boil. Reduce heat; simmer 8 to 10 minutes or until sauce is slightly thickened, stirring occasionally.

3. Carefully stir cooked ravioli into sauce mixture. Spoon onto serving platter. Sprinkle with cheese.

Nutrition Information Per Serving: Serving Size: 1⅓ Cups • Calories 590 • Calories from Fat 240 • % Daily Value: Total Fat 27 g 42% • Saturated Fat 12 g 60% • Cholesterol 115 mg 38% • Sodium 1,630 mg 68% • Total Carbohydrate 57 g 19% • Dietary Fiber 6 g 24% • Sugars 3 g • Protein 29 g • Vitamin A 20% • Vitamin C 15% • Calcium 40% • Iron 20%
Dietary Exchanges: 4 Starch, 2½ High-Fat Meat, 1 Fat OR 4 Carbohydrate, 2½ High-Fat Meat, 1 Fat

Skillet Pizza Potatoes

Pork sausage and tomato sauce give the distinctive flavors of sausage pizza to this easy stove-top cheese and potato dish.

Yield: 5 (1½-cup) servings

1 lb. bulk Italian pork sausage

½ cup pepperoni slices (about 3 oz.)

1 (14-oz.) jar pizza sauce

½ cup water

1 (28-oz.) pkg. frozen potatoes O'Brien with onions and peppers

4 oz. (1 cup) shredded Italian cheese blend

1. Brown sausage in Dutch oven or 12-inch nonstick skillet over medium-high heat until no longer pink, stirring frequently. Add pepperoni; cook 2 minutes. Drain.

2. Add pizza sauce and water; mix well. Add potatoes; stir to mix. Reduce heat to medium; cover and cook 10 to 15 minutes or until potatoes are tender, stirring occasionally.

3. Sprinkle with cheese. Remove from heat; cover and let stand 5 minutes or until cheese is melted.

Nutrition Information Per Serving: Serving Size: 1½ Cups • Calories 540 • Calories from Fat 300 • % Daily Value: Total Fat 33 g 51% • Saturated Fat 13 g 65% • Cholesterol 80 mg 27% • Sodium 1,710 mg 71% • Total Carbohydrate 35 g 12% • Dietary Fiber 4 g 16% • Sugars 7 g • Protein 26 g • Vitamin A 15% • Vitamin C 25% • Calcium 20% • Iron 20%
Dietary Exchanges: 2 Starch, ½ Fruit, 3 High-Fat Meat, 1½ Fat OR 2½ Carbohydrate, 3 High-Fat Meat, 1½ Fat

SKILLET PIZZA POTATOES

Romaine lettuce with sliced olives and vinaigrette

Chocolate cookies

While the potato mixture simmers, rinse and drain the greens (unless you've purchased pre-washed romaine) and slice in the olives. Or, in the supermarket, look for jars of "salad olives"—broken pieces that are perfect when you don't need whole olives.

Pork with Peachy Plum Sauce

Plum sauce, available in Asian markets and the supermarket's international aisle, brings tangy sweetness to an easy pork entree.

Yield: 4 servings

2 cups uncooked regular long-grain white rice

4 cups water

1/2 cup purchased Chinese plum sauce

1/4 cup apple juice

1 tablespoon soy sauce

2 teaspoons cornstarch

1 tablespoon oil

1 lb. pork tenderloin, halved lengthwise, thinly sliced

2 garlic cloves, minced

3/4 cup cut (1-inch) green onions

1/2 green bell pepper, cut into thin strips

2 medium peaches, peeled, sliced

1 tablespoon lemon juice

1. Cook rice in water as directed on package.

2. Meanwhile, in small bowl, combine plum sauce, apple juice, soy sauce and cornstarch; blend well. Set aside.

3. Heat oil in large skillet or wok over medium-high heat until hot. Add pork and garlic; cook and stir 4 minutes. Add onions and bell pepper; cook and stir 2 to 3 minutes or until vegetables are crisp-tender and pork is no longer pink in center.

4. Stir cornstarch mixture until smooth. Add to skillet; cook and stir until sauce is bubbly and thickened. Stir in peaches and lemon juice; cook until thoroughly heated. Serve over rice.

menu

PORK WITH PEACHY PLUM SAUCE

Green peas

Coffee ice cream drizzled with chocolate syrup

Start the rice; then slice the pork and prepare the garlic, green onions and bell pepper. Peel and slice the peaches and toss them with the lemon juice to prevent discoloration. While the pork is cooking, heat the peas.

Nutrition Information Per Serving: Serving Size: 1/4 of Recipe • Calories 620 • Calories from Fat 70 • % Daily Value: Total Fat 8 g 12% • Saturated Fat 2 g 10% • Cholesterol 65 mg 22% • Sodium 790 mg 33% • Total Carbohydrate 105 g 35% • Dietary Fiber 3 g 12% • Sugars 26 g • Protein 31 g • Vitamin A 8% • Vitamin C 20% • Calcium 6% • Iron 30%
Dietary Exchanges: 5 Starch, 2 Fruit, 2 Lean Meat OR 7 Carbohydrate, 2 Lean Meat

menu

PORK WITH ORANGE-GLAZED ONIONS AND PEA PODS

Carrot sticks

Couscous

Navel oranges

Peel and cut the carrots, or rinse baby-cut carrots. Slice the pork and onions; trim the snow peas. While the pork cooks, prepare the couscous. Slice or section the oranges and arrange on individual small plates.

Pork with Orange-Glazed Onions and Pea Pods

For a pleasing presentation, lay overlapping slices of pork tenderloin on a bed of couscous; spoon the chili-flecked sweet sauce and snow peas over the meat.

Yield: 4 (1-cup) servings

2 tablespoons oil

1 lb. pork tenderloin, cut crosswise into ¼-inch slices

½ cup orange marmalade

2 tablespoons chili sauce

8 oz. (2 cups) fresh snow pea pods, trimmed

2 small onions, sliced, separated into rings

1. Heat oil in large skillet or wok over medium-high heat until hot. Add pork; cook and stir 3 to 4 minutes or until pork is no longer pink in center. Remove from skillet; cover to keep warm.

2. Reduce heat to medium. In same skillet, combine all remaining ingredients; cook and stir 3 to 5 minutes or until vegetables are crisp-tender. Return pork to skillet; cook and stir 1 to 2 minutes or until thoroughly heated.

Nutrition Information Per Serving: Serving Size: 1 Cup • Calories 340 • Calories from Fat 100 • % Daily Value: Total Fat 11 g 17% • Saturated Fat 2 g 10% • Cholesterol 65 mg 22% • Sodium 190 mg 8% • Total Carbohydrate 35 g 12% • Dietary Fiber 2 g 8% • Sugars 25 g • Protein 26 g • Vitamin A 4% • Vitamin C 45% • Calcium 6% • Iron 15%
Dietary Exchanges: 2 Fruit, 1 Vegetable, 3 Lean Meat, ½ Fat OR 2 Carbohydrate, 1 Vegetable, 3 Lean Meat, ½ Fat

Sweet-and-Sour Pork

Double this fruity-tangy recipe, if you wish, and you'll have zesty leftovers for a satisfying lunch.

Yield: 4 servings

2/3 cup uncooked regular long-grain white rice

1 1/3 cups water

1 lb. pork tenderloin, cut crosswise into thin slices

1 green bell pepper, cut into 1-inch squares

1 (20-oz.) can pineapple chunks in unsweetened juice, drained

1/2 cup purchased sweet-and-sour sauce

1/4 teaspoon ginger

---

1. Cook rice in water as directed on package.

2. Meanwhile, spray large skillet with nonstick cooking spray. Heat over medium-high heat until hot. Add pork; cook and stir 3 to 5 minutes or until no longer pink in center.

3. Add bell pepper; cook and stir 4 to 6 minutes or until crisp-tender.

4. Stir in pineapple, sweet-and-sour sauce and ginger; cook and stir until thoroughly heated. Serve over rice.

Nutrition Information Per Serving: Serving Size: 1/4 of Recipe • Calories 320 • Calories from Fat 35 • % Daily Value: Total Fat 4 g 6% • Saturated Fat 1 g 5% • Cholesterol 65 mg 22% • Sodium 150 mg 6% • Total Carbohydrate 44 g 15% • Dietary Fiber 2 g 8% • Sugars 19 g • Protein 26 g • Vitamin A 2% • Vitamin C 30% • Calcium 4% • Iron 15%
Dietary Exchanges: 2 Starch, 1 Fruit, 2 Lean Meat OR 3 Carbohydrate, 2 Lean Meat

menu

SWEET-AND-SOUR PORK
Fresh sugar snap peas
Fortune cookies

Start the rice; then trim the sugar-snap peas, remove the string running along one side and place them in a serving dish. Then slice the pork and cut the pepper.

Pork & Lamb **87**

Lime-Marinated
Pork Tenderloins

Butterflying the pork tenderloin (cutting the meat
in half lengthwise and flattening it) speeds cooking time and allows more absorption of the glaze.
Marinate the meat in a plastic bag or nonmetal
container because the acidity of the lime juice will
react with metal, giving the food a tinny taste.

Yield: 6 servings

2 (¾-lb.) pork tenderloins

¼ cup frozen limeade concentrate, thawed

1 tablespoon oil

2 garlic cloves, minced

½ teaspoon salt

¼ teaspoon seasoned pepper blend

1. Cut each pork tenderloin in half lengthwise,
cutting to but not through bottom; open and
flatten. Place tenderloins in food storage plastic
bag or shallow nonmetal dish.

2. In small bowl, combine all remaining ingredients; mix well. Pour over tenderloins; turn to
coat. Seal bag or cover dish; let stand at room
temperature for 10 minutes to marinate.

3. Line 13x9-inch pan with foil. Place tenderloins, cut side up, in foil-lined pan. Broil 4 to
6 inches from heat for 12 to 15 minutes or until
pork is no longer pink in center, turning once.
Cut into slices.

Nutrition Information Per Serving: Serving Size: ⅙ of Recipe • Calories 170 •
Calories from Fat 50 • % Daily Value: Total Fat 6 g 9% • Saturated Fat 2 g 10% •
Cholesterol 65 mg 22% • Sodium 240 mg 10% • Total Carbohydrate 6 g 2% •
Dietary Fiber 0 g 0% • Sugars 5 g • Protein 24 g • Vitamin A 0% • Vitamin C 2% •
Calcium 0% • Iron 6%
Dietary Exchanges: ½ Fruit, 3½ Very Lean Meat, ½ Fat OR ½ Carbohydrate,
3½ Very Lean Meat, ½ Fat

Braised Pork Chops in Sour Cream Sauce

The creamy sauce surrounding these skillet-browned pork chops is actually very low in fat, thanks to skim milk and nonfat sour cream.

Yield: 6 servings

6 (4-oz.) boneless pork loin chops

¼ teaspoon salt

⅛ teaspoon pepper

¾ cup beef broth

1 tablespoon barbecue sauce

⅓ cup evaporated skim milk

⅓ cup nonfat sour cream

3 tablespoons all-purpose flour

1. Sprinkle pork chops with salt and pepper. Spray large nonstick skillet with nonstick cooking spray. Heat over medium-high heat until hot. Add pork chops; cover and cook 4 to 6 minutes or until golden brown, turning once.

2. In small bowl, mix ½ cup of the broth and the barbecue sauce. Pour over pork chops; cover tightly. Reduce heat to medium-low; simmer 5 to 10 minutes or until pork is no longer pink in center. Remove pork chops from skillet; cover.

3. In same small bowl, combine remaining ¼ cup broth, milk, sour cream and flour; beat until smooth. Pour into same skillet; cook and stir over medium heat for 2 to 3 minutes or until bubbly and thickened. Serve sauce over pork chops.

Nutrition Information Per Serving: Serving Size: ⅙ of Recipe • Calories 200 • Calories from Fat 70 • % Daily Value: Total Fat 8 g 12% • Saturated Fat 3 g 15% • Cholesterol 70 mg 23% • Sodium 300 mg 13% • Total Carbohydrate 6 g 2% • Dietary Fiber 0 g 0% • Sugars 3 g • Protein 27 g • Vitamin A 4% • Vitamin C 0% • Calcium 8% • Iron 6%
Dietary Exchanges: ½ Starch, 3½ Lean Meat OR ½ Carbohydrate, 3½ Lean Meat

menu

BRAISED PORK CHOPS IN SOUR CREAM SAUCE

Sweet potatoes

Broccoli-cauliflower-carrot combination

Rocky road ice cream

Canned sweet potatoes make an easy, colorful side dish, or scrub and trim small, fresh sweet potatoes and cook them in the microwave before cooking the pork. Cook the vegetable mixture while the pork chops simmer.

menu

SKILLET HAM STEAK

Green beans

Buttered bread

Chocolate chip cookies and chocolate chip ice cream

For dessert, put a slice of ice cream between two cookies to improvise an ice cream sandwich. If you make them ahead, roll the edges in mini-chocolate chips or chocolate sprinkles. Wrap tightly and freeze. While the ham steaks cook, butter the bread slices.

Skillet Ham Steak

Spiced orange juice and brown sugar make an easy glaze for ham steaks. If you wish, garnish the plate with a fresh orange slice.

Yield: 4 servings

---

2 tablespoons frozen orange juice concentrate

2 tablespoons brown sugar

¼ teaspoon allspice

1 (¾-lb.) fully cooked center-cut ham steak (¾ inch thick)

---

1. In small bowl, combine orange juice concentrate, brown sugar and allspice; blend well.

2. Spray large nonstick skillet with nonstick cooking spray. Heat over medium-high heat until hot. Place ham in skillet; cook 4 minutes. Turn ham; brush with orange juice mixture. Cook an additional 4 to 6 minutes or until thoroughly heated.

Nutrition Information Per Serving: Serving Size: ¼ of Recipe • Calories 140 • Calories from Fat 35 • % Daily Value: Total Fat 4 g 6% • Saturated Fat 1 g 5% • Cholesterol 40 mg 13% • Sodium 1,080 mg 45% • Total Carbohydrate 10 g 3% • Dietary Fiber 0 g 0% • Sugars 10 g • Protein 17 g • Vitamin A 0% • Vitamin C 45% • Calcium 0% • Iron 6%
Dietary Exchanges: ½ Fruit, 2½ Lean Meat, ½ Fat OR ½ Carbohydrate, 2½ Lean Meat, ½ Fat

Teriyaki Pork and Vegetables

Grocery stores offer fresh vegetables trimmed and chopped to eliminate time-consuming preparation. Here, the vegetables team up with bite-sized strips of pork and ramen noodles.

Yield: 4 (1½-cup) servings

¾ lb. boneless pork loin chops, cut into thin bite-sized strips

2 garlic cloves, minced

1½ cups water

1 (3- or 3.5-oz.) pkg. pork or chicken-flavor ramen noodle soup mix

1 (16-oz.) pkg. (4 cups) fresh stir-fry vegetables

¼ cup purchased teriyaki baste and glaze

1. Spray large nonstick skillet with nonstick cooking spray. Heat over medium-high heat until hot. Add pork; cook and stir 3 to 5 minutes or until pork is no longer pink in center. Add garlic; cook 30 seconds, stirring constantly. Remove pork and garlic from skillet.

2. Add water to same skillet; increase heat to high. Bring to a boil. Break noodles into small pieces; add to water. Add 1 teaspoon of the seasoning from soup mix seasoning packet and stir-fry vegetables; mix well. (Discard or reserve remaining seasoning from packet.) Cover; cook 3 to 5 minutes or until vegetables are crisp-tender and noodles are tender, stirring occasionally.

3. Return pork and garlic to skillet. Stir in teriyaki baste and glaze. Cook and stir 1 to 2 minutes or until thoroughly heated.

TERIYAKI PORK AND VEGETABLES

Melon wedges

Pecan pie

If you have time early in the day, cut the melon and chill it. When it's time to prepare dinner, cut the meat into thin, bite-sized strips, and refrigerate, tightly wrapped, until cooking time.

Nutrition Information Per Serving: Serving Size: 1½ Cups • Calories 270 • Calories from Fat 90 • % Daily Value: Total Fat 10 g 15% • Saturated Fat 4 g 20% • Cholesterol 50 mg 17% • Sodium 810 mg 34% • Total Carbohydrate 25 g 8% • Dietary Fiber 3 g 12% • Sugars 5 g • Protein 21 g • Vitamin A 130% • Vitamin C 40% • Calcium 10% • Iron 15%
Dietary Exchanges: 1 Starch, 2 Vegetable, 2 Lean Meat, ½ Fat OR 1 Carbohydrate, 2 Vegetable, 2 Lean Meat, ½ Fat

tip

To broil pork tenderloins, place on broiler pan; broil 4 to 6 inches from heat using times in recipe as a guide, turning once and spooning remaining sauce over pork.

Barbecued Pork Tenderloin

Tenderloin, a premium pork cut, grills up quickly into a moist, succulent entree.

Yield: 4 servings

¼ cup ketchup

¼ cup chili sauce

1 tablespoon brown sugar

2 tablespoons finely chopped onion

⅛ teaspoon celery seed

Dash garlic powder

1½ teaspoons cider vinegar

1½ teaspoons Worcestershire sauce

1 teaspoon prepared mustard

⅛ teaspoon liquid smoke

2 (½-lb.) pork tenderloins

1. In small saucepan, combine all ingredients except pork; mix well. Bring to a boil. Reduce heat; simmer 5 minutes. Cool slightly.

2. Heat grill. Cut each pork tenderloin in half lengthwise, cutting to but not through bottom; open and flatten.

3. When ready to grill, place flattened pork on gas grill over medium-high heat or on charcoal grill 4 to 6 inches from medium-high coals. Spoon half of sauce over pork; cook 5 to 7 minutes. Turn pork; spoon remaining sauce over pork. Cook an additional 5 to 7 minutes or until pork is no longer pink in center.

Nutrition Information Per Serving: Serving Size: ¼ of Recipe • Calories 180 • Calories from Fat 35 • % Daily Value: Total Fat 4 g 6% • Saturated Fat 1 g 5% • Cholesterol 65 mg 22% • Sodium 520 mg 22% • Total Carbohydrate 13 g 4% • Dietary Fiber 0 g 0% • Sugars 9 g • Protein 24 g • Vitamin A 8% • Vitamin C 6% • Calcium 0% • Iron 10%
Dietary Exchanges: ½ Fruit, 3 Lean Meat OR ½ Carbohydrate, 3 Lean Meat

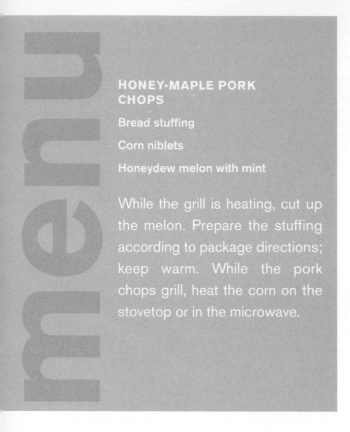

Honey-Maple Pork Chops

Allspice, which flavors the glaze for these pork chops, sounds and tastes like a blend of spices but is actually the dried, ground berry of a single plant. In American cooking, it's most often used in sweet baked goods. Here, it adds verve to the meat.

Yield: 4 servings

2 tablespoons honey

2 tablespoons microwave-ready maple-flavored syrup

⅛ teaspoon allspice

4 (6-oz.) pork loin chops (¾ inch thick)

¼ teaspoon salt

⅛ teaspoon pepper

1. Heat grill. In small bowl, combine honey, syrup and allspice; mix well. Sprinkle pork chops with salt and pepper.

2. When ready to grill, brush pork chops with honey mixture. Place chops on gas grill over medium heat or on charcoal grill 4 to 6 inches from medium coals. Cook 8 to 10 minutes or until pork is no longer pink in center, turning once and brushing occasionally with sauce.

Nutrition Information Per Serving: Serving Size: ¼ of Recipe • Calories 200 • Calories from Fat 80 • % Daily Value: Total Fat 9 g 14% • Saturated Fat 3 g 15% • Cholesterol 75 mg 25% • Sodium 190 mg 8% • Total Carbohydrate 4 g 1% • Dietary Fiber 0 g 0% • Sugars 3 g • Protein 26 g • Vitamin A 0% • Vitamin C 0%; Calcium 0% • Iron 6%
Dietary Exchange: 3½ Lean Meat

Peach-Dijon Pork Chops

This recipe gets its name from the French city famous for its winey mustard. The condiment rounds out the salty-sweet flavors of a sauce made with peach preserves and soy.

Yield: 4 servings

½ cup peach preserves, large pieces finely chopped

2 tablespoons Dijon mustard

2 tablespoons soy sauce

¼ teaspoon dried marjoram leaves

4 (6-oz.) pork loin chops (¾ inch thick)

¼ teaspoon salt

⅛ teaspoon pepper

1. Heat grill. In small saucepan, combine preserves, mustard, soy sauce and marjoram; mix well. Cook over low heat until preserves are melted, stirring frequently.

2. When ready to grill, sprinkle both sides of pork chops with salt and pepper. Place chops on gas grill over medium heat or on charcoal grill 4 to 6 inches from medium coals. Cook 12 to 15 minutes or until pork is no longer pink in center, turning once and brushing with preserves mixture during last 2 minutes of cooking time.

3. To serve, bring any remaining preserves mixture to a boil. Serve with pork chops.

Nutrition Information Per Serving: Serving Size: ¼ of Recipe • Calories 260 • Calories from Fat 60 • % Daily Value: Total Fat 7 g 11% • Saturated Fat 2 g 10% • Cholesterol 60 mg 20% • Sodium 900 mg 38% • Total Carbohydrate 27 g 9% • Dietary Fiber 1 g 4% • Sugars 20 g • Protein 22 g • Vitamin A 0% • Vitamin C 6% • Calcium 4% • Iron 8%
Dietary Exchanges: 2 Fruit, 3 Very Lean Meat, 1 Fat OR 2 Carbohydrate, 3 Very Lean Meat, 1 Fat

menu

PEACH-DIJON PORK CHOPS

Frozen mixed vegetables

Cornbread

Butter pecan ice cream

If you have time earlier in the day, prepare cornbread from scratch or a mix if you haven't purchased it ready to serve. Cook the vegetables while the pork is grilling.

tip

To broil pork chops, place on broiler pan; broil 4 to 6 inches from heat using times in recipe as a guide, turning once and brushing occasionally with preserves mixture.

Grilled Pork Kabobs

Fruit and pork are a traditional pairing because the sweetness and acidity of the fruit balances the richness of the meat. Here, apricot preserves infuse the glaze with subtle sweetness; the sugar content of the preserves promotes a nicely browned exterior, too.

Yield: 4 servings

---

4 (½- to ¾-inch-thick) boneless pork loin chops (1 lb.)

½ teaspoon seasoned salt or dried pork seasoning

2 small zucchini, cut into 12 (1-inch) pieces

8 medium mushrooms

1 medium red bell pepper, cut into 12 pieces

½ cup apricot preserves

1 tablespoon cider vinegar

---

1. Heat grill. Sprinkle both sides of each pork chop with seasoned salt; cut each chop into 4 pieces. Alternately thread pork pieces, zucchini, mushrooms and bell pepper evenly onto four 12- to 14-inch metal skewers. In small bowl, combine preserves and vinegar; blend well.

2. When ready to grill, place kabobs on gas grill over medium heat or on charcoal grill 4 to 6 inches from medium coals. Brush with preserves mixture. Cook 5 minutes. Turn kabobs; brush with remaining preserves mixture. Cook an additional 5 to 7 minutes or until pork is no longer pink in center. If desired, serve over hot cooked rice.

Nutrition Information Per Serving: Serving Size: ¼ of Recipe • Calories 290 • Calories from Fat 70 • % Daily Value: Total Fat 8 g 12% • Saturated Fat 3 g 15% • Cholesterol 65 mg 22% • Sodium 260 mg 11% • Total Carbohydrate 29 g 10% • Dietary Fiber 2 g 8% • Sugars 21 g • Protein 25 g • Vitamin A 25% • Vitamin C 50% • Calcium 4% • Iron 10%
Dietary Exchanges: 1½ Fruit, 1 Vegetable, 3 Lean Meat OR 1½ Carbohydrate, 1 Vegetable, 3 Lean Meat

menu

GRILLED PORK KABOBS

Relish tray

Instant rice

Fresh cherries

Rinse and drain fresh Bing or golden cherries or a combination. Heat the grill, assemble the kabobs and measure the water for the rice. While the kabobs cook, cook the rice and compose a relish tray of ripe olives, cherry tomatoes, baby carrots and pickle spears.

tip

To broil kabobs, place on broiler pan; broil 4 to 6 inches from heat using times in recipe as a guide, turning and brushing once with preserves mixture.

Nutrition Information Per Serving: Serving Size: 1/4 of Recipe • Calories 240 • Calories from Fat 60 • % Daily Value: Total Fat 7 g 11% • Saturated Fat 1 g 5% • Cholesterol 20 mg 7% • Sodium 560 mg 23% • Total Carbohydrate 31 g 10% • Dietary Fiber 3 g 12% • Sugars 5 g • Protein 14 g • Vitamin A 25% • Vitamin C 20% • Calcium 8% • Iron 15%
Dietary Exchanges: 2 Starch, 1 Lean Meat, 1/2 Fat OR 2 Carbohydrate, 1 Lean Meat, 1/2 Fat

tip

To broil pork and vegetables, place on broiler pan; broil 4 to 6 inches from heat using times in recipe as a guide, turning once.

Chili-Charred Fajita Kabobs

Meat cut into chunks cooks more quickly than a large piece. Use flat or twisted skewers, not perfectly round—ingredients are less likely to slip off.

Yield: 4 servings

1 teaspoon garlic powder

1 1/2 teaspoons cumin

2 teaspoons paprika

1 1/2 teaspoons dried oregano leaves

1/4 to 1/2 teaspoon ground red pepper (cayenne)

4 boneless pork loin chops, cut into 1-inch cubes

1 small green bell pepper, cut into 16 pieces

8 cherry tomatoes

1 small onion, cut into 8 pieces

Nonstick cooking spray

8 (6-inch) flour tortillas, heated

3/4 cup salsa

1. Heat grill. In medium bowl, combine garlic powder, cumin, paprika, oregano and ground red pepper; mix well. Add pork; toss to coat well.

2. On eight 8- to 10-inch metal skewers, alternately thread pork, bell pepper, tomatoes and onion. Spray kabobs lightly with nonstick cooking spray.

3. When ready to grill, place kabobs on gas grill over medium heat or on charcoal grill 4 to 6 inches from medium coals. Cook 6 to 10 minutes or until pork is no longer pink in center, turning once.

4. To serve, wrap a warm tortilla around each kabob; pull pork and vegetables off skewer into tortilla. Serve with salsa.

Skillet Pork Stew

Keep a supply of mixed frozen vegetables in the freezer—they add quick color and nutrients to meals on nights when you don't have time for peeling and chopping.

Yield: 4 (1¼-cup) servings

3 boneless pork loin chops (about 1 lb.), cut into ½-inch cubes

1 medium onion, chopped

1 (1-lb.) pkg. frozen broccoli florets, carrots and cauliflower

¼ cup water

2 tablespoons tomato paste

1 (12-oz.) jar seasoned gravy for pork

1. Spray large nonstick skillet with nonstick cooking spray. Heat over high heat until hot. Add pork and onion; cook 3 to 5 minutes or until pork is no longer pink and onion is crisp-tender, stirring occasionally.

2. Meanwhile, place frozen vegetables in colander or strainer; rinse with warm water until thawed. Drain well.

3. Add vegetables, water, tomato paste and gravy to pork mixture. Bring to a boil. Reduce heat to medium; cover and cook 5 to 8 minutes or until vegetables are crisp-tender, stirring occasionally. If desired, add salt and pepper to taste.

Nutrition Information Per Serving: Serving Size: 1¼ Cups • Calories 250 • Calories from Fat 80 • % Daily Value: Total Fat 9 g 14% • Saturated Fat 3 g 15% • Cholesterol 70 mg 23% • Sodium 600 mg 25% • Total Carbohydrate 14 g 5% • Dietary Fiber 3 g 12% • Sugars 4 g • Protein 28 g • Vitamin A 60% • Vitamin C 35% • Calcium 4% • Iron 8%
Dietary Exchanges: ½ Starch, 1 Vegetable, 3½ Lean Meat OR ½ Carbohydrate, 1 Vegetable, 3½ Lean Meat

SKILLET PORK STEW

Refrigerated garlic breadsticks

Apple sampler platter with Cheddar cheese

Preheat the oven for the breadsticks. Cube the pork and chop the onion for the stew. Bake the breadsticks while the stew cooks. For dessert, cut into wedges four apples of different varieties, such as Granny Smith, Golden Delicious, Red Delicious and Braeburn. Serve the apple sampler with sliced cheese.

Ham and Potato Chowder

"Chowder" comes from the French word for "kettle." This creamy, chunky dinner-in-a-bowl puts a packaged potato mix to creative use.

Yield: 4 (1½-cup) servings

1 (7.8-oz.) pkg. au gratin potato mix

1½ cups diced cooked ham

½ cup shredded carrot

¼ teaspoon pepper

3 cups water

2 cups milk

¼ cup chopped fresh parsley

1. In large saucepan, combine potato slices, contents of sauce mix packet from potatoes, ham, carrot, pepper, water and milk. Bring to a boil.

2. Reduce heat to medium; cook 15 minutes or until potatoes are tender. Do not drain. Stir in parsley.

Nutrition Information Per Serving: Serving Size: 1½ Cups • Calories 340 • Calories from Fat 60 • % Daily Value: Total Fat 7 g 11% • Saturated Fat 3 g 15% • Cholesterol 35 mg 12% • Sodium 1,910 mg 80% • Total Carbohydrate 51 g 17% • Dietary Fiber 3 g 12% • Sugars 9 g • Protein 19 g • Vitamin A 90% • Vitamin C 10% • Calcium 20% • Iron 8%
Dietary Exchanges: 3 Starch, ½ Fruit, 1½ Lean Meat OR 3½ Carbohydrate, 1½ Lean Meat

HAM AND POTATO CHOWDER

Rustic rye or wheat bread

Banana splits

Dice the ham, shred the carrot and chop the parsley before beginning the soup. At dessert time, make the banana splits by slicing the bananas if you're serving the treat in a dish or by cutting them into long spears for traditional boat-shaped dishes. Add 2 or 3 scoops of ice cream, favorite toppings and whipped cream.

menu

CABBAGE, POTATO AND SAUSAGE SOUP

Buttered pumpernickel bread

Canned plums

Gingerbread cookies

While the soup cooks, butter the bread and put the plums into the refrigerator to chill. When the soup is done, if you wish, swirl a spoonful of sour cream, plain yogurt or heavy cream into each bowl of soup just before serving.

Cabbage, Potato and Sausage Soup

This nourishing soup hints at German fare with its cabbage and sausage ingredients, and it proves thoroughly satisfying on a cold night.

Yield: 6 (1½-cup) servings

1 lb. cooked kielbasa or Polish sausage, cut in half lengthwise, sliced

1 (16-oz.) pkg. coleslaw blend

2 (14½-oz.) cans ready-to-serve chicken broth

3 cups water

1 teaspoon minced garlic in water (from 4.5-oz. jar)

¼ teaspoon salt

¼ teaspoon pepper

2 cups mashed potato flakes

1. In Dutch oven, combine all ingredients except mashed potato flakes; mix well. Bring to a boil over medium-high heat, stirring occasionally.

2. Reduce heat to medium-low; simmer 5 to 10 minutes or until cabbage is almost tender.

3. Remove Dutch oven from heat. Stir in mashed potato flakes.

Nutrition Information Per Serving: Serving Size: 1½ Cups • Calories 370 • Calories from Fat 200 • % Daily Value: Total Fat 22 g 34% • Saturated Fat 8 g 40% • Cholesterol 50 mg 17% • Sodium 1,490 mg 62% • Total Carbohydrate 26 g 9% • Dietary Fiber 2 g 8% • Sugars 5 g • Protein 16 g • Vitamin A 45% • Vitamin C 30% • Calcium 8% • Iron 10%
Dietary Exchanges: 1½ Starch, 1 Vegetable, 1½ High-Fat Meat, 2 Fat OR 1½ Carbohydrate, 1 Vegetable, 1½ High-Fat Meat, 2 Fat

Creamy Bacon-Spinach Soup

Cooking the mushrooms, onion and garlic together with the bacon lets the delicious, smoky flavor permeate the soup.

Yield: 4 (1½-cup) servings

6 slices bacon, cut into 1-inch pieces

1½ cups sliced fresh mushrooms

¼ cup chopped onion

1 garlic clove, minced

2 (14½-oz.) cans ready-to-serve chicken broth

1 (9-oz.) pkg. frozen spinach in a pouch, thawed, squeezed to drain well

1½ cups milk

6 tablespoons all-purpose flour

1. In Dutch oven, combine bacon, mushrooms, onion and garlic; cook over medium-high heat until bacon is cooked and vegetables are tender. Drain.

2. Add broth and spinach; simmer 5 minutes.

3. In small bowl, combine milk and flour; beat with wire whisk until well blended. Stir flour mixture into soup. Simmer until mixture boils and thickens, stirring constantly.

Nutrition Information Per Serving: Serving Size: 1½ Cups • Calories 200 • Calories from Fat 70 • % Daily Value: Total Fat 8 g 12% • Saturated Fat 3 g 15% • Cholesterol 15 mg 5% • Sodium 1,000 mg 42% • Total Carbohydrate 18 g 6% • Dietary Fiber 2 g 8% • Sugars 5 g • Protein 14 g • Vitamin A 45% • Vitamin C 20% • Calcium 20% • Iron 10%
Dietary Exchanges: 1 Starch, 1 Vegetable, 1 High-Fat Meat OR 1 Carbohydrate, 1 Vegetable, 1 High-Fat Meat

menu

CREAMY BACON-SPINACH SOUP

Toasted whole-grain rolls
Crumb cake

If you have time early in the day, make the crumb cake from scratch or a mix, if you haven't purchased it ready to serve. Just before the soup is done, warm the rolls and set the butter out on the table.

TOASTED HAM AND GOUDA SANDWICHES

Tomato-basil soup

Pickles

Gingerbread topped with whipped cream and minced, candied ginger

If you have time earlier in the day, prepare the gingerbread from a mix or purchase soft ginger cookies. Start the soup heating; then prepare the sandwiches. To intensify the ginger flavor of the dessert, top each serving with a dollop of whipped cream and sprinkle with minced, candied ginger.

Toasted Ham and Gouda Sandwiches

Here's a new take on the traditional ham and cheese, using Gouda instead of Swiss cheese and adding mustard-mayonnaise sauce.

Yield: 4 sandwiches

8 slices pumpernickel bread

¼ cup creamy mustard-mayonnaise sauce

2 tablespoons chopped fresh chives

8 oz. thinly sliced cooked ham

1 medium tomato, sliced

8 oz. Gouda cheese, sliced

3 tablespoons butter, softened

1. Spread each bread slice with mustard-mayonnaise sauce. Sprinkle 4 slices with chives; top with ham, tomato and cheese. Cover with remaining bread slices, sauce side down. Using 1 tablespoon of the butter, spread on tops of sandwiches.

2. Melt remaining 2 tablespoons butter in 12-inch skillet over low heat. Add sandwiches, buttered side up; cover and cook 3 to 4 minutes or until toasted.

3. Turn sandwiches; cover and cook an additional 3 to 4 minutes or until toasted and cheese is melted.

Nutrition Information Per Serving: Serving Size: 1 Sandwich • Calories 560 • Calories from Fat 290 • % Daily Value: Total Fat 32 g 49% • Saturated Fat 18 g 90% • Cholesterol 115 mg 38% • Sodium 1,960 mg 82% • Total Carbohydrate 37 g 12% • Dietary Fiber 5 g 20% • Sugars 4 g • Protein 31 g • Vitamin A 20% • Vitamin C 8% • Calcium 45% • Iron 15%
Dietary Exchanges: 2½ Starch, 3½ Lean Meat, 4 Fat OR 2½ Carbohydrate, 3½ Lean Meat, 4 Fat

Bratwurst and Mozzarella Sandwiches

Here's a twist on the sausage and pepper hero, with German bratwurst substituting for Italian sausage. If you wish, sprinkle the sandwich with shredded mozzarella in place of the cheese slices.

Yield: 6 sandwiches

6 cooked bratwurst

1 medium green bell pepper, cut into 6 pieces

1 medium red bell pepper, cut into 6 pieces

¾ cup refrigerated marinara sauce

6 brat buns, split

6 (1-oz.) slices mozzarella cheese

1. Heat grill. When ready to grill, place bratwurst and bell peppers on gas grill over medium heat or on charcoal grill 4 to 6 inches from medium coals. Cook 8 to 12 minutes or until bell peppers are crisp-tender and bratwurst are thoroughly heated, turning frequently.

2. Meanwhile, heat marinara sauce in small saucepan over medium heat until thoroughly heated.

3. To toast buns, place, cut side down, on grill during last 1 to 2 minutes of cooking time. Layer bell peppers, marinara sauce, bratwurst and cheese in buns.

Nutrition Information Per Serving: Serving Size: 1 Sandwich • Calories 490 • Calories from Fat 270 • % Daily Value: Total Fat 30 g 46% • Saturated Fat 12 g 60% • Cholesterol 65 mg 22% • Sodium 1,020 mg 43% • Total Carbohydrate 31 g 10% • Dietary Fiber 2 g 8% • Sugars 9 g • Protein 25 g • Vitamin A 25% • Vitamin C 40% • Calcium 35% • Iron 20%
Dietary Exchanges: 2 Starch, 2½ High-Fat Meat, 2 Fat OR 2 Carbohydrate, 2½ High-Fat Meat, 2 Fat

menu

BRATWURST AND MOZZARELLA SANDWICHES

Deli coleslaw

Chocolate chip cookies

While the grill heats, cut the bell peppers. For easy handling, skewer the pepper pieces or place them in an oiled grill basket of woven wire or perforated metal. While the sausage and peppers cook, spoon the coleslaw into a serving dish.

BARBECUE PORK BURGERS

Tomato and cucumber slices

Deli potato salad

Pistachio ice cream

While the grill is heating, slice the tomatoes and cucumbers and arrange them on a plate, garnished with a sprig of fresh parsley or basil, if you like. (Cucumbers from the garden or farmers' market can simply be scrubbed and sliced; waxed supermarket cucumbers need to be peeled.)

tip

To broil patties, place on broiler pan; broil 4 to 6 inches from heat using times in recipe as a guide, turning once. Meanwhile, place pineapple slices and buns, cut side up, on broiler pan; broil 1 to 2 minutes. Turn pineapple slices; broil an additional 1 to 2 minutes.

Barbecue Pork Burgers

Juicy ground pork, a nice change of pace from beef burgers, takes on a smoky, salty-sweet flavor from barbecue sauce spiked with maple syrup and liquid smoke.

Yield: 4 sandwiches

3 tablespoons barbecue sauce

2 tablespoons microwave-ready maple-flavored syrup

¼ teaspoon liquid smoke, if desired

1 lb. ground pork

1 (8-oz.) can pineapple slices, drained

4 sesame seed burger buns, split

1. Heat grill. In small bowl, combine barbecue sauce, syrup and liquid smoke; mix well.

2. In medium bowl, combine ground pork and 3 tablespoons of the barbecue sauce mixture; mix well. Shape mixture into 4 patties, ½ inch thick.

3. When ready to grill, place patties on gas grill over medium heat or on charcoal grill 4 to 6 inches from medium coals. Cook 10 to 12 minutes or until patties are no longer pink in center, turning once.

4. Meanwhile, place pineapple slices and buns, cut side down, on grill. Cook 1 to 2 minutes or until buns are lightly toasted. Turn pineapple slices; cook an additional 1 to 2 minutes. Place patties and pineapple slices on bottom halves of buns; drizzle with remaining barbecue sauce mixture. Cover with top halves of buns.

Nutrition Information Per Serving: Serving Size: 1 Sandwich • Calories 400 • Calories from Fat 170 • % Daily Value: Total Fat 19 g 29% • Saturated Fat 7 g 35% • Cholesterol 75 mg 25% • Sodium 410 mg 17% • Total Carbohydrate 34 g 11% • Dietary Fiber 2 g 8% • Sugars 13 g • Protein 24 g • Vitamin A 2% • Vitamin C 6% • Calcium 8% • Iron 15%
Dietary Exchanges: 1½ Starch, 1 Fruit, 2½ High-Fat Meat OR 2½ Carbohydrate, 2½ High-Fat Meat

Lamb and Asparagus Stir-Fry

Two ingredients that traditionally herald spring, lamb and asparagus, mingle in a rosemary-scented mixture served over noodles.

Yield: 6 servings

13½ oz. (6 cups) uncooked medium egg noodles

½ cup ready-to-serve vegetable broth

2 teaspoons cornstarch

¾ teaspoon dried rosemary leaves, crushed

¼ teaspoon salt

¼ teaspoon coarse ground black pepper

2 teaspoons olive oil

1 lb. boneless lean lamb sirloin or round steak, cut into thin strips

1 large onion, halved, thinly sliced

1 lb. fresh asparagus spears, cut diagonally into 1-inch pieces

1 small red bell pepper, cut into 2 × ¼ × ¼-inch strips

1. Cook noodles to desired doneness as directed on package. Drain; cover to keep warm.

2. Meanwhile, in small bowl or jar with tight-fitting lid, combine broth, cornstarch, rosemary, salt and pepper. Blend or shake well; set aside.

3. Heat oil in large nonstick skillet or wok over medium-high heat until hot. Add lamb; cook and stir 3 minutes. Add onion and asparagus; cook and stir an additional 3 minutes or until onion is tender and lamb is no longer pink in center.

4. Add bell pepper; cook and stir 1 minute. Add broth mixture; cook until thickened, stirring constantly. Serve over noodles.

menu

LAMB AND ASPARAGUS STIR-FRY

Strawberry ice cream with sliced fresh strawberries

Prepare and chill the strawberries. Start the water cooking for the pasta, then cut the meat and the stir-fry ingredients so you can easily add them in sequence when the skillet is hot.

Nutrition Information Per Serving: Serving Size: ⅙ of Recipe • Calories 390 • Calories from Fat 80 • % Daily Value: Total Fat 9 g 14% • Saturated Fat 2 g 10% • Cholesterol 105 mg 35% • Sodium 230 mg 10% • Total Carbohydrate 53 g 18% • Dietary Fiber 4 g 16% • Sugars 6 g • Protein 25 g • Vitamin A 20% • Vitamin C 30% • Calcium 4% • Iron 25%
Dietary Exchanges: 3 Starch, 1 Vegetable, 2 Lean Meat, ½ Fat OR 3 Carbohydrate, 1 Vegetable, 2 Lean Meat, ½ Fat

Grilled Lamb Chops with Rosemary and Black Pepper

Rosemary and lamb are a classic pairing, and every bite of these succulent chops proves why.

Yield: 4 servings

8 (4-oz.) lamb loin chops

½ cup dry red wine

2 tablespoons Worcestershire sauce

1 teaspoon dried rosemary leaves

4 garlic cloves, minced

Freshly ground black pepper

¼ teaspoon salt

1. Heat grill. Pierce lamb chops all over with fork. Place in shallow dish; add wine. Let stand at room temperature for 15 minutes to marinate.

2. Meanwhile, in small bowl, combine Worcestershire sauce, rosemary and garlic; mix well. Set aside.

3. When ready to grill, remove lamb from marinade; discard marinade. Place lamb on gas grill over medium heat or on charcoal grill 4 to 6 inches from medium coals. Spoon half of sauce mixture evenly over chops; sprinkle generously with pepper. Cook 4 to 5 minutes or until browned.

4. Turn chops. Spoon remaining sauce over lamb; sprinkle with pepper. Cook an additional 4 to 5 minutes or until of desired doneness. Sprinkle lamb with salt.

Nutrition Information Per Serving: Serving Size: ¼ of Recipe • Calories 190 • Calories from Fat 80 • % Daily Value: Total Fat 9 g 14% • Saturated Fat 3 g 15% • Cholesterol 80 mg 27% • Sodium 270 mg 11% • Total Carbohydrate 2 g 1% • Dietary Fiber 0 g 0% • Sugars 0 g • Protein 25 g • Vitamin A 0% • Vitamin C 0% • Calcium 2% • Iron 15%
Dietary Exchanges: 3½ Lean Meat

menu

GRILLED LAMB CHOPS WITH ROSEMARY AND BLACK PEPPER

Steamed broccoli and cauliflower florets

Watermelon slices

While the grill heats, marinate the lamb. Slice and chill the watermelon. While the lamb cooks on the grill, cook the broccoli and cauliflower.

tip

To broil lamb chops, place on broiler pan; broil 4 to 6 inches from heat using times in recipe as a guide, turning once and spooning sauce over chops as directed.

**APRICOT-GLAZED
LAMB CHOPS**

Curry-flavored couscous

Buttered French-cut green beans

Cheesecake

To streamline preparation, use an ovenproof pan for browning the chops on the stove top and finishing the dish in the oven. While the chops are in the oven, prepare the couscous and heat the beans. Just before serving, drain the beans and toss them with butter.

Apricot-Glazed Lamb Chops

The apricot glaze caramelizes during baking, yielding beautifully browned chops.

Yield: 4 servings

¼ cup apricot preserves or jam, large pieces finely chopped

2 teaspoons chopped fresh tarragon or ½ teaspoon dried tarragon leaves

¼ teaspoon Dijon mustard

8 lean lamb rib chops (about 1 ¼ lb.)

¼ teaspoon salt

⅛ teaspoon pepper

1. Heat oven to 450° F. Line 15x10x1-inch baking pan with foil. In small bowl, combine preserves, tarragon and mustard; mix well. Set aside.

2. Spray large nonstick skillet with nonstick cooking spray. Heat over medium-high heat until hot. Sprinkle both sides of lamb chops with salt and pepper; place in hot skillet. Cook 4 to 6 minutes or until browned, turning once. Place chops in foil-lined pan; spoon apricot mixture evenly over chops.

3. Bake at 450° F. for 7 to 10 minutes or until of desired doneness.

Nutrition Information Per Serving: Serving Size: ¼ of Recipe • Calories 170 • Calories from Fat 60 • % Daily Value: Total Fat 7 g 11% • Saturated Fat 2 g 10% • Cholesterol 45 mg 15% • Sodium 190 mg 8% • Total Carbohydrate 13 g 4% • Dietary Fiber 0 g 0% • Sugars 10 g • Protein 13 g • Vitamin A 0% • Vitamin C 4% • Calcium 0% • Iron 6%
Dietary Exchanges: 1 Fruit, 2 Lean Meat OR 1 Carbohydrate, 2 Lean Meat

Skewered Hot-Curry Lamb with Pineapple

These spicy lamb meatballs are a nice change of pace from ordinary ground beef meatballs. The suggested rice soaks up the wonderful sauce.

Yield: 4 servings

8 (7- to 10-inch) bamboo skewers

½ cup orange marmalade

1 (8-oz.) can pineapple chunks in unsweetened juice, drained, reserving ⅓ cup liquid

2 tablespoons soy sauce

1 teaspoon cornstarch

1 lb. ground lamb loin

2 slices white or whole wheat bread, toasted, crumbled*

2 teaspoons curry powder

¼ to ½ teaspoon crushed red pepper flakes

1 medium green bell pepper, cut into 1-inch pieces

1. Soak bamboo skewers in water for 15 minutes. Meanwhile, in small bowl, combine orange marmalade and reserved ⅓ cup pineapple liquid; blend well. Set aside.

2. In medium bowl, combine soy sauce and cornstarch; blend well. Add lamb, bread crumbs, curry powder and pepper flakes; mix well. Shape mixture into 32 meatballs.

3. Spray broiler pan with nonstick cooking spray. Spray bamboo skewers with nonstick cooking spray. Alternately thread meatballs, bell pepper pieces and pineapple chunks onto skewers. Place kabobs on sprayed pan.

4. Broil 4 to 6 inches from heat for 3 to 4 minutes or until meatballs are browned. Turn kabobs; spoon some of marmalade mixture over meatballs. Broil an additional 3 to 4 minutes or until meatballs are no longer pink in center.

5. To serve, place kabobs on serving platter; spoon remaining marmalade mixture over meatballs, bell pepper and pineapple.

Nutrition Information Per Serving: Serving Size: ¼ of Recipe • Calories 280 • Calories from Fat 45 • % Daily Value: Total Fat 5 g 8% • Saturated Fat 2 g 10% • Cholesterol 40 mg 13% • Sodium 640 mg 27% • Total Carbohydrate 44 g 15% • Dietary Fiber 2 g 8% • Sugars 29 g • Protein 15 g • Vitamin A 25% • Vitamin C 50% • Calcium 6% • Iron 15%
Dietary Exchanges: ½ Starch, 2½ Fruit, 2 Lean Meat OR 3 Carbohydrate, 2 Lean Meat

SKEWERED HOT-CURRY LAMB WITH PINEAPPLE

menu

Basmati rice

Shredded romaine with lemon juice vinaigrette

Orange sherbet

Start the rice and place the bamboo skewers in water to soak; then prepare the lettuce and blend the meat mixture. Serve the skewers on a bed of rice. Toss the lettuce with the dressing at the last minute.

*If desired, coarsely chop toasted bread in food processor or blender.

chicken

OPPOSITE PAGE:
Asian Cashew Chicken, page 135

● Kid-Pleasing Recipe
● 20-Minutes-or-Less Recipe

ALFREDO CHICKEN DIVAN

Seasoned mixed wild and white rice

Cantaloupe wedges

Spumoni ice cream

Start the rice mix; then prepare the 3-ingredient chicken dish. While the chicken cooks, slice the cantaloupe.

Alfredo Chicken Divan

Boneless chicken breasts, a staple for the time-pressed cook, are poached with broccoli and topped with creamy Alfredo sauce.

Yield: 2 servings

2 boneless skinless chicken breast halves

1 cup frozen cut broccoli

½ cup purchased Alfredo sauce

1. Place chicken in large skillet; cover with water. Bring to a boil. Cover; boil 7 to 8 minutes. Add broccoli; boil 3 to 5 minutes or until broccoli is crisp-tender, and chicken is fork-tender and juices run clear. Drain.

2. Meanwhile, in small saucepan, heat sauce over low heat until hot.

3. Place chicken on serving plates. Top with broccoli and sauce.

Nutrition Information Per Serving: Serving Size: ½ of Recipe • Calories 390; Calories from Fat 210 • % Daily Value: Total Fat 23 g 35% • Saturated Fat 12 g 60% • Cholesterol 135 mg 45% • Sodium 350 mg 15% • Total Carbohydrate 6 g 2% • Dietary Fiber 1 g 4% • Sugars 2 g • Protein 40 g • Vitamin A 6% • Vitamin C 20% • Calcium 15% • Iron 8%
Dietary Exchanges: 1 Vegetable, 5 Very Lean Meat, 4 Fat

Cheesy Chicken à la King

The classic white sauce—milk thickened with butter and flour—is still an ideal starting point for homespun meals. This interpretation adds vegetables, chicken and cheese, resulting in a creamy classic.

Yield: 5 servings

1 (10.8-oz.) can (5 biscuits) large refrigerated flaky biscuits

3 tablespoons margarine or butter

3 tablespoons all-purpose flour

¼ teaspoon salt

⅛ teaspoon pepper

1½ cups milk

2 cups frozen mixed vegetables, cooked, drained

1½ cups cubed cooked chicken

4 oz. pasteurized prepared cheese product, cubed (1 cup)

1. Bake biscuits as directed on can.

2. Meanwhile, melt margarine in medium saucepan over medium heat. Stir in flour, salt and pepper. Gradually add milk, stirring constantly. Cook over medium-high heat until mixture boils and thickens, stirring constantly.

3. Stir in vegetables, chicken and cheese. Cook and stir until cheese is melted and mixture is thoroughly heated.

4. Split warm biscuits; place on serving plates. Spoon hot chicken mixture over biscuits.

Nutrition Information Per Serving: Serving Size: ⅕ of Recipe • Calories 490 • Calories from Fat 230 • % Daily Value: Total Fat 26 g 40% • Saturated Fat 8 g 40% • Cholesterol 55 mg 18% • Sodium 1,130 mg 47% • Total Carbohydrate 40 g 13% • Dietary Fiber 2 g 8% • Sugars 10 g • Protein 25 g • Vitamin A 30% • Vitamin C 6% • Calcium 25% • Iron 15%
Dietary Exchanges: 2 Starch, ½ Fruit, 2½ Medium-Fat Meat, 2½ Fat OR 2½ Carbohydrate, 2½ Medium-Fat Meat, 2½ Fat

menu

CHEESY CHICKEN À LA KING

Gelatin fruit salad on leaf lettuce leaves

Peanut butter cookies

Make the gelatin fruit salad ahead of time if you haven't purchased a molded salad. Preheat the oven for the biscuits and prepare the ingredients for the entree; start cooking the sauce when the biscuits go into the oven.

Chicken à la King

Served over buttermilk biscuits, chicken and peas in cream sauce resembles an upside-down chicken pot pie. It's just right for a hearty dinner.

Yield: 5 servings

1 (12-oz.) can refrigerated fluffy buttermilk biscuits

¼ cup margarine or butter

⅓ cup all-purpose flour

1 (10½-oz.) can condensed chicken broth

1¼ cups milk

2 cups cubed cooked chicken

1 cup frozen sweet peas

1 (4-oz.) can mushroom pieces and stems, drained

1 (2-oz.) jar diced pimientos, drained

¼ teaspoon salt

¼ teaspoon pepper

1. Bake biscuits as directed on can.

2. Meanwhile, melt margarine in large saucepan over medium-low heat. Add flour; blend well. Add broth and milk. Cook, stirring constantly, until mixture boils and thickens.

3. Add all remaining ingredients; simmer 5 to 10 minutes or until thoroughly heated.

4. Split warm biscuits; place on serving plates. Spoon hot chicken mixture over biscuits.

Nutrition Information Per Serving: Serving Size: ⅕ of Recipe • Calories 500 • Calories from Fat 210 • % Daily Value: Total Fat 23 g 35% • Saturated Fat 6 g 30% • Cholesterol 55 mg 18% • Sodium 1,600 mg 67% • Total Carbohydrate 44 g 15% • Dietary Fiber 3 g 12% • Sugars 9 g • Protein 28 g • Vitamin A 20% • Vitamin C 20% • Calcium 10% • Iron 20%
Dietary Exchanges: 3 Starch, 2½ Lean Meat, 2½ Fat OR 3 Carbohydrate, 2½ Lean Meat, 2½ Fat

menu

CHICKEN À LA KING
Sliced apples and grape clusters
Brownies topped with caramel sauce

Preheat the oven, and cut up the cooked chicken. Start the sauce for the chicken when the biscuits go into the oven. Slice the apples and rinse the grapes while the sauce simmers.

menu

**CHEESY
TOMATO-CHICKEN
SKILLET**

Mixed spinach and leaf lettuce salad with orange segments and balsamic vinaigrette

Soft breadsticks and butter

Cantaloupe wedges topped with vanilla frozen yogurt

While waiting for the pasta water to boil and the oven to preheat for the breadsticks, chop the tomatoes and basil. Assemble the salad, but wait to dress it until just before serving. Put the breadsticks in the oven when you begin to cook the chicken.

Cheesy Tomato-Chicken Skillet

Garnish each plate with fresh basil leaves to complement the herb mixed with the pasta.

Yield: 4 (1¼-cup) servings

7 oz. (2 cups) uncooked pasta nuggets (radiatore)

¾ lb. chicken breast strips for stir-frying

1 (10¾-oz.) can condensed cream of chicken soup

1½ cups (5 to 6 medium) chopped Italian plum tomatoes

½ cup milk

2 tablespoons chopped fresh basil

4 oz. (1 cup) shredded mozzarella cheese

1. Cook pasta to desired doneness as directed on package. Drain; cover to keep warm.

2. Meanwhile, spray large nonstick skillet with nonstick cooking spray. Heat over medium-high heat until hot. Add chicken strips; cook and stir 4 to 6 minutes or until chicken is no longer pink in center. Reduce heat to medium. Add soup, tomatoes, milk and basil; mix well.

3. Add cooked pasta; cook and stir until bubbly and thoroughly heated. Sprinkle with cheese. Remove from heat. Cover; let stand 2 to 3 minutes or until cheese is melted.

Nutrition Information Per Serving: Serving Size: 1¼ Cups • Calories 450 • Calories from Fat 120 • % Daily Value: Total Fat 13 g 20% • Saturated Fat 5 g 25% • Cholesterol 75 mg 25% • Sodium 820 mg 34% • Total Carbohydrate 48 g 16% • Dietary Fiber 2 g 8% • Sugars 5 g • Protein 36 g • Vitamin A 20% • Vitamin C 15% • Calcium 30% • Iron 20%
Dietary Exchanges: 3 Starch, 4 Lean Meat OR 3 Carbohydrate, 4 Lean Meat

Creamy Swiss Chicken and Noodles

Swiss families have long delighted in dipping chunks of bread into a shared pot of warm cheese sauce spiked with white wine. Our fondue-inspired recipe pairs a similar sauce with chicken and broccoli.

Yield: 5 (1½-cup) servings

6 oz. (3 cups) uncooked wide egg noodles

2 teaspoons oil

1 lb. boneless skinless chicken breast halves, cut into
    ½-inch pieces

3 cups frozen broccoli florets

½ cup white wine

1 (10¾-oz.) can condensed cream of onion soup

4 oz. (1 cup) shredded Swiss cheese

2 teaspoons Dijon mustard

⅛ teaspoon pepper

1. Cook noodles to desired doneness as directed on package. Drain; cover to keep warm.

2. Meanwhile, heat oil in 12-inch nonstick skillet over medium-high heat until hot. Add chicken; cook 2 to 3 minutes or until browned, stirring frequently. Add broccoli; cook 3 to 4 minutes or until hot, stirring occasionally.

3. Reduce heat to medium-low; stir in wine. Cover; cook 4 to 5 minutes or until chicken is no longer pink in center and broccoli is tender.

4. Add cooked noodles, soup, cheese, mustard and pepper; mix well. Cook until thoroughly heated and cheese is melted.

**CREAMY SWISS
CHICKEN AND NOODLES**

Deli mixed fruit salad

Pita or foccacia

Bakery or frozen cherry turnovers

Prepare the chicken and noodles in advance, if you like, and refrigerate them separately until it's time to combine and reheat them for supper. Briefly warm the pita or foccacia in the oven or toaster oven while the entree cooks. Sprinkle the bread with cheese if desired. Heat the turnovers as necessary while you eat dinner.

Nutrition Information Per Serving: Serving Size: 1½ Cups • Calories 380 • Calories from Fat 120 • % Daily Value: Total Fat 13 g 20% • Saturated Fat 5 g 25% • Cholesterol 105 mg 35% • Sodium 700 mg 29% • Total Carbohydrate 31 g 10% • Dietary Fiber 2 g 8% • Sugars 5 g • Protein 34 g • Vitamin A 8% • Vitamin C 20% • Calcium 25% • Iron 15%
Dietary Exchanges: 2 Starch, 4 Very Lean Meat, 2 Fat OR 2 Carbohydrate, 4 Very Lean Meat, 2 Fat

CHICKEN AND NOODLE
SUPPER

Whole-grain rolls with butter and
preserves

Fresh strawberries and blueberries
with whipped cream

Prepare the berries and chill
them until dessert time. Briefly
warm the rolls in a toaster oven
while the main course cooks.

Chicken and Noodle Supper

The characteristic chicken, noodles and vegetables found in soup team up in a similarly comforting stew.

Yield: 4 (1¼-cup) servings

2½ cups water

2 (3-oz.) pkg. chicken-flavor ramen noodle soup mix

1½ cups cubed cooked chicken

1 cup frozen peas and carrots

2 tablespoons chopped onion or 2 teaspoons instant chopped onion

1 (2.5-oz.) jar sliced mushrooms, drained

1. Bring water to a boil in large saucepan. Add ramen noodles, contents of soup mix seasoning packets, chicken, peas and carrots, and onion; mix well. Cook over medium-high heat for 4 to 6 minutes or until vegetables are tender.

2. Stir in mushrooms; cook until thoroughly heated.

Nutrition Information Per Serving: Serving Size: 1¼ Cups • Calories 320 • Calories from Fat 110 • % Daily Value: Total Fat 12 g 18% • Saturated Fat 5 g 25% • Cholesterol 45 mg 15% • Sodium 800 mg 33% • Total Carbohydrate 32 g 11% • Dietary Fiber 2 g 8% • Sugars 3 g • Protein 21 g • Vitamin A 70% • Vitamin C 4% • Calcium 4% • Iron 10%
Dietary Exchanges: 2 Starch, 2 Very Lean Meat, 2 Fat OR 2 Carbohydrate, 2 Very Lean Meat, 2 Fat

Golden Rice and Chicken Pilaf

Curry powder gives the chicken and rice a golden tint and infuses them with spicy flavor. Curry powder is a spice blend, not a single ingredient.

Yield: 4 (1½-cup) servings

2 teaspoons oil

1 lb. fresh chicken tenders

½ cup chopped onion

1 cup uncooked regular long-grain white rice

½ cup shredded carrot

¼ cup golden raisins

1 teaspoon curry powder

1 teaspoon coriander

¼ teaspoon salt

1 (14½-oz.) can ready-to-serve chicken broth

½ cup water

¼ cup slivered almonds, toasted if desired

1. Heat oil in large nonstick skillet over medium-high heat until hot. Add chicken and onion; cook 5 minutes or until chicken is browned and onion is tender, stirring occasionally.

2. Add all remaining ingredients except almonds; mix well. Bring to a boil. Reduce heat to medium-low; cover and cook 15 to 20 minutes or until chicken is no longer pink, rice is tender and liquid is absorbed. Top each serving with almonds.

Nutrition Information Per Serving: Serving Size: 1½ Cups • Calories 410 • Calories from Fat 90 • % Daily Value: Total Fat 10 g 15% • Saturated Fat 2 g 10% • Cholesterol 65 mg 22% • Sodium 530 mg 22% • Total Carbohydrate 49 g 16% • Dietary Fiber 3 g 12% • Sugars 8 g • Protein 32 g • Vitamin A 80% • Vitamin C 4% • Calcium 6% • Iron 20%
Dietary Exchanges: 3 Starch, ½ Fruit, 3 Very Lean Meat, 1 Fat OR 3½ Carbohydrate, 3 Very Lean Meat, 1 Fat

GOLDEN RICE AND CHICKEN PILAF

Mango chutney

Banana bread

Custard pudding

Make the banana bread from scratch or a mix early in the day if you haven't purchased it ready to serve. Present it plain, or spread it with whipped cream cheese. Set out the chutney while the chicken is cooking.

menu

CHICKEN STRIPS ITALIANO WITH LINGUINE

Broccoli spears with butter and garlic-pepper blend

Lemon bars

Cut the chicken into strips while the oven preheats. Cook the broccoli while the chicken cooks. Drain the broccoli and toss it with butter and garlic-pepper blend.

Nutrition Information Per Serving: Serving Size: ½ of Recipe • Calories 700 • Calories from Fat 280 • % Daily Value: Total Fat 31 g 48% • Saturated Fat 6 g 30% • Cholesterol 75 mg 25% • Sodium 1,190 mg 50% • Total Carbohydrate 66 g 22% • Dietary Fiber 4 g 16% • Sugars 5 g • Protein 40 g • Vitamin A 15% • Vitamin C 15% • Calcium 20% • Iron 30%
Dietary Exchanges: 4½ Starch, 3½ Very Lean Meat, 5 Fat OR 4½ Carbohydrate, 3½ Very Lean Meat, 5 Fat

Chicken Strips Italiano with Linguine

Bottled Italian dressing makes a quick, flavorful marinade for chicken strips with linguine and red sauce.

Yield: 2 servings

---

4 oz. uncooked linguine

¼ cup grated Parmesan cheese

¼ cup Italian style dry bread crumbs

¼ cup purchased Italian salad dressing

½ lb. boneless skinless chicken breast halves, cut into 1-inch-thick strips

1 tablespoon oil

1 cup spaghetti sauce

Chopped fresh parsley

---

1. Cook linguine to desired doneness as directed on package. Drain.

2. Meanwhile, in small bowl, combine cheese and bread crumbs; mix well. Place salad dressing in another small bowl. Dip chicken strips in salad dressing; place in bread crumb mixture. Toss to coat evenly.

3. Heat oil in large skillet over medium heat until hot. Add chicken strips; cook 8 to 10 minutes or until chicken is lightly browned and no longer pink in center, turning occasionally.

4. Place spaghetti sauce in small microwave-safe bowl; cover with waxed paper. Microwave on HIGH for 2 to 3 minutes or until thoroughly heated, stirring once.

5. Serve hot spaghetti sauce and chicken strips over linguine. Sprinkle with parsley.

Chicken and Spinach Tetrazzini

If you're tired of seeing red (sauce, that is), try this classic pasta dish featuring spinach and chicken.

Yield: 4 servings

8 oz. uncooked spaghetti

3 tablespoons margarine or butter

¼ cup chopped onion

1 garlic clove, minced

2 tablespoons all-purpose flour

½ teaspoon salt

¼ teaspoon dried oregano leaves

¼ teaspoon dried basil leaves

Dash pepper

2 cups milk

½ cup grated Parmesan cheese

1½ cups cubed cooked chicken

1 cup frozen cut leaf spinach, thawed

1 large carrot, cut into ¼-inch slices, cooked

1 tablespoon grated Parmesan cheese

1. Cook spaghetti to desired doneness as directed on package. Drain.

2. Meanwhile, melt margarine in large saucepan over medium heat. Add onion and garlic; cook 2 to 3 minutes or until tender. Stir in flour, salt, oregano, basil and pepper; cook until mixture is smooth and bubbly. Gradually add milk, stirring constantly, until mixture boils and thickens.

3. Add ½ cup cheese, chicken, spinach and carrot; cook 2 to 3 minutes or until spinach is tender, stirring constantly.

4. Serve chicken mixture over spaghetti. Sprinkle with 1 tablespoon cheese.

menu

CHICKEN AND SPINACH TETRAZZINI

Caesar salad

Whole-grain Italian rolls

Chocolate ice cream and almond biscotti cookies

Start the water for the pasta. Defrost the spinach in the microwave or by setting it in a bowl of hot water. Prepare the salad, but wait to add the dressing until the last minute. Prepare the ingredients for the tetrazzini recipe. Once the sauce is under way, warm the rolls in the toaster oven.

Nutrition Information Per Serving: Serving Size: ¼ of Recipe • Calories 520 • Calories from Fat 170 • % Daily Value: Total Fat 19 g 29% • Saturated Fat 6 g 30% • Cholesterol 65 mg 22% • Sodium 740 mg 31% • Total Carbohydrate 55 g 18% • Dietary Fiber 3 g 12% • Sugars 8 g • Protein 32 g • Vitamin A 190% • Vitamin C 10% • Calcium 35% • Iron 20%
Dietary Exchanges: 3½ Starch, 3 Lean Meat, 1½ Fat OR 3½ Carbohydrate, 3 Lean Meat, 1½ Fat

CHICKEN RAVIOLI MARINARA

Chopped mixed vegetable salad with ranch salad dressing

Sliced fresh peaches

Chocolate candy with almonds

Ahead of time, or while the sauce heats up, chop an assortment of fresh vegetables, including bell pepper, celery, carrot, cucumber, snow pea pods, onion and tomato. Toss them with ranch dressing just before serving. Slice the peaches when you're ready for dessert so they don't discolor, or toss them with lemon or orange juice if you are preparing them ahead.

Chicken Ravioli Marinara

For an all-in-one dinner, cook the zucchini half-moons right in the marinara sauce that gets tossed with ravioli.

Yield: 6 servings

1 (25-oz.) pkg. frozen chicken or cheese-filled ravioli

3 to 4 small zucchini, halved lengthwise, sliced

1 (26-oz.) jar marinara or spaghetti sauce

1. Cook ravioli to desired doneness as directed on package. Drain; arrange on serving platter or return to saucepan. Cover to keep warm.

2. Meanwhile, in large saucepan, combine zucchini and marinara sauce; cook and stir over medium-high heat for 6 to 7 minutes or until zucchini is crisp-tender and sauce is thoroughly heated.

3. Spoon zucchini mixture over cooked ravioli, or add zucchini mixture to ravioli and toss gently. If desired, garnish with grated fresh Romano or Parmesan cheese.

Nutrition Information Per Serving: Serving Size: 1/6 of Recipe • Calories 320 • Calories from Fat 80 • % Daily Value: Total Fat 9 g 14% • Saturated Fat 2 g 10% • Cholesterol 15 mg 5% • Sodium 680 mg 28% • Total Carbohydrate 47 g 16% • Dietary Fiber 5 g 20% • Sugars 12 g • Protein 12 g • Vitamin A 20% • Vitamin C 8% • Calcium 6% • Iron 20%
Dietary Exchanges: 3 Starch, 1 Lean Meat, 1 Fat OR 3 Carbohydrate, 1 Lean Meat, 1 Fat

Quick and Spicy Chicken and Rice

No fancy technique or laborious chopping
required here; simply stir four ingredients (plus
salt and water) together and heat for a saucy,
cheesy entree. For a slightly different flavor
nuance, use smoked chicken instead of plain.

Yield: 4 (1½-cup) servings

2 cups water

¼ teaspoon salt

2 cups uncooked instant rice

3 cups frozen cut broccoli

1 (8-oz.) jar jalapeño pasteurized process cheese sauce

½ lb. cooked chicken breast (from deli), cut into ½-inch
        cubes (1½ cups)

1. In large saucepan, bring water and salt to a
boil. Add rice and broccoli; return to a boil. Boil
1 minute. Remove from heat; cover and let stand
5 minutes.

2. Stir in cheese sauce and chicken; cook over
low heat for 2 to 4 minutes or until thoroughly
heated, stirring occasionally.

Nutrition Information Per Serving: Serving Size: 1½ Cups • Calories 410 •
Calories from Fat 120 • % Daily Value: Total Fat 13 g 20% • Saturated Fat 10 g 50% •
Cholesterol 65 mg 22% • Sodium 1,560 mg 65% • Total Carbohydrate 48 g 16% •
Dietary Fiber 2 g 8% • Sugars 5 g • Protein 24 g • Vitamin A 15% • Vitamin C 35% •
Calcium 20% • Iron 15%
Dietary Exchanges: 3 Starch, 1 Vegetable, 2 Medium-Fat Meat OR 3 Carbohydrate,
1 Vegetable, 2 Medium-Fat Meat

Garden Chicken Sauté

Ramen noodles are always fun to eat, and they're delightful in this savory skillet dinner of chicken and vegetables.

Yield: 4 (1¼-cup) servings

2 teaspoons olive or vegetable oil

2 boneless skinless chicken breast halves, cut into 1-inch pieces

2 garlic cloves, minced

2 cups water

1 cup fresh baby carrots, halved crosswise

1 teaspoon dried Italian seasoning

2 (3-oz.) pkg. chicken-flavor ramen noodle soup mix

2 cups sliced zucchini

1. Heat oil in large nonstick skillet over medium-high heat until hot. Add chicken and garlic; cook and stir 4 to 5 minutes or until chicken is browned.

2. Stir in water, carrots, Italian seasoning and contents of 1 of the soup mix seasoning packets. (Discard remaining seasoning packet or reserve for a later use.) Bring to a boil. Reduce heat; cover and cook 6 to 7 minutes or until carrots are crisp-tender.

3. Gently break each block of ramen noodles in half; add noodles and zucchini to skillet. Bring to a boil. Boil, uncovered, 5 to 6 minutes or until zucchini is tender and noodles are cooked, separating noodles gently as they soften.

Nutrition Information Per Serving: Serving Size: 1¼ Cups • Calories 320 • Calories from Fat 110 • % Daily Value: Total Fat 12 g 18% • Saturated Fat 5 g 25% • Cholesterol 35 mg 12% • Sodium 710 mg 30% • Total Carbohydrate 33 g 11% • Dietary Fiber 2 g 8% • Sugars 4 g • Protein 19 g • Vitamin A 180% • Vitamin C 10% • Calcium 6% • Iron 10%
Dietary Exchanges: 2 Starch, 1 Vegetable, 1½ Very Lean Meat, 2 Fat OR 2 Carbohydrate, 1 Vegetable, 1½ Very Lean Meat, 2 Fat

menu

GARDEN CHICKEN SAUTÉ

Warm mozzarella cheese bread

Sliced oranges and fresh strawberries drizzled with strawberry yogurt

Cut up the oranges and strawberries and chill until dessert; wait to drizzle the yogurt until serving time. Cut up the chicken and vegetables for the main course. Warm the bread while the chicken is cooking.

Dilled Chicken-Potato Hash

Serve this herbed blend of chicken, potato, peppers and onions for dinner or Sunday brunch. If you like hot, spicy foods, add one or two chopped cherry peppers to the mixture.

Yield: 4 (1¼-cup) servings

2 teaspoons margarine or butter

1 lb. fresh chicken breast tenders, cut into 1-inch pieces

2 cups frozen bell pepper and onion stir-fry

1 (16-oz.) pkg. frozen southern-style hash-brown potatoes

1 teaspoon dried dill weed

½ teaspoon salt

¼ teaspoon cracked black pepper

½ cup chicken broth

1. Melt margarine in large nonstick skillet over medium-high heat. Add chicken; cook and stir 5 to 7 minutes or until chicken is no longer pink in center.

2. Add bell pepper and onion stir-fry; cook and stir 2 minutes. Add potatoes, dill, salt and pepper; cook and stir 5 minutes or until potatoes are lightly browned and mixture is hot.

3. Stir in broth; cook 1 minute.

Nutrition Information Per Serving: Serving Size: 1¼ Cups • Calories 260 • Calories from Fat 50 • % Daily Value: Total Fat 6 g 9% • Saturated Fat 1 g 5% • Cholesterol 65 mg 22% • Sodium 480 mg 20% • Total Carbohydrate 23 g 8% • Dietary Fiber 3 g 12% • Sugars 2 g • Protein 28 g • Vitamin A 6% • Vitamin C 20% • Calcium 2% • Iron 10%
Dietary Exchanges: 1 Starch, 1 Vegetable, 3 Very Lean Meat, 1 Fat OR 1 Carbohydrate, 1 Vegetable, 3 Very Lean Meat, 1 Fat

DILLED CHICKEN-POTATO HASH

Toasted English muffins with preserves

Fresh orange wedges

Chocolage pudding

Prepare instant pudding if you haven't purchased it ready to serve. Cut the oranges. Toward the end of the hash's cooking time, toast the English muffins and spread them with preserves.

menu

CREAMY CHICKEN-TOPPED POTATOES

Shredded romaine, red onion and cucumber salad with Italian dressing

Frosted ginger cookies

Assemble the salad, but wait to toss with dressing until serving time. Chop the chicken early in the day, if you wish. Refrigerate the salad and chicken separately, tightly covered, until suppertime. Start the potatoes and the chicken. Toss the salad with dressing just before you're ready to serve.

Creamy Chicken-Topped Potatoes

The creaminess of chicken and vegetables Alfredo crowns the hot baked potato.

Yield: 2 servings

---

2 medium baking potatoes

1 (9-oz.) pkg. frozen broccoli, peas, carrots and low-fat creamy Alfredo sauce

1 cup chopped cooked chicken

1 tablespoon diced pimientos

½ cup sour cream

¼ cup grated Parmesan cheese

---

1. Pierce potatoes several times with fork. Place on microwave-safe paper towel in microwave oven. Microwave on HIGH for 6 to 8 minutes or until tender, turning potatoes over and re-arranging halfway through cooking. Let stand 3 minutes.

2. Meanwhile, open pouch of vegetables; pour into medium saucepan. Add chicken and pimientos; cook over medium-low heat until vegetables are tender and mixture is thoroughly heated, stirring frequently. Stir in sour cream and 2 tablespoons of the cheese. Cook until thoroughly heated.

3. To serve, cut potatoes in half lengthwise; place on individual plates. Mash potatoes slightly with fork. Spoon vegetable mixture over potatoes. Top with remaining cheese. If desired, add salt and pepper to taste.

Nutrition Information Per Serving: Serving Size: ½ of Recipe • Calories 530 • Calories from Fat 220 • % Daily Value: Total Fat 24 g 37% • Saturated Fat 13 g 65% • Cholesterol 105 mg 35% • Sodium 820 mg 34% • Total Carbohydrate 44 g 15% • Dietary Fiber 6 g 24% • Sugars 8 g • Protein 34 g • Vitamin A 60% • Vitamin C 50% • Calcium 35% • Iron 20%
Dietary Exchanges: 2½ Starch, 1 Vegetable, 3½ Lean Meat, 2½ Fat OR 2½ Carbohydrate, 1 Vegetable, 3½ Lean Meat, 2½ Fat

Stir-Fry Chicken and Peppers

Sherry and soy sauce laced with fresh ginger makes a delicious sauce for chicken and a colorful array of vegetables.

Yield: 4 servings

1⅓ cups uncooked regular long-grain white rice

2⅔ cups water

¼ cup dry sherry

¼ cup water

3 tablespoons soy sauce

2 teaspoons cornstarch

½ teaspoon grated gingerroot

1 tablespoon oil

1 lb. chicken breast strips for stir-frying

1 medium onion, cut into 8 wedges

1 medium green bell pepper, cut into thin bite-sized strips

1 medium yellow bell pepper, cut into thin bite-sized strips

2 medium tomatoes, cut into 8 wedges

1. Cook rice in 2⅔ cups water as directed on package.

2. Meanwhile, in small bowl, combine sherry, ¼ cup water, soy sauce, cornstarch and ginger-root; blend well. Set aside.

3. Heat oil in large skillet or wok over medium-high heat until hot. Add chicken strips; cook and stir 3 minutes. Add onion and bell peppers; cook and stir 4 to 6 minutes or until chicken is no longer pink in center and vegetables are crisp-tender.

4. Stir cornstarch mixture until smooth. Add to skillet; cook and stir 2 to 3 minutes or until sauce is bubbly and thickened. Add tomatoes; cook and stir until thoroughly heated. Serve over rice.

STIR-FRY CHICKEN AND PEPPERS

Mixed fruit platter

Chocolate frozen yogurt

Start the rice; then arrange rinsed whole fruits on a platter, or choose assorted cut-up fruits that won't brown, such as fresh pineapple or canned pineapple chunks, orange slices, melon slices or chunks, fresh berries, kiwi and starfruit slices. Chill the fruit; and then cut up everything you need for the entree and stir-fry it.

Nutrition Information Per Serving: Serving Size: ¼ of Recipe • Calories 430 • Calories from Fat 60 • % Daily Value: Total Fat 7 g 11% • Saturated Fat 1 g 5% • Cholesterol 65 mg 22% • Sodium 920 mg 38% • Total Carbohydrate 60 g 20% • Dietary Fiber 3 g 12% • Sugars 5 g • Protein 31 g • Vitamin A 10% • Vitamin C 70% • Calcium 4% • Iron 25%
Dietary Exchanges: 3½ Starch, 1 Vegetable, 2½ Very Lean Meat, 1 Fat OR 3½ Carbohydrate, 1 Vegetable, 2½ Very Lean Meat, 1 Fat

Easy Chinese Chicken

Toss the cooked, drained noodles with peanut oil or sesame oil to prevent them from sticking while the chicken and vegetables are stir-fried.

Yield: 4 servings

---

1 (6-oz.) pkg. uncooked rice noodles

2 teaspoons light sesame or vegetable oil

4 boneless skinless chicken breast halves, cut into thin bite-sized strips

2 cups fresh bean sprouts

1 (9-oz.) pkg. frozen cut broccoli in a pouch, thawed, drained

1 (8-oz.) can bamboo shoots, drained

½ cup water

2 tablespoons soy sauce

4 teaspoons cornstarch

1 teaspoon sugar

½ teaspoon chicken-flavor instant bouillon

---

1. Cook noodles to desired doneness as directed on package. Drain; cover to keep warm.

2. Meanwhile, heat oil in large skillet over medium-high heat until hot. Add chicken; cook and stir 3 to 6 minutes or until chicken is no longer pink in center. Add bean sprouts, broccoli and bamboo shoots; cook and stir about 5 minutes or until vegetables are tender.

3. In small bowl, combine all remaining ingredients; blend well. Stir into chicken mixture; cook and stir until bubbly and thickened. Serve chicken mixture over noodles.

Nutrition Information Per Serving: Serving Size: ¼ of Recipe • Calories 370 • Calories from Fat 50 • % Daily Value: Total Fat 6 g 9% • Saturated Fat 1 g 5% • Cholesterol 75 mg 25% • Sodium 820 mg 34% • Total Carbohydrate 48 g 16% • Dietary Fiber 3 g 12% • Sugars 3 g • Protein 31 g • Vitamin A 6% • Vitamin C 45% • Calcium 6% • Iron 15%
Dietary Exchanges: 3 Starch, 1 Vegetable, 3 Very Lean Meat OR 3 Carbohydrate, 1 Vegetable, 3 Very Lean Meat

CHICKEN CHOW MEIN

Deli Asian cabbage salad

Egg roll bites

Raspberry sherbet topped with fresh raspberries

Preheat the oven; then start the rice. Warm the frozen or deli-bought egg rolls while the rice cooks and you prepare the chow mein. To give some crunch to the finished chow mein, top each serving with crisp chow mein noodles, dry-roasted peanuts or minced fresh celery.

Chicken Chow Mein

Long before fiery dishes from China's Hunan and Szechuan provinces became known here, chow mein (an American invention) gave folks a comforting balance of the exotic and the familiar.

Yield: 4 servings

2/3 cup uncooked regular long-grain white rice

1 1/3 cups water

1 1/2 cups cubed cooked chicken

1 cup sliced celery

1 (14 1/2-oz.) can ready-to-serve chicken broth

2 tablespoons cornstarch

2 tablespoons soy sauce

1 (14-oz.) can chow mein vegetables, drained

1 (2.5-oz.) jar sliced mushrooms, drained

1. Cook rice in water as directed on package.

2. Meanwhile, in large saucepan, combine all remaining ingredients; mix well. Bring to a boil, stirring constantly. Reduce heat; simmer 15 minutes, stirring frequently.

3. Serve chicken mixture over rice.

Nutrition Information Per Serving: Serving Size: 1/4 of Recipe • Calories 250 • Calories from Fat 45 • % Daily Value: Total Fat 5 g 8% • Saturated Fat 1 g 5% • Cholesterol 45 mg 15% • Sodium 1,220 mg 51% • Total Carbohydrate 31 g 10% • Dietary Fiber 2 g 8% • Sugars 1 g • Protein 21 g • Vitamin A 8% • Vitamin C 8% • Calcium 6% • Iron 15%
Dietary Exchanges: 1 1/2 Starch, 1 Vegetable, 2 Lean Meat OR 1 1/2 Carbohydrate, 1 Vegetable, 2 Lean Meat

Asian Cashew Chicken

Asian ingredients to keep on hand include canned water chestnuts and bamboo shoots. They easily round out this meal of breaded chicken strips with sugar snap peas and cashews.

Yield: 4 servings

1⅓ cups uncooked regular long-grain white rice

2⅔ cups water

10 frozen fully cooked breaded chicken breast strips, each cut diagonally into thirds

¼ cup cashew pieces

2 teaspoons oil

1 (9-oz.) pkg. frozen sugar snap peas in a pouch

1 (8-oz.) can whole water chestnuts, drained, quartered

1 (8-oz.) can sliced bamboo shoots, drained

1 cup chicken broth

2 tablespoons teriyaki sauce

2 tablespoons hoisin sauce

1 tablespoon cornstarch

1. Cook rice in water as directed on package.

2. Meanwhile, heat oven to 400° F. Place chicken in single layer on ungreased cookie sheet. Bake at 400° F. for 10 to 15 minutes or until crisp and thoroughly heated, adding cashews to cookie sheet during last 3 minutes of baking time.

3. Heat oil in large skillet over medium-high heat until hot. Add sugar snap peas; cook and stir 3 minutes or until crisp-tender. Stir in water chestnuts and bamboo shoots.

4. In small bowl, combine broth, teriyaki sauce, hoisin sauce and cornstarch; blend well. Add to vegetables; cook until mixture boils and thickens, stirring occasionally. Fold in cooked chicken; sprinkle with cashews. Serve over rice.

ASIAN CASHEW CHICKEN

Sliced fresh oranges

Egg rolls with hot mustard sauce

Fortune cookies

Slice the oranges and chill until serving time. If you wish, make this chicken dish in advance, but wait to add the cashews until serving time to make sure they remain crisp. Start the rice and preheat the oven; then assemble all the ingredients for the stir-fry so you'll be ready to add them in sequence. Heat the egg rolls in the oven while the chicken bakes.

Nutrition Information Per Serving: Serving Size: ¼ of Recipe • Calories 620 • Calories from Fat 170 • % Daily Value: Total Fat 19 g 29% • Saturated Fat 4 g 20% • Cholesterol 35 mg 12% • Sodium 1,290 mg 54% • Total Carbohydrate 88 g 29% • Dietary Fiber 5 g 20% • Sugars 12 g • Protein 23 g • Vitamin A 2% • Vitamin C 8% • Calcium 8% • Iron 25%
Dietary Exchanges: 4½ Starch, 1 Fruit, 1 Lean Meat, 2½ Fat OR 5½ Carbohydrate, 1 Lean Meat, 2½ Fat

SWEET-AND-SOUR SESAME CHICKEN AND NOODLES

Refrigerated breadsticks

Mixed green salad with Asian salad dressing

Chocolate cream pie

Purchase the pie ahead of time, or make it by pouring instant pudding into a graham cracker pie shell and chilling it until dessert. Assemble the salad, except for the dressing; then prepare the entree. Bake the breadsticks while the chicken cooks, or use purchased breadsticks.

Sweet-and-Sour Sesame Chicken and Noodles

This dish is best prepared just before serving so the chicken's coating stays crisp.

Yield: 4 (1½-cup) servings

20 frozen fully cooked breaded chicken nuggets

1 (1-lb.) pkg. frozen broccoli florets, carrots and water chestnuts

1 (2.8-oz.) pkg. any flavor ramen noodle soup mix

1 (8-oz.) can pineapple chunks in juice, undrained

½ cup water

¾ cup purchased sweet-and-sour sauce

1 tablespoon sesame seed, toasted if desired

1. Heat chicken nuggets as directed on package.

2. Meanwhile, spray large nonstick skillet with nonstick cooking spray. Heat over medium-high heat until hot. Add vegetables; cover and cook 2 to 3 minutes or until thawed.

3. Reserve for a future use or discard seasoning packet from soup mix. Break noodles into pieces. Add noodles, pineapple with liquid and water to skillet. Reduce heat to medium; cover and cook 4 to 6 minutes or until vegetables are crisp-tender and noodles are tender.

4. Stir in sweet-and-sour sauce. Fold in hot chicken nuggets; cook and stir until thoroughly heated. Sprinkle with sesame seed.

Nutrition Information Per Serving: Serving Size: 1½ Cups • Calories 450 • Calories from Fat 150 • % Daily Value: Total Fat 17 g 26% • Saturated Fat 4 g 20% • Cholesterol 10 mg 3% • Sodium 990 mg 41% • Total Carbohydrate 60 g 20% • Dietary Fiber 5 g 20% • Sugars 22 g • Protein 13 g • Vitamin A 60% • Vitamin C 30% • Calcium 8% • Iron 10%
Dietary Exchanges: 2 Starch, 1½ Fruit, 1½ Vegetable, ½ Medium-Fat Meat, 2½ Fat OR 3½ Carbohydrate, 1½ Vegetable, ½ Medium-Fat Meat, 2½ Fat

Quick Italian Chicken and Rice

This speedy version of chicken and rice with tomatoes can easily be doubled for a bigger crowd. Garnish each serving with fresh basil leaves or a sprig of parsley.

Yield: 3 (1²/₃-cup) servings

3 (4-oz.) pkg. refrigerated tomato and herb with basil-seasoned boneless skinless chicken breast fillet

2 teaspoons oil

1 (14.5-oz.) can Italian-style stewed tomatoes, undrained

¾ cup water

1½ cups uncooked instant white rice

1. Cut chicken fillets into small bite-sized strips.

2. Heat oil in large nonstick skillet over medium-high heat until hot. Add chicken; cook and stir 4 to 5 minutes or until browned and no longer pink in center.

3. Add tomatoes and water; mix well. Bring to a boil. Stir in rice. Cover; remove from heat. Let stand 5 minutes or until liquid is absorbed.

Nutrition Information Per Serving: Serving Size: 1²/₃ Cups • Calories 350 • Calories from Fat 35 • % Daily Value: Total Fat 4 g 6% • Saturated Fat 0 g 0% • Cholesterol 55 mg 18% • Sodium 1,120 mg 47% • Total Carbohydrate 51 g 17% • Dietary Fiber 2 g 8% • Sugars 3 g • Protein 27 g • Vitamin A 15% • Vitamin C 20% • Calcium 8% • Iron 25%
Dietary Exchanges: 3 Starch, 1 Vegetable, 2½ Very Lean Meat OR 3 Carbohydrate, 1 Vegetable, 2½ Very Lean Meat

QUICK ITALIAN CHICKEN AND RICE

Deli mixed Italian vegetable salad

Crusty French bread

Fudge brownies drizzled with melted vanilla chips

While the chicken cooks, set out the salad and slice the bread. Whether you have homemade or bakery brownies, dress them up at dessert time by drizzling them with melted white vanilla chips.

CHICKEN, PINEAPPLE AND BROCCOLI SUPREME

Roasted sweet potato cubes

Corn muffins

Butterscotch pudding

Bake the corn muffins in advance and warm them while the chicken cooks, or purchase muffins that are ready to serve. Prepare instant pudding if you haven't purchased it ready to serve. Toss the sweet potato with a little olive oil and chopped apple, and roast or microwave until it is tender while you prepare the entree.

Chicken, Pineapple and Broccoli Supreme

This recipe is a supremely delicious dish that will become a mainstay of a time-crunched cook.

Yield: 4 servings

1 (9-oz.) pkg. frozen broccoli spears in a pouch

4 boneless skinless chicken breast halves

3 tablespoons all-purpose flour

½ teaspoon salt

⅛ teaspoon white pepper

2 tablespoons margarine or butter

1 (8-oz.) can pineapple slices, drained

4 oz. (4 slices) Monterey Jack cheese

1. Cook broccoli as directed on package. Drain; cover to keep warm.

2. Meanwhile, place 1 chicken breast half, boned side up, between 2 pieces of plastic wrap or waxed paper. Working from center, gently pound chicken with flat side of meat mallet or rolling pin until about ¼ inch thick; remove wrap. Repeat with remaining chicken breast halves.

3. In shallow pan, combine flour, salt and pepper. Coat chicken with flour mixture.

4. Melt margarine in large skillet. Add chicken; cook 10 to 12 minutes or until chicken is fork-tender and juices run clear, turning once.

5. Place pineapple slice on each chicken breast half. Top each pineapple slice with ¼ of broccoli spears and 1 cheese slice. Cover; cook an additional minute or until cheese is melted.

Nutrition Information Per Serving: Serving Size: ¼ of Recipe • Calories 350 • Calories from Fat 160 • % Daily Value: Total Fat 18 g 28% • Saturated Fat 7 g 35% • Cholesterol 100 mg 33% • Sodium 630 mg 26% • Total Carbohydrate 12 g 4% • Dietary Fiber 2 g 8% • Sugars 6 g • Protein 36 g • Vitamin A 15% • Vitamin C 30% • Calcium 25% • Iron 10%
Dietary Exchanges: ½ Fruit, 1 Vegetable, 5 Very Lean Meat, 3 Fat OR ½ Carbohydrate, 1 Vegetable, 5 Very Lean Meat, 3 Fat

Chicken and Shrimp Stir-Fry

Cutting stir-fry ingredients into small, uniformly sized pieces is a technique that originated in China, where a way to shorten cooking times was made necessary by a shortage of cooking fuel.

Yield: 4 servings

1⅓ cups uncooked regular long-grain white rice

3 cups water

3 tablespoons soy sauce

2 tablespoons dry sherry

2 teaspoons cornstarch

1 garlic clove, minced

1 tablespoon oil

½ lb. chicken breast strips for stir-frying

1 (1-lb.) pkg. frozen broccoli florets, carrots and water chestnuts

½ lb. shelled deveined uncooked medium shrimp, tails removed

1. Cook rice in 2⅔ cups of the water as directed on package.

2. Meanwhile, in small bowl, combine remaining ⅓ cup water, soy sauce, sherry, cornstarch and garlic; blend well. Set aside.

3. Heat oil in 12-inch skillet or wok over medium-high heat until hot. Add chicken strips; cook and stir 4 to 6 minutes or until chicken is no longer pink in center.

4. Stir in frozen vegetables. Cover; cook 3 to 4 minutes or until vegetables are thawed, stirring once. Add shrimp. Cover; cook 3 to 4 minutes or until shrimp turn pink, stirring once.

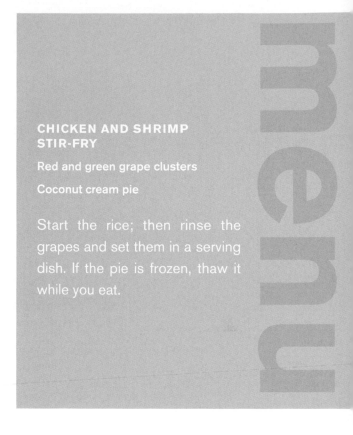

menu

CHICKEN AND SHRIMP STIR-FRY

Red and green grape clusters

Coconut cream pie

Start the rice; then rinse the grapes and set them in a serving dish. If the pie is frozen, thaw it while you eat.

5. Stir cornstarch mixture until smooth. Add to skillet; cook and stir until sauce is bubbly and thickened. Serve over rice.

Nutrition Information Per Serving: Serving Size: ¼ of Recipe • Calories 410 • Calories from Fat 50 • % Daily Value: Total Fat 6 g 9% • Saturated Fat 1 g 5% • Cholesterol 115 mg 38% • Sodium 980 mg 41% • Total Carbohydrate 60 g 20% • Dietary Fiber 3 g 12% • Sugars 4 g • Protein 28 g • Vitamin A 60% • Vitamin C 25% • Calcium 6% • Iron 25%
Dietary Exchanges: 3½ Starch, 1 Vegetable, 2½ Lean Meat, ½ Fat OR 3½ Carbohydrate, 1 Vegetable, 2½ Lean Meat, ½ Fat

Chicken Lo Mein

Angel hair pasta, delicate and quick-cooking, stands in for Chinese lo mein noodles. Cooked in broth along with the chicken, ginger, soy and vegetables, the noodles absorb the flavors.

Yield: 4 (1½-cup) servings

---

1 tablespoon oil

2 boneless skinless chicken breast halves, cut into thin bite-sized strips

1 garlic clove, minced

¼ teaspoon ginger

½ cup water

2 tablespoons soy sauce

1 (10½-oz.) can condensed chicken broth

4 oz. uncooked angel hair pasta (capellini), broken into thirds

1 (1-lb.) pkg. frozen broccoli florets, carrots and water chestnuts

---

1. Heat oil in large skillet or wok over medium-high heat until hot. Add chicken and garlic; cook and stir 4 to 5 minutes or until chicken is no longer pink in center.

2. Add ginger, water, soy sauce and broth. Bring to a boil. Stir in pasta. Add frozen vegetables; stir gently. Return to a boil. Reduce heat to medium-low; cover and simmer 5 to 8 minutes or until pasta and vegetables are tender, stirring occasionally.

Nutrition Information Per Serving: Serving Size: 1½ Cups • Calories 280 • Calories from Fat 60 • % Daily Value: Total Fat 7 g 11% • Saturated Fat 1 g 5% • Cholesterol 35 mg 12% • Sodium 1,050 mg 44% • Total Carbohydrate 30 g 10% • Dietary Fiber 3 g 12% • Sugars 4 g • Protein 23 g • Vitamin A 60% • Vitamin C 25% • Calcium 4% • Iron 15%
Dietary Exchanges: 1½ Starch, 1 Vegetable, 2½ Very Lean Meat, 1 Fat OR 1½ Carbohydrate, 1 Vegetable, 2½ Very Lean Meat, 1 Fat

menu

LEMON-GINGER CHICKEN

White rice

Steamed snow pea pods

Lemon sherbet and almond cookies

Start the rice, and then prepare the chicken. While the chicken is cooking, trim the snow peas; steam them briefly just before you begin microwaving the sauce.

tip

*When a recipe calls for citrus peel or "zest," remove the colored part of the skin only, not the bitter white pith underneath.

Lemon-Ginger Chicken

While the chicken sautés on the stove top, the tangy-sweet sauce—bright with the flavors of lemon and ginger—warms in the microwave oven.

Yield: 4 servings

4 boneless skinless chicken breast halves

2 teaspoons ginger

1/3 cup water

1/2 teaspoon grated lemon peel*

3 tablespoons lemon juice

3 tablespoons honey

2 tablespoons orange juice

2 teaspoons cornstarch

1. Rub chicken breast halves with ginger. Spray large nonstick skillet with nonstick cooking spray. Heat over medium-high heat until hot. Add chicken; cover and cook 8 to 12 minutes or until chicken is fork-tender and juices run clear, turning once.

2. Meanwhile, in small microwave-safe bowl, combine all remaining ingredients; blend well. Microwave on HIGH for 1½ to 2 minutes or until sauce has thickened.

3. To serve, spoon sauce over chicken. If desired, serve with lemon slices and green onions.

Nutrition Information Per Serving: Serving Size: ¼ of Recipe • Calories 200 • Calories from Fat 25 • % Daily Value: Total Fat 3 g 5% • Saturated Fat 1 g 5% • Cholesterol 75 mg 25% • Sodium 65 mg 3% • Total Carbohydrate 17 g 6% • Dietary Fiber 0 g 0% • Sugars 14 g • Protein 27 g • Vitamin A 0% • Vitamin C 10% • Calcium 0% • Iron 6%
Dietary Exchanges: 1 Fruit, 4 Very Lean Meat OR 1 Carbohydrate, 4 Very Lean Meat

Pecan Chicken with Creamy Honey-Mustard Sauce

The sauce—a mixture of honey-mustard salad dressing, sour cream and sliced green onions—is also delicious on grilled chicken or fish, especially salmon.

Yield: 2 servings

Chicken

2 boneless skinless chicken breast halves

2 tablespoons all-purpose flour

⅓ cup purchased honey mustard salad dressing

½ cup finely chopped pecans

2 tablespoons butter

Sauce

2 tablespoons purchased honey mustard salad dressing

⅓ cup sour cream

1 teaspoon sliced green onions

1. Place 1 chicken breast half, boned side up, between 2 pieces of plastic wrap or waxed paper. Working from center, gently pound chicken with flat side of meat mallet or rolling pin until about ¼ inch thick; remove wrap. Repeat with remaining chicken breast half.

2. Place flour, ⅓ cup dressing and pecans in 3 separate small flat dishes. Coat each chicken breast half with flour. Dip in dressing to coat well. Dip in pecans, coating both sides.

3. Melt butter in medium nonstick skillet over medium-low heat. Add chicken; cook 4 to 6 minutes or until chicken is fork-tender and juices run clear, turning once. Remove chicken from skillet; place on serving platter. Cover to keep warm.

PECAN CHICKEN WITH CREAMY HONEY-MUSTARD SAUCE

Rice pilaf

Fresh or frozen asparagus spears with butter and marjoram

Strawberry shortcakes

Chop the pecans and assemble the other ingredients for the entree; then start the rice and trim the asparagus. The chicken, rice and asparagus can cook at the same time. If you're using fresh strawberries, rinse and slice them for dessert; otherwise, defrost the frozen berries while you're having dinner.

4. To drippings in skillet, add 2 tablespoons dressing and sour cream; cook and stir until mixture boils and thickens. Pour over chicken. Sprinkle with onions.

Nutrition Information Per Serving: Serving Size: ½ of Recipe • Calories 720 • Calories from Fat 470 • % Daily Value: Total Fat 52 g 80% • Saturated Fat 16 g 80% • Cholesterol 120 mg 40% • Sodium 620 mg 26% • Total Carbohydrate 32 g 11% • Dietary Fiber 5 g 20% • Sugars 21 g • Protein 32 g • Vitamin A 15% • Vitamin C 0% • Calcium 6% • Iron 10%
Dietary Exchanges: 2 Starch, 3½ Very Lean Meat, 9½ Fat OR 2 Carbohydrate, 3½ Very Lean Meat, 9½ Fat

Grilled Teriyaki-Apricot Chicken

Evidence that low-fat does *not* always equal low flavor, each serving has just 3 grams of fat. The apricot- and ginger-enhanced teriyaki baste guarantees that each forkful will be tantalizing.

Yield: 4 servings

4 boneless skinless chicken breast halves

¼ teaspoon salt

¼ teaspoon coarse ground black pepper

⅓ cup apricot preserves, large pieces finely chopped

3 tablespoons purchased teriyaki baste and glaze

½ teaspoon grated gingerroot

1. Heat grill. Sprinkle chicken with salt and pepper. In small bowl, combine all remaining ingredients; mix well. Set aside.

2. When ready to grill, place chicken on gas grill over medium heat or on charcoal grill 4 to 6 inches from medium coals. Cook 15 to 20 minutes or until chicken is fork-tender and juices run clear, turning once and brushing with teriyaki-apricot mixture during last 5 minutes of cooking time.

Nutrition Information Per Serving: Serving Size: ¼ of Recipe • Calories 220 • Calories from Fat 25 • % Daily Value: Total Fat 3 g 5% • Saturated Fat 1 g 5% • Cholesterol 75 mg 25% • Sodium 510 mg 21% • Total Carbohydrate 21 g 7% • Dietary Fiber 0 g 0% • Sugars 16 g • Protein 27 g • Vitamin A 0% • Vitamin C 2% • Calcium 4% • Iron 8%
Dietary Exchanges: 1 ½ Fruit, 4 Very Lean Meat OR 1 ½ Carbohydrate, 4 Very Lean Meat

menu

GRILLED TERIYAKI-APRICOT CHICKEN

White rice

Green beans

Chocolate sorbet or frozen yogurt

While waiting for the grill to heat, get the green beans ready and start the rice.

tip

To broil chicken, place on broiler pan; broil 4 to 6 inches from heat using times in recipe as a guide, turning once and brushing with mixture as directed.

menu

SIMPLE CHICKEN PARMIGIANA

Refrigerated linguine or fettuccine

Buttered broccoli cuts

Chocolate cake

Bring the water to a boil for the refrigerated pasta, and then prepare the chicken recipe. Start the broccoli and the spaghetti sauce when the chicken is added to the skillet.

Simple Chicken Parmigiana

"Parmigiana" means Parmesan, but the name tells only half the cheese story. Melted mozzarella completes the recipe.

Yield: 4 servings

¼ cup unseasoned dry bread crumbs

2 tablespoons grated Parmesan cheese

2 tablespoons chopped fresh Italian parsley

4 boneless skinless chicken breast halves

1 egg, beaten

2 tablespoons olive or vegetable oil

⅔ cup spaghetti sauce

2 oz. (½ cup) shredded mozzarella cheese

1. In medium bowl, combine bread crumbs, Parmesan cheese and parsley; mix well. Dip chicken in beaten egg; coat with bread crumb mixture.

2. Heat oil in large nonstick skillet over medium-high heat until hot. Add chicken; reduce heat to medium. Cook 20 to 23 minutes or until chicken is fork-tender and juices run clear, turning once.

3. Meanwhile, heat spaghetti sauce. Sprinkle chicken with mozzarella cheese; cover skillet to melt cheese. Serve sauce with chicken. Garnish as desired.

Nutrition Information Per Serving: Serving Size: ¼ of Recipe • Calories 320 • Calories from Fat 140 • % Daily Value: Total Fat 16 g 25% • Saturated Fat 4 g 20% • Cholesterol 135 mg 45% • Sodium 420 mg 18% • Total Carbohydrate 9 g 3% • Dietary Fiber 1 g 3% • Sugars 1 g • Protein 35 g • Vitamin A 10% • Vitamin C 6% • Calcium 20% • Iron 10%
Dietary Exchanges: ½ Starch, 4½ Very Lean Meat, 2½ Fat OR ½ Carbohydrate, 4½ Very Lean Meat, 2½ Fat

Light Chicken Parmesan

Breaded and sautéed to a lovely golden brown, chicken breasts are combined with spaghetti sauce and melted cheese.

Yield: 4 servings

1 cup spaghetti sauce

4 boneless skinless chicken breast halves

3 tablespoons Italian-style dry bread crumbs

1 tablespoon grated Parmesan cheese

1 tablespoon margarine or butter, melted

¼ cup shredded reduced-fat 6-cheese Italian-recipe
     cheese blend

2 tablespoons chopped fresh parsley

1. Heat spaghetti sauce in small saucepan over low heat until thoroughly heated. Cover to keep warm.

2. Meanwhile, place 1 chicken breast half, boned side up, between 2 pieces of plastic wrap or waxed paper. Working from center, gently pound chicken with flat side of meat mallet or rolling pin until about ¼ inch thick; remove wrap. Repeat with remaining chicken breast halves.

3. In shallow bowl, combine bread crumbs, Parmesan cheese and margarine; mix well. Coat chicken with crumb mixture.

4. Spray large nonstick skillet with nonstick cooking spray. Heat over medium-high heat until hot. Add chicken; cook 4 to 6 minutes or until fork-tender and juices run clear, turning once.

5. To serve, place cooked chicken on serving platter; sprinkle with shredded cheese. Pour warm spaghetti sauce over chicken. Sprinkle with parsley.

LIGHT CHICKEN PARMESAN

Spaghetti

Green beans

Biscotti cookies

Bring the water to a boil for the pasta. Pound the chicken breasts before cooking to help tenderize the meat and promote even cooking. Cook the green beans while the chicken cooks. Serve the biscotti with coffee or hot chocolate for dipping.

Nutrition Information Per Serving: Serving Size: ¼ of Recipe • Calories 240 • Calories from Fat 80 • % Daily Value: Total Fat 9 g 14% • Saturated Fat 2 g 10% • Cholesterol 75 mg 25% • Sodium 500 mg 21% • Total Carbohydrate 9 g 3% • Dietary Fiber 1 g 4% • Sugars 0 g • Protein 31 g • Vitamin A 10% • Vitamin C 8% • Calcium 10% • Iron 10%
Dietary Exchanges: ½ Fruit, 4½ Very Lean Meat, 1 Fat OR ½ Carbohydrate, 4½ Very Lean Meat, 1 Fat

menu

**LEMON-PEPPER
CHICKEN STEW**

Crisp breadsticks

**Cantaloupe wedges with raspberry
sherbet**

Slice and chill the cantaloupe;
then cut up the chicken and prepare the entree. If you're serving
melon wedges with the skin on,
set out serrated-edge grapefruit
spoons for easier eating.

Lemon-Pepper Chicken Stew

Here's a dish whose ease of preparation and
short ingredient list belies the elegant meal that
results.

Yield: 4 (1½-cup) servings

1 tablespoon oil

1 lb. boneless skinless chicken breast halves, cut into
        1-inch pieces

1 (1 lb. 10-oz.) pkg. frozen potato, carrots, broccoli and
        cauliflower with lemon-pepper seasoning meal
        starter

1 cup water

1 (10¾-oz.) can condensed cream of chicken soup

1. Heat oil in large saucepan over medium-high
heat until hot. Add chicken; cook 4 to 5 minutes
or until browned, stirring occasionally.

2. Add frozen vegetables, contents of seasoning
packet from meal starter and water; mix well.
Bring to a boil. Reduce heat to medium; cover
and cook 6 to 8 minutes or until chicken is no
longer pink in center and vegetables are tender,
stirring occasionally.

3. Add soup; mix well. Cook an additional 2 to
3 minutes or until thoroughly heated.

Nutrition Information Per Serving: Serving Size: 1½ Cups • Calories 370 •
Calories from Fat 100 • % Daily Value: Total Fat 11 g 17% • Saturated Fat 2 g 10% •
Cholesterol 75 mg 25% • Sodium 2,050 mg 85% • Total Carbohydrate 38 g 13% •
Dietary Fiber 5 g 20% • Sugars 8 g • Protein 30 g • Vitamin A 60% • Vitamin C 35% •
Calcium 8% • Iron 10%
Dietary Exchanges: 2 Starch, 2 Vegetable, 3 Very Lean Meat, 1½ Fat OR
2 Carbohydrate, 2 Vegetable, 3 Very Lean Meat, 1½ Fat

Winter Chicken Stew

When the weather is brisk, a stew of chicken and vegetables brings a warm ending to the day.

Yield: 4 (1½-cup) servings

1 teaspoon onion powder

1 lb. fresh chicken breast tenders, cut in half crosswise

3 medium Yukon gold or russet potatoes, cut into 1-inch cubes (about 3½ cups)

1 cup fresh baby carrots

1 (8-oz.) pkg. fresh whole mushrooms, halved

1 (14½-oz.) can ready-to-serve fat-free chicken broth with ⅓ less sodium

1 tablespoon tomato paste

½ teaspoon salt

½ teaspoon dried thyme leaves

¼ cup water

2 tablespoons cornstarch

1. Sprinkle onion powder evenly over chicken; toss to coat. Spray nonstick Dutch oven with nonstick cooking spray. Heat over medium-high heat until hot. Add chicken; cook until browned.

2. Add all remaining ingredients except water and cornstarch. Bring to a boil. Reduce heat to low; cover and simmer 15 minutes or until vegetables are tender and chicken is no longer pink in center.

3. In small bowl, combine water and cornstarch; blend well. Add to chicken mixture; mix well. Bring to a boil. Cook and stir until thickened.

Nutrition Information Per Serving: Serving Size: 1½ Cups • Calories 300 • Calories from Fat 25 • % Daily Value: Total Fat 3 g 5% • Saturated Fat 1 g 5% • Cholesterol 65 mg 22% • Sodium 620 mg 26% • Total Carbohydrate 38 g 13% • Dietary Fiber 4 g 16% • Sugars 4 g • Protein 30 g • Vitamin A 160% • Vitamin C 25% • Calcium 4% • Iron 20%
Dietary Exchanges: 2½ Starch, 3 Very Lean Meat OR 2½ Carbohydrate, 3 Very Lean Meat

WINTER CHICKEN STEW

Lettuce wedge salad with Thousand Island dressing and fresh chives

Whole wheat bread

Apple dumplings with maple syrup

Assemble and prepare all of the ingredients for the stew, but wait to cut up the potatoes until last—the cut surfaces will discolor if exposed to air for too long. Cut up the lettuce, and chop some fresh chives while the entree cooks. Just before serving, drizzle the lettuce with dressing and sprinkle with chives. While you're having dinner, heat the dumplings as needed.

**VEGETABLE CHICKEN
SOUP**

Grilled cheddar cheese sandwiches

Ice cream bars

Grill the sandwiches in the toaster oven or a sauté pan while the soup heats.

tip

*Small pasta shapes are best for soup—easier to eat with a spoon. Good choices include minia-ture shells, mafalda (mini lasagna noodles), ditalini and tubettini (little tubes), orzo (rice-shaped pasta) and alphabet macaroni.

Vegetable Chicken Soup

Purchased broth makes a steaming and satisfying bowlful for supper when chock-full of chicken, vegetables, and pasta.

Yield: 4 (1¼-cup) servings

2 (14½-oz.) cans ready-to-serve chicken broth

2 cups water

1 cup frozen mixed vegetables

3 oz. (¾ cup) uncooked small shell pasta or specialty shaped pasta*

1½ cups cubed cooked chicken

¼ teaspoon dried thyme leaves

¼ teaspoon salt

⅛ teaspoon pepper

2 tablespoons chopped fresh parsley, if desired

1. In large saucepan, bring broth and water to a boil. Add vegetables; return to a boil.

2. Add pasta, chicken, thyme, salt and pepper; return to a boil. Cook 7 to 9 minutes or until pasta and vegetables are tender. Sprinkle with parsley.

Nutrition Information Per Serving: Serving Size: 1¼ Cups • Calories 220 • Calories from Fat 45 • % Daily Value: Total Fat 5 g 8% • Saturated Fat 1 g 5% • Cholesterol 45 mg 15% • Sodium 850 mg 35% • Total Carbohydrate 21 g 7% • Dietary Fiber 1 g 4% • Sugars 1 g • Protein 23 g • Vitamin A 15% • Vitamin C 6% • Calcium 4% • Iron 10%
Dietary Exchanges: 1½ Starch, 2½ Very Lean Meat, ½ Fat OR 1½ Carbohydrate, 2½ Very Lean Meat, ½ Fat

Spicy Chicken Chili

Ground chicken is part of a lighter chili that's a nice alternative to ground-beef versions.

Yield: 2 (1¾-cup) servings

½ lb. ground chicken*

¼ cup chopped onion

2 garlic cloves, minced

1 (15-oz.) can spicy chili beans, undrained

1 (10-oz.) can diced tomatoes with green chiles, undrained

1 teaspoon chili powder

1. In large saucepan, combine ground chicken, onion and garlic; cook 5 to 8 minutes or until chicken is no longer pink, stirring frequently. Drain.

2. Stir in all remaining ingredients. Bring to a boil. Reduce heat; cover and simmer 15 minutes, stirring occasionally.

Nutrition Information Per Serving: Serving Size: 1¾ Cups • Calories 440 • Calories from Fat 120 • % Daily Value: Total Fat 13 g 20% • Saturated Fat 3 g 15% • Cholesterol 85 mg 28% • Sodium 1,230 mg 51% • Total Carbohydrate 47 g 16% • Dietary Fiber 11 g 44% • Sugars 6 g • Protein 33 g • Vitamin A 30% • Vitamin C 25% • Calcium 15% • Iron 25%
Dietary Exchanges: 3 Starch, 3½ Lean Meat OR 3 Carbohydrate, 3½ Lean Meat

menu

SPICY CHICKEN CHILI

Refrigerated cornbread sticks

Green salad with shredded carrot

Warm apple pie drizzled with caramel sauce

Prepare the salad greens and carrot but wait to dress the salad until just before serving time. Heat the oven for the cornbread, then start the chili. Put the pie in the oven to warm up once the cornbread is done.

tip

*Ground chicken, like other ground meats, is more perishable than whole cuts of meat. Check the "sell-by" date on the package at the store, and use or freeze it the same day you purchase it.

Caesar Chicken Wraps

A restaurant-quality Caesar salad is as close as your supermarket's produce section. Packaged Caesar salad mix—lettuce, dressing and croutons—is ready to toss and serve.

Yield: 4 wraps

1 (7.5-oz.) pkg. complete Caesar salad mix

1 cup chopped cooked chicken*

4 (8- to 9-inch) garden vegetable or plain flour tortillas

2 tablespoons shredded fresh Parmesan cheese

1. Crush croutons from salad mix; set aside. In large bowl, combine remaining Caesar salad mix ingredients and chicken; mix well.

2. Spoon salad mixture evenly onto tortillas; spread to within 1 inch of edges. Sprinkle each with shredded cheese and crushed croutons. Roll up each tortilla.

Nutrition Information Per Serving: Serving Size: 1 Wrap • Calories 330 • Calories from Fat 130 • % Daily Value: Total Fat 14 g 22% • Saturated Fat 3 g 15% • Cholesterol 35 mg 12% • Sodium 760 mg 32% • Total Carbohydrate 32 g 11% • Dietary Fiber 2 g 8% • Sugars 1 g • Protein 18 g • Vitamin A 6% • Vitamin C 2% • Calcium 10% • Iron 15%
Dietary Exchanges: 1½ Starch, 1½ Vegetable, 1½ Lean Meat, 2 Fat OR 1½ Carbohydrate, 1½ Vegetable, 1½ Lean Meat, 2 Fat

menu

CAESAR CHICKEN WRAPS

Minestrone soup

Grape clusters

Blonde brownies

Wash the grapes, and then heat the soup while you chop the chicken and assemble the wraps.

tip

*When a recipe calls for cooked chicken, there are several options. Use chicken (or turkey) left from a previous meal or buy a chunk of chicken or a whole chicken from the deli. Cans of cooked chicken are also available.

menu

ASIAN CHICKEN WRAPS

Carrot, celery and cucumber sticks with flavored sour cream dip

Rainbow sherbet with almond cookies

Make the chicken salad in advance, if you wish, and wrap it in the tortillas just before serving; the veggie sticks can also be prepared early in the day and refrigerated.

Asian Chicken Wraps

Wrapped in a tortilla, this supper is a cross-cultural version of a chicken salad sandwich. This wrap also makes a nice choice for a brown-bag lunch.

Yield: 4 wraps

---

1 1/2 cups chopped cooked chicken

1 cup shredded Chinese (napa) cabbage

1/2 cup sliced water chestnuts

1/4 cup slivered almonds

1/2 red bell pepper, cut into thin strips

1/3 cup purchased sweet-and-sour sauce

4 (7- or 8-inch) flour tortillas

---

1. In medium bowl, combine all ingredients except tortillas; mix well.

2. Spoon chicken mixture evenly down center of each tortilla; roll up.

Nutrition Information Per Serving: Serving Size: 1 Wrap • Calories 300 • Calories from Fat 90 • % Daily Value: Total Fat 10 g 15% • Saturated Fat 2 g 10% • Cholesterol 45 mg 15% • Sodium 350 mg 15% • Total Carbohydrate 32 g 11% • Dietary Fiber 3 g 12% • Sugars 7 g • Protein 20 g • Vitamin A 20% • Vitamin C 45% • Calcium 10% • Iron 10%
Dietary Exchanges: 2 Starch, 2 Lean Meat, 1/2 Fat OR 2 Carbohydrate, 2 Lean Meat, 1/2 Fat

Spicy Chinese Chicken Tacos

Many professional chefs combine ingredients and techniques from around the world in bold ways. In that spirit, this recipe features a thoroughly Chinese chicken preparation—complete with soy and ginger—served Mexican-style in taco shells.

Yield: 12 tacos; 6 servings

12 white or yellow corn taco shells

3 boneless skinless chicken breast halves, cut into thin bite-sized strips

1 teaspoon grated gingerroot

1 small garlic clove, minced

2 tablespoons soy sauce

1 tablespoon honey

1 large green onion, sliced

1/2 teaspoon crushed red pepper flakes

1 1/2 cups shredded lettuce

1. Heat taco shells as directed on package.

2. Meanwhile, spray large nonstick skillet with nonstick cooking spray. Heat over medium-high heat until hot. Add chicken, gingerroot and garlic; cook and stir 3 to 5 minutes or until lightly browned.

3. Reduce heat to low. Add soy sauce, honey, onion and crushed red pepper flakes; stir to coat. Cover; cook 5 minutes or until chicken is no longer pink in center, stirring occasionally.

4. Place about 1/4 cup chicken mixture in each taco shell. Top each with lettuce.

SPICY CHINESE CHICKEN TACOS

Deli Asian cabbage or lettuce salad

Chocolate pudding and fresh strawberry parfaits

Cut up the ingredients for the tacos before cooking. To prepare the fresh ginger, peel off its brown skin before you grate it. Assemble the parfaits in advance or while the chicken cooks, and chill them until dessert time.

Nutrition Information Per Serving: Serving Size: 1/6 of Recipe • Calories 180 • Calories from Fat 50 • % Daily Value: Total Fat 6 g 9% • Saturated Fat 1 g 5% • Cholesterol 35 mg 12% • Sodium 470 mg 20% • Total Carbohydrate 17 g 6% • Dietary Fiber 1 g 4% • Sugars 3 g • Protein 15 g • Vitamin A 2% • Vitamin C 2% • Calcium 4% • Iron 6%
Dietary Exchanges: 1 Starch, 1 1/2 Very Lean Meat, 1 Fat OR 1 Carbohydrate, 1 1/2 Very Lean Meat, 1 Fat

Grilled Chicken Club Sandwiches

The traditional triple-decker's bread slices are replaced here with kaiser rolls split into three layers. Use a serrated knife to cut the rolls cleanly.

Yield: 2 sandwiches

2 boneless skinless chicken breast halves

4 thin slices Canadian bacon

2 kaiser rolls, cut horizontally into thirds

3 tablespoons mayonnaise or salad dressing

4 lettuce leaves

2 slices tomato

1. Heat grill. Place 1 chicken breast half, boned side up, between 2 pieces of plastic wrap or waxed paper. Working from center, gently pound chicken with flat side of meat mallet or rolling pin until about G inch thick; remove wrap. Repeat with remaining chicken breast half.

2. When ready to grill, carefully oil grill rack. Place chicken on gas grill over medium heat or on charcoal grill 4 to 6 inches from medium coals. Cook 6 to 8 minutes or until fork-tender and juices run clear, turning once. Add bacon during last 5 minutes of cooking time; turn once. If desired, toast kaiser rolls, cut side down, during last 3 minutes of cooking time.

3. Spread all cut sides of rolls with mayonnaise. Cut each chicken breast half into 2 pieces. On bottom section of each roll, place 2 chicken pieces, overlapping if necessary. Top with lettuce, tomato and middle section of roll. Place 2 Canadian bacon slices on top of middle section. Top with lettuce and top of roll. Press each sandwich slightly; spear each with 2 long toothpicks. Cut sandwiches in half between toothpicks.

GRILLED CHICKEN CLUB SANDWICHES

Dill pickle spears

Potato salad

Chocolate chip cookies

While the chicken is on the grill, slice the rolls and tomatoes. Set out the pickles and the potato salad. Garnish the potato salad, if you wish, with a sprinkling of fresh parsley, chives or paprika.

Nutrition Information Per Serving: Serving Size: 1 Sandwich • Calories 540 • Calories from Fat 230 • % Daily Value: Total Fat 26 g 40% • Saturated Fat 5 g 25% • Cholesterol 115 mg 38% • Sodium 1,290 mg 54% • Total Carbohydrate 32 g 11% • Dietary Fiber 2 g 8% • Sugars 3 g • Protein 44 g • Vitamin A 4% • Vitamin C 4% • Calcium 8% • Iron 20%
Dietary Exchanges: 2 Starch, 5½ Very Lean Meat, 4 Fat OR 2 Carbohydrate, 5½ Very Lean Meat, 4 Fat

To broil chicken and Canadian bacon, place on oiled broiler pan; broil 4 to 6 inches from heat using times in recipe as a guide, turning once.

Chicken **157**

menu

BBQ CHICKENWICHES

Creamy coleslaw

Corn on the cob

Frozen fruit bars

Assemble the chicken mixture ahead of time, if you wish, and refrigerate it in the medium saucepan until ready to heat and eat. At suppertime, peel the corn and boil it in a pot with an inch or two of water. While the chicken and corn cook, toss the coleslaw blend with bottled dressing if you're not using a purchased salad.

BBQ Chickenwiches

Yesterday's roasted chicken appears in this sandwich as a "makeover," not merely a "leftover." Mixed with barbecue sauce and onion, the chicken takes on a whole new starring role.

Yield: 4 sandwiches

---

2 cups shredded cooked chicken

3/4 cup barbecue sauce

1 tablespoon chopped onion

1 tablespoon prepared mustard

4 kaiser rolls, split

1 oz. (1/4 cup) shredded colby-Monterey Jack cheese blend

---

1. In medium saucepan, combine chicken, barbecue sauce, onion and mustard; cook over medium heat for 15 minutes, stirring occasionally.

2. Spoon about ½ cup chicken mixture onto bottom half of each roll. Top each with 1 tablespoon cheese. Cover with top halves of rolls.

Nutrition Information Per Serving: Serving Size: 1 Sandwich • Calories 360 • Calories from Fat 100 • % Daily Value: Total Fat 11 g 17% • Saturated Fat 4 g 20% • Cholesterol 70 mg 23% • Sodium 840 mg 35% • Total Carbohydrate 36 g 12% • Dietary Fiber 2 g 8% • Sugars 2 g • Protein 28 g • Vitamin A 10% • Vitamin C 4% • Calcium 10% • Iron 20%

Dietary Exchanges: 2 Starch, 1/2 Fruit, 3 Lean Meat OR 2 1/2 Carbohydrate, 3 Lean Meat

Buffalo Chicken Pita Folds

The original buffalo chicken recipe paired spicy wings with palate-cooling celery and blue cheese dressing. Substituting chicken breast strips speeds up the meal considerably.

Yield: 4 sandwiches

---

1 tablespoon oil

¾ lb. chicken breast strips for stir-frying

⅓ cup purchased hot wings sauce

2 cups purchased coleslaw blend (from 16-oz. pkg.)

4 pita fold breads

4 tablespoons purchased blue cheese salad dressing

4 tablespoons crumbled blue cheese

---

1. Heat oil in large skillet or wok over medium-high heat until hot. Add chicken strips; cook and stir 4 to 6 minutes or until chicken is no longer pink in center. Add sauce; cook and stir until bubbly. Remove skillet from heat. Add coleslaw blend; toss to coat with sauce.

2. Spoon chicken mixture down center of each pita fold bread. Top each with 1 tablespoon salad dressing and 1 tablespoon cheese. Fold pita bread around filling; secure with toothpick or wrap in napkin.

Nutrition Information Per Serving: Serving Size: 1 Sandwich • Calories 460 • Calories from Fat 150 • % Daily Value: Total Fat 17 g 26% • Saturated Fat 4 g 20% • Cholesterol 60 mg 20% • Sodium 980 mg 41% • Total Carbohydrate 48 g 16% • Dietary Fiber 2 g 8% • Sugars 5 g • Protein 28 g • Vitamin A 25% • Vitamin C 15% • Calcium 15% • Iron 15%
Dietary Exchanges: 3 Starch, 2½ Very Lean Meat, 3 Fat OR 3 Carbohydrate, 2½ Very Lean Meat, 3 Fat

menu

BUFFALO CHICKEN PITA FOLDS

Vegetable pasta salad

Fresh blueberries and cream

Toss cooked leftover pasta with chopped vegetables and bottled dressing, or scoop deli pasta salad into a serving dish. Pick over, rinse and drain the blueberries while the chicken cooks.

**BUFFALO CHICKEN
SANDWICHES**

Tortilla chips

Marinated vegetables

German chocolate cake

While the chicken bakes, pour
the chips and the marinated
vegetables into serving dishes.

Buffalo Chicken Sandwiches

Between the spiciness of the hot pepper sauce
and the creamy richness of the blue cheese, this
recipe proves that opposites attract. To add one
more dimension, serve the patties on onion rolls.

Yield: 4 sandwiches

---

1 tablespoon margarine or butter, melted

1 tablespoon hot pepper sauce

4 frozen breaded chicken patties

4 leaves leaf lettuce

4 sandwich buns, split

4 tablespoons purchased blue cheese salad dressing

---

1. Heat oven to 400° F. In small cup, combine
margarine and hot pepper sauce; mix well. Brush
margarine mixture over chicken patties; place on
ungreased cookie sheet.

2. Bake at 400° F. for 12 to 15 minutes or until
thoroughly heated.

3. Place lettuce on bottom halves of buns. Top
each with chicken patty and blue cheese dressing.
Cover with top halves of buns. If desired, serve
with celery sticks.

Nutrition Information Per Serving: Serving Size: 1 Sandwich • Calories 520 •
Calories from Fat 290 • % Daily Value: Total Fat 32 g 49% • Saturated Fat 6 g 30% •
Cholesterol 45 mg 15% • Sodium 460 mg 19% • Total Carbohydrate 38 g 13% •
Dietary Fiber 4 g 16% • Sugars 8 g • Protein 19 g • Vitamin A 4% • Vitamin C 0% •
Calcium 8% • Iron 10%
Dietary Exchanges: 2½ Starch, 1½ High-Fat Meat, 4 Fat OR 2½ Carbohydrate,
1½ High-Fat Meat, 4 Fat

Mexican Subs

Some of the ingredients most associated with Mexican fare—refried beans, salsa, cheese, sour cream and cilantro—join forces in this casual meal.

Yield: 4 sandwiches

2 teaspoons oil

¾ lb. chicken breast strips for stir-frying

1 small onion, sliced

½ medium green bell pepper, cut into thin bite-sized strips

⅓ cup salsa

4 hoagie buns, split, toasted

½ cup refried beans, heated

4 oz. (1 cup) shredded hot pepper Monterey Jack cheese

¼ cup coarsely chopped fresh cilantro

¼ cup sour cream

1. Heat oil in large skillet or wok over medium-high heat until hot. Add chicken strips and onion; cook and stir 3 minutes. Add bell pepper; cook and stir 2 to 3 minutes or until bell pepper is crisp-tender and chicken is no longer pink in center. Stir in salsa. Remove from heat.

2. Spread bottom half of each bun with warm refried beans. Spoon chicken mixture onto each. Sprinkle with cheese and cilantro. Spread top halves of buns with sour cream; place over cheese and cilantro.

Nutrition Information Per Serving: Serving Size: 1 Sandwich • Calories 560 • Calories from Fat 190 • % Daily Value: Total Fat 21 g 32% • Saturated Fat 10 g 50% • Cholesterol 85 mg 28% • Sodium 1,150 mg 48% • Total Carbohydrate 58 g 19% • Dietary Fiber 5 g 20% • Sugars 4 g • Protein 35 g • Vitamin A 10% • Vitamin C 10% • Calcium 35% • Iron 20%
Dietary Exchanges: 4 Starch, 3 Lean Meat, 2 Fat OR 4 Carbohydrate, 3 Lean Meat, 2 Fat

MEXICAN SUBS

Tortilla chips and guacamole

Vanilla pudding drizzled with caramel

Before you fry the chicken, cut up the onion, bell pepper and cilantro, shred the cheese and begin heating the refried beans. While the chicken cooks, open the bag of chips and container of guacamole. Prepare instant pudding if you haven't purchased it ready to serve.

Grilled Chicken Melts

Thick slices of onion and red pepper add crunch to this grilled chicken breast sandwich with ranch dressing and melted cheese.

Yield: 4 sandwiches

---

4 (½-inch-thick) onion slices

4 (½-inch-thick) red bell pepper rings

4 boneless skinless chicken breast halves

½ cup purchased ranch salad dressing

4 oz. (1 cup) shredded colby-Monterey Jack cheese blend

4 large kaiser rolls, split

---

1. Heat grill. Brush onion, bell pepper and chicken breast halves with salad dressing.

2. When ready to grill, place onion, bell pepper and chicken on gas grill over medium-high heat or on charcoal grill 4 to 6 inches from medium-high coals. Cook vegetables 3 to 4 minutes or until lightly browned, turning once. Remove from grill; set aside. Cook chicken 10 to 14 minutes or until chicken is fork-tender and juices run clear, turning once. During last 1 to 2 minutes of cooking, sprinkle cheese on chicken.

3. While cheese is melting, place kaiser rolls, cut side down, on grill; toast 1 to 2 minutes.

4. Place chicken on bottom halves of toasted rolls. Top each with bell pepper ring and onion slice. Cover with top halves of rolls. If desired, serve with additional salad dressing.

Nutrition Information Per Serving: Serving Size: 1 Sandwich • Calories 520 • Calories from Fat 280 • % Daily Value: Total Fat 31 g 48% • Saturated Fat 9 g 45% • Cholesterol 65 mg 22% • Sodium 760 mg 32% • Total Carbohydrate 34 g 11% • Dietary Fiber 2 g 8% • Sugars 3 g • Protein 26 g • Vitamin A 15% • Vitamin C 20% • Calcium 25% • Iron 15%
Dietary Exchanges: 2½ Starch, 2½ Lean Meat, 4½ Fat OR 2½ Carbohydrate, 2½ Lean Meat, 4½ Fat

Lemon Grilled Chicken Sandwiches

The cucumber sauce, so good with the lemon and oregano in this recipe, also does wonders for grilled fish or turkey.

Yield: 2 sandwiches

Cucumber Sauce

¼ cup plain yogurt

⅓ cup finely chopped seeded cucumber

1 tablespoon sliced green onions

1 teaspoon grated lemon peel

Dash salt and pepper

Sandwiches

2 teaspoons lemon juice

1 teaspoon olive or vegetable oil

¼ teaspoon dried oregano leaves

2 boneless skinless chicken breast halves

2 whole wheat sandwich buns, split

1 small tomato, sliced

2 thin slices red onion

1. Heat grill. In small bowl, combine all cucumber sauce ingredients; mix well. Set aside. (Sauce may become watery if it stands longer than 30 minutes.)

2. In another small bowl, combine lemon juice, oil and oregano; mix well. Brush lemon mixture over chicken, coating all sides. If desired, sprinkle with salt and pepper.

3. When ready to grill, place chicken on gas grill over medium heat or on charcoal grill 4 to 6 inches from medium coals. Cook 15 to 20 minutes or until chicken is fork-tender and juices run clear, turning once. Place buns, cut side down, on gas grill over medium heat or on charcoal grill 4

to 6 inches from medium coals. Cook 1 to 2 minutes or until buns are lightly toasted.

4. Place chicken, tomato and onion on bottom halves of buns. Top with cucumber sauce. Cover with top halves of buns.

Nutrition Information Per Serving: Serving Size: 1 Sandwich • Calories 300 • Calories from Fat 70 • % Daily Value: Total Fat 8 g 12% • Saturated Fat 2 g 10% • Cholesterol 70 mg 23% • Sodium 360 mg 15% • Total Carbohydrate 27 g 9% • Dietary Fiber 4 g 16% • Sugars 6 g • Protein 31 g • Vitamin A 6% • Vitamin C 15% • Calcium 15% • Iron 15%
Dietary Exchanges: 2 Starch, 3 Very Lean Meat, 1 Fat OR 2 Carbohydrate, 3 Very Lean Meat, 1 Fat

LEMON GRILLED CHICKEN SANDWICHES

Three-bean salad

Watermelon wedges

Use deli bean salad or toss together bottled vinaigrette with a combination of rinsed, drained beans, such as kidney beans, green beans and chickpeas. Slice the watermelon while the chicken cooks.

tip

To broil chicken, place on broiler pan; broil 4 to 6 inches from heat using times in recipe as a guide, turning once. Place buns, cut side up, on broiler pan; broil 1 to 2 minutes.

turkey

OPPOSITE PAGE:
Turkey-Vegetable-Cheddar Soup, page 190

☺ Kid-Pleasing Recipe
🕐 20-Minutes-or-Less Recipe

menu

LEMON-WALNUT TURKEY AND LINGUINE

Spinach salad with orange segments, dried cranberries and poppy seed dressing

Refrigerated crescent rolls

Pumpkin bars

Make the pumpkin bars from scratch or a mix ahead of time, or buy them at the bakery. Set the pasta water to boil, and preheat the oven for the rolls. Assemble the salad, but don't dress it until just before serving. Bake the rolls while the turkey cooks.

Lemon-Walnut Turkey and Linguine

Fresh pasta, sold in the refrigerator case at the supermarket, cooks more quickly than dried pasta. The tender noodles are perfect with this delicate lemon sauce.

Yield: 3 (2-cup) servings

---

1 (9-oz.) pkg. refrigerated linguine

1 (3/4-lb.) fresh turkey breast tenderloin, cut into thin bite-sized strips

1/2 teaspoon peppered seasoned salt

2 tablespoons olive or vegetable oil

3/4 cup coarsely chopped walnuts

1 teaspoon grated lemon peel

1/2 cup chicken broth

2 to 4 tablespoons chopped fresh parsley

---

1. Cook linguine to desired doneness as directed on package. Drain.

2. Meanwhile, sprinkle turkey strips with seasoned salt. Heat oil in large skillet over medium-high heat until hot. Add turkey and walnuts; cook and stir 2 to 3 minutes or until turkey is no longer pink.

3. Add lemon peel, broth and cooked linguine; stir to combine. Cook over medium heat for 1 to 2 minutes or until thoroughly heated. Sprinkle with parsley.

Nutrition Information Per Serving: Serving Size: 2 Cups • Calories 860 • Calories from Fat 440 • % Daily Value: Total Fat 49 g 75% • Saturated Fat 5 g 25% • Cholesterol 135 mg 45% • Sodium 460 mg 19% • Total Carbohydrate 58 g 19% • Dietary Fiber 6 g 24% • Sugars 3 g • Protein 46 g • Vitamin A 8% • Vitamin C 15% • Calcium 10% • Iron 35%
Dietary Exchanges: 4 Starch, 5 Very Lean Meat, 8 Fat OR 4 Carbohydrate, 5 Very Lean Meat, 8 Fat

Turkey Pasta Alfredo

Turkey and peas enhance the creamy pasta classic to make a hearty meal that, much to the cook and cleanup crew's pleasure, only uses one saucepan.

Yield: 4 (1½-cup) servings

8 oz. (3½ cups) uncooked bow tie pasta (farfalle)

1 (10-oz.) container refrigerated Alfredo sauce

¼ cup milk

2 cups cubed cooked turkey

1 cup frozen sweet peas

1. In large saucepan or Dutch oven, cook pasta to desired doneness as directed on package. Drain in colander; cover to keep warm.

2. In same saucepan, combine Alfredo sauce, milk, turkey and peas. Cook over medium heat until peas are tender and mixture is thoroughly heated, stirring frequently.

3. Stir in cooked pasta. Cook until thoroughly heated.

Nutrition Information Per Serving: Serving Size: 1½ Cups • Calories 600 • Calories from Fat 240 • % Daily Value: Total Fat 27 g 42% • Saturated Fat 14 g 70% • Cholesterol 100 mg 33% • Sodium 420 mg 18% • Total Carbohydrate 54 g 18% • Dietary Fiber 4 g 16% • Sugars 5 g • Protein 35 g • Vitamin A 4% • Vitamin C 8% • Calcium 20% • Iron 20%
Dietary Exchanges: 3½ Starch, 3½ Lean Meat, 3 Fat OR 3½ Carbohydrate, 3½ Lean Meat, 3 Fat

TURKEY PASTA ALFREDO

Garlic bread

Banana and strawberry slices with chocolate syrup

While the water for the pasta is coming to a boil, cut the turkey and prepare the garlic bread for heating. Slice the strawberries before supper, if you like, but wait until serving time to cut the bananas for best color and texture.

SKILLET TURKEY AND DRESSING

Cranberry jelly

Butternut or buttercup squash

Green peas

Deep dish apple pie with cinnamon ice cream

Cut the squash in half and scoop out its seeds. Rub the cut side with oil, place it cut-side-down on a plate and cook it in the microwave on HIGH until squash is tender, about 7 to 9 minutes. Start the turkey cooking; then heat the peas. Warm the pie before serving and top each slice with a scoop of ice cream.

menu

Skillet Turkey and Dressing

Whether you call it "stuffing" or "dressing," this sage-flavored side dish is delicious with gravy and turkey breast slices.

Yield: 4 servings

4 fresh turkey breast slices (about ¾ lb.)

½ cup chopped green bell pepper

2 tablespoons water

1 (12-oz.) jar fat-free turkey gravy

1 cup ready-to-serve fat-free chicken broth with ⅓ less sodium (from 14½-oz. can)

3 cups dry cubed sage and onion stuffing

1 (6-oz.) pkg. dried fruit bits

1. Spray large nonstick skillet with nonstick cooking spray. Heat over medium-high heat until hot. Add turkey breast slices; if desired, sprinkle with salt and pepper. Cook 2 to 4 minutes or until turkey is golden brown and no longer pink in center, turning once. Remove turkey from skillet; cover to keep warm.

2. In same skillet, combine bell pepper and water; cover and cook 1 to 2 minutes. Reserve ¼ cup gravy. Add remaining gravy and broth to skillet; mix well. Bring to a boil. Remove skillet from heat. Stir in stuffing and fruit bits until well moistened.

3. Return turkey to skillet; drizzle with reserved gravy. Cover; let stand 5 minutes before serving.

Nutrition Information Per Serving: Serving Size: ¼ of Recipe • Calories 390 • Calories from Fat 20 • % Daily Value: Total Fat 2 g 3% • Saturated Fat 0 g 0% • Cholesterol 55 mg 18% • Sodium 1,220 mg 51% • Total Carbohydrate 65 g 22% • Dietary Fiber 7 g 28% • Sugars 18 g • Protein 29 g • Vitamin A 20% • Vitamin C 15% • Calcium 6% • Iron 20%
Dietary Exchanges: 2½ Starch, 1½ Fruit, 3 Very Lean Meat OR 4 Carbohydrate, 3 Very Lean Meat

Lemony Turkey Primavera Skillet

"Primavera" is Italian for "springtime," which is well-represented here with asparagus and baby vegetables.

Yield: 6 (1½-cup) servings

5 oz. (1½ cups) uncooked bow tie pasta (farfalle)

½ lb. fresh asparagus spears, trimmed, cut into 1½-inch pieces (about 2 cups)

6 oz. (1⅓ cups) fresh baby carrots, halved lengthwise

1 cup chicken broth

4 teaspoons cornstarch

½ teaspoon garlic-pepper blend

1 lb. fresh turkey breast slices, cut into thin bite-sized strips

1 cup fresh whole mushrooms, quartered

1 (14-oz.) can whole baby corn, drained, rinsed

1 teaspoon grated lemon peel

1. In Dutch oven or large saucepan, cook pasta to desired doneness as directed on package, adding asparagus and carrots during last 2 to 4 minutes of cooking time. Cook until asparagus is crisp-tender. Drain.

2. Meanwhile, in small bowl, combine broth, cornstarch and garlic-pepper blend; mix well. Set aside.

3. Spray 12-inch nonstick skillet with nonstick cooking spray. Heat over medium-high heat until hot. Add turkey and mushrooms; cook 3 to 5 minutes or until turkey is lightly browned and no longer pink in center, stirring frequently.

4. Add broth mixture; cook and stir just until mixture begins to thicken. Add cooked pasta and vegetables, corn and lemon peel; cook and stir until thoroughly heated. If desired, add salt and pepper to taste.

menu

LEMONY TURKEY PRIMAVERA SKILLET

Whole-grain rolls

Sugar cookies

If you have time early in the day, cut the turkey into strips and get the vegetables ready. The carrots and asparagus will cook together and can be stored together; refrigerate the turkey and mushrooms separately. Otherwise, prepare the vegetables and turkey while waiting for the pasta water to boil.

Nutrition Information Per Serving: Serving Size: 1½ Cups • Calories 210 • Calories from Fat 20 • % Daily Value: Total Fat 2 g 3% • Saturated Fat 1 g 5% • Cholesterol 50 mg 17% • Sodium 210 mg 9% • Total Carbohydrate 25 g 8% • Dietary Fiber 3 g 12% • Sugars 3 g • Protein 23 g • Vitamin A 160% • Vitamin C 10% • Calcium 4% • Iron 15%
Dietary Exchanges: 1½ Starch, 1 Vegetable, 2 Very Lean Meat OR 1½ Carbohydrate, 1 Vegetable, 2 Very Lean Meat

Turkey Tortellini Divan

Divine divan, a dish that typically includes poultry with broccoli or asparagus in a creamy sauce, gets a new twist from the inclusion of cheese-filled tortellini. Pass Parmesan cheese at the table, if you like.

Yield: 4 (1¼-cup) servings

1 (14½-oz.) can ready-to-serve chicken broth

2 tablespoons all-purpose flour

1 (9-oz.) pkg. frozen cut broccoli in a pouch

1 (9-oz.) pkg. refrigerated cheese-filled tortellini

2 cups cubed smoked turkey breast (from deli)

½ cup sour cream

1. In small bowl, combine ¼ cup of the broth and the flour; blend until smooth. Set aside.

2. In medium saucepan, bring remaining broth to a boil over medium-high heat. Add broccoli; return to a boil. Stir in tortellini. Cook 3 to 5 minutes or until broccoli and tortellini are tender.

3. Stir in turkey. Add flour mixture; cook an additional 2 to 3 minutes, stirring constantly. Reduce heat to medium-low; stir in sour cream. Cook and stir until thoroughly heated.

Nutrition Information Per Serving: Serving Size: 1¼ Cups • Calories 370 • Calories from Fat 120 • % Daily Value: Total Fat 13 g 20% • Saturated Fat 6 g 30% • Cholesterol 70 mg 23% • Sodium 1,290 mg 54% • Total Carbohydrate 38 g 13% • Dietary Fiber 3 g 12% • Sugars 3 g • Protein 25 g • Vitamin A 10% • Vitamin C 35% • Calcium 15% • Iron 10%
Dietary Exchanges: 2½ Starch, 2½ Lean Meat, 1 Fat OR 2½ Carbohydrate, 2½ Lean Meat, 1 Fat

Rosemary Turkey and Vegetables with Parmesan Couscous

Fresh rosemary has a pungent, almost piney flavor. If you're using the fresh herb, strip the needle-like leaves from the stem and chop them finely.

Yield: 4 servings

1 (5.9-oz.) pkg. uncooked Parmesan-flavored couscous

1/2 cup dry white wine or chicken broth

2 teaspoons cornstarch

2 tablespoons olive or vegetable oil

2 garlic cloves, minced

1 lb. fresh turkey breast slices, cut into 1/4-inch-thick strips

3/4 teaspoon salt

1/8 teaspoon pepper

1 red bell pepper, thinly sliced

1 medium zucchini, julienne-cut (2 × 1/8 × 1/8-inch)

3 Italian plum tomatoes, thinly sliced

1 to 2 teaspoons chopped fresh rosemary or 1/4 to
   3/4 teaspoon dried rosemary leaves, crushed

1. Cook couscous as directed on package. Cover to keep warm.

2. Meanwhile, in small bowl, combine wine and cornstarch; blend well. Set aside.

3. Heat oil in large skillet or wok over medium-high heat until hot. Add garlic; cook and stir 30 seconds. Add turkey, salt and pepper; cook and stir 5 to 7 minutes or until turkey is no longer pink in center.

4. Add bell pepper and zucchini; cook and stir 3 to 4 minutes or until crisp-tender.

5. Stir wine mixture until smooth. Add wine mixture, tomatoes and rosemary to skillet; cook and stir until sauce is bubbly and thickened. Serve with couscous.

Nutrition Information Per Serving: Serving Size: 1/4 of Recipe • Calories 400 • Calories from Fat 100 • % Daily Value: Total Fat 11 g 17% • Saturated Fat 3 g 15% • Cholesterol 85 mg 28% • Sodium 850 mg 35% • Total Carbohydrate 37 g 12% • Dietary Fiber 3 g 12% • Sugars 5 g • Protein 34 g • Vitamin A 30% • Vitamin C 50% • Calcium 6% • Iron 15%
Dietary Exchanges: 2 Starch, 1 Vegetable, 4 Very Lean Meat, 1 1/2 Fat OR 2 Carbohydrate, 1 Vegetable, 4 Very Lean Meat, 1 1/2 Fat

---

menu

ROSEMARY TURKEY AND VEGETABLES WITH PARMESAN COUSCOUS

Broccoli spears

Date muffins with butter

Raspberries and cream

Prepare the muffins early in the day from scratch or a mix, or get them at the bakery; warm the muffins while the turkey cooks. Begin cooking the broccoli about halfway through the cooking time for the turkey, steaming it either in the microwave or on the stove top.

Rigatoni with Sausage and Vegetables

Italian plum tomatoes, thick-skinned and meaty, are especially good in this filling entree.

Yield: 4 (2-cup) servings

8 oz. (3 cups) uncooked rigatoni (pasta tubes with ridges)

1 lb. Italian turkey sausage links, cut into 1/2-inch slices

1 small onion, cut into thin wedges

1 garlic clove, minced

1 (9-oz.) pkg. frozen sugar snap peas in a pouch, thawed

1 medium yellow bell pepper, cut into 1-inch pieces

1/2 cup chicken broth

1 teaspoon dried basil leaves or 1 tablespoon chopped fresh basil

1/2 teaspoon salt

1/8 teaspoon pepper

4 Italian plum tomatoes, coarsely chopped

2 tablespoons olive or vegetable oil

Shredded mozzarella cheese

1. In Dutch oven or large saucepan, cook rigatoni to desired doneness as directed on package. Drain; return to Dutch oven. Cover to keep warm.

2. Meanwhile, cook sausage in large skillet over medium-high heat for 5 minutes, stirring occasionally. Drain.

3. Add onion and garlic; cook and stir 3 minutes. Add sugar snap peas, bell pepper, broth, basil, salt and pepper; mix well. Bring to a boil. Reduce heat; simmer 3 to 5 minutes or until sugar snap peas are crisp-tender and sausage is no longer pink.

RIGATONI WITH SAUSAGE AND VEGETABLES

Crusty Italian rolls drizzled with olive oil and Italian seasoning

Spumoni ice cream with chocolate biscotti cookies

Prepare the vegetables for the rigatoni while waiting for the pasta water to boil. Heat the rolls, seasoned with olive oil and herbs, in the oven shortly before the main dish is finished cooking.

4. Add tomatoes and oil; cook over medium-low heat for 3 to 5 minutes or until mixture is bubbly, stirring occasionally.

5. Add to cooked rigatoni; toss gently to mix. Sprinkle with cheese.

Nutrition Information Per Serving: Serving Size: 2 Cups • Calories 550 • Calories from Fat 190 • % Daily Value: Total Fat 21 g 32% • Saturated Fat 5 g 25% • Cholesterol 65 mg 22% • Sodium 1,220 mg 51% • Total Carbohydrate 58 g 19% • Dietary Fiber 5 g 20% • Sugars 8 g • Protein 31 g • Vitamin A 8% • Vitamin C 60% • Calcium 15% • Iron 35%
Dietary Exchanges: 3 1/2 Starch, 1 Vegetable, 2 1/2 Lean Meat, 2 1/2 Fat OR 3 1/2 Carbohydrate, 1 Vegetable, 2 1/2 Lean Meat, 2 1/2 Fat

Quick Turkey Stroganoff

Diced pimiento brings a touch of scarlet to a creamy turkey entree. Pimientos, sold in jars, are prepared from a pepper that's similar to bell pepper, but heart-shaped and with thicker flesh.

Yield: 4 servings

---

8 oz. (4 cups) uncooked egg noodles

2 cups cubed cooked turkey

1 (4.5-oz.) jar sliced mushrooms, drained

1 (10¾-oz.) can condensed cream of mushroom soup

1 cup sour cream

1 (2-oz.) jar diced pimientos, drained

---

1. Cook noodles to desired doneness as directed on package. Drain.

2. Meanwhile, in large skillet, combine turkey, mushrooms and soup; mix well. Cook over medium heat until bubbly, stirring frequently. Stir in sour cream and pimientos. Cook until thoroughly heated. DO NOT BOIL.

3. Serve turkey mixture over noodles.

Nutrition Information Per Serving: Serving Size: ¼ of Recipe • Calories 550 • Calories from Fat 220 • % Daily Value: Total Fat 24 g 37% • Saturated Fat 11 g 55% • Cholesterol 135 mg 45% • Sodium 810 mg 34% • Total Carbohydrate 51 g 17% • Dietary Fiber 3 g 12% • Sugars 6 g • Protein 33 g • Vitamin A 20% • Vitamin C 25% • Calcium 15% • Iron 25%
Dietary Exchanges: 3½ Starch, 3 Very Lean Meat, 4 Fat OR 3½ Carbohydrate, 3 Very Lean Meat, 4 Fat

Sweet Red Pepper-Turkey Lo Mein

Strips of tender turkey take on Asian flair when paired with noodles and colorful vegetables in a lemony stir-fry sauce.

Yield: 4 servings

8 oz. uncooked lo mein noodles

½ cup chicken broth

½ cup purchased stir-fry sauce

1 tablespoon cornstarch

1 teaspoon grated lemon peel

1 tablespoon oil

1 (¾-lb.) fresh turkey breast tenderloin, cut lengthwise into 2-inch-wide strips, thinly sliced

⅛ teaspoon salt

2 cups frozen cut broccoli

2 medium red bell peppers, cut into 1-inch pieces

1 medium onion, sliced

1. Cook noodles to desired doneness as directed on package. Drain.

2. Meanwhile, in small bowl, combine broth, stir-fry sauce, cornstarch and lemon peel; blend well. Set aside.

3. Heat oil in large skillet or wok over medium-high heat until hot. Add turkey strips; sprinkle with salt. Cook and stir 3 to 5 minutes or until turkey is no longer pink. Remove turkey from skillet; cover to keep warm.

4. Add broccoli, bell peppers and onion to same skillet; cook and stir 4 to 5 minutes or until vegetables are crisp-tender. Return turkey to skillet.

5. Stir cornstarch mixture until smooth. Add to skillet; cook and stir until sauce is bubbly and thickened. Serve over noodles.

SWEET RED PEPPER-TURKEY LO MEIN

Napa Cabbage Salad with Vinaigrette Dressing

Frozen Egg Rolls

Fortune Cookies

Lemon Sherbet

Preheat the oven for the egg rolls and start the water to boiling for the noodles. Shred the cabbage for the salad, then assemble and prepare all the ingredients for the stir-fry. Begin stir-frying while the noodles are cooking. For easiest scooping, set the sherbet on the counter 5 to 10 minutes before you'll be ready to serve dessert.

Nutrition Information Per Serving: Serving Size: ¼ of Recipe • Calories 400 • Calories from Fat 45 • % Daily Value: Total Fat 5 g 8% • Saturated Fat 1 g 5% • Cholesterol 55 mg 18% • Sodium 1,370 mg 57% • Total Carbohydrate 57 g 19% • Dietary Fiber 4 g 16% • Sugars 8 g • Protein 32 g • Vitamin A 45% • Vitamin C 110% • Calcium 4% • Iron 20%
Dietary Exchanges: 3 Starch, ½ Fruit, 1 Vegetable, 3 Very Lean Meat OR 3½ Carbohydrate, 1 Vegetable, 3 Very Lean Meat

SPICY SAUSAGE AND PEPPERS RIGATONI

Mixed romaine and leaf lettuce salad with marinated artichoke hearts and Italian dressing

Chocolate mousse or pudding with whipped cream and chocolate curls

While you wait for the pasta water to boil, chop the bell peppers for the rigatoni and assemble the salad; wait to toss it with the dressing until serving time. For a finishing touch on the dessert, take a block of sweetened chocolate and shave off curls using a vegetable peeler, paring knife or citrus zester.

Spicy Sausage and Peppers Rigatoni

Rigatoni's shape allows it to catch bits of the chunky sauce, but the dish would also be excellent with shell pasta, radiatore or bow ties.

Yield: 2 servings

---

4 oz. uncooked rigatoni (pasta tubes with ridges)

2 (3-oz.) hot Italian turkey sausage links, sliced

½ cup chopped red bell pepper

½ cup chopped green bell pepper

1 cup low-fat chunky spaghetti sauce

2 tablespoons grated Parmesan cheese, if desired

---

1. Cook rigatoni to desired doneness as directed on package. Drain; cover to keep warm.

2. Meanwhile, cook sausage in medium nonstick skillet over medium heat for 10 minutes or until no longer pink, stirring frequently. Drain.

3. Add bell peppers; cook and stir 3 to 5 minutes or until bell peppers are tender.

4. Stir in spaghetti sauce; cook 1 minute or until thoroughly heated. Serve sausage mixture over rigatoni. Sprinkle with cheese.

Nutrition Information Per Serving: Serving Size: ½ of Recipe • Calories 440 • Calories from Fat 110 • % Daily Value: Total Fat 12 g 18% • Saturated Fat 4 g 20% • Cholesterol 50 mg 17% • Sodium 1,040 mg 43% • Total Carbohydrate 58 g 19% • Dietary Fiber 4 g 16% • Sugars 12 g • Protein 26 g • Vitamin A 40% • Vitamin C 100% • Calcium 15% • Iron 30%
Dietary Exchanges: 3½ Starch, 1 Vegetable, 2 Lean Meat, 1 Fat OR 3½ Carbohydrate, 1 Vegetable, 2 Lean Meat, 1 Fat

Bayou Sausage Jambalaya

Jambalaya, a signature dish of Louisiana, is a spicy stew sometimes made with shrimp. Our quick version uses turkey kielbasa and chicken breast with salsa-spiked rice.

Yield: 4 (1½-cup) servings

¼ lb. smoked turkey kielbasa, cut into ½-inch-thick slices

2 boneless skinless chicken breast halves, cut into bite-sized pieces

2 cups salsa

1½ cups uncooked instant white rice

1 cup water

Hot pepper sauce, if desired

1. Spray large nonstick skillet or Dutch oven with nonstick cooking spray. Heat over medium-high heat until hot. Add kielbasa and chicken; cook and stir 5 to 8 minutes or until chicken is no longer pink.

2. Add salsa, rice and water; mix well. Bring to a boil. Reduce heat; cover and simmer 5 to 10 minutes or until rice is tender. If desired, add salt and pepper to taste. Serve with hot pepper sauce.

Nutrition Information Per Serving: Serving Size: 1½ Cups • Calories 280 • Calories from Fat 25 • % Daily Value: Total Fat 3 g 5% • Saturated Fat 1 g 5% • Cholesterol 55 mg 18% • Sodium 1,280 mg 53% • Total Carbohydrate 41 g 14% • Dietary Fiber 2 g 8% • Sugars 5 g • Protein 23 g • Vitamin A 10% • Vitamin C 10% • Calcium 6% • Iron 15%
Dietary Exchanges: 2 Starch, ½ Fruit, 2½ Very Lean Meat OR 2½ Carbohydrate, 2½ Very Lean Meat

BAYOU SAUSAGE JAMBALAYA

Sautéed zucchini, yellow squash, garlic and onions

Cantaloupe slices

Gingerbread drizzled with whipped topping

To start, cut up the turkey kielbasa and chicken. Julienne the zucchini, yellow squash and onions for faster sautéing; mince the garlic. While the jambalaya cooks, heat a little oil in a skillet; when hot, sauté the squash mixture until tender—adding a pinch of dried tarragon or oregano. Cut the cantaloupe in advance or at serving time.

menu

SPEEDY TURKEY CUTLETS AND ZUCCHINI

New potatoes

Marinated Italian salad

Marble cake

Choose potatoes of uniform size, scrub and trim them, and rub them with a little olive oil. Microwave the potatoes until tender. Slice the zucchini and the mushrooms for the cutlets while the cutlets cook. Make the cake in advance from scratch or a mix, and spread it with prepared frosting, or purchase a cake from a bakery.

Speedy Turkey Cutlets and Zucchini

Cook the zucchini with the skin on to preserve nutrients and the bright green color that plays well against the basil-flecked turkey slices.

Yield: 4 servings

2 tablespoons tarragon vinegar

1 teaspoon dried basil leaves

2 garlic cloves, minced

1 lb. fresh turkey cutlets or turkey breast slices

3 tablespoons oil

4 cups sliced zucchini (3 to 4 medium)

1½ cups sliced fresh mushrooms

1. In small bowl, combine vinegar, basil and garlic; mix well. Brush over both sides of turkey.

2. Heat 2 tablespoons of the oil in large nonstick skillet over medium-high heat until hot. Add turkey cutlets; cook about 4 minutes or until turkey is no longer pink in center, turning once. Remove from skillet; place on serving platter. Cover to keep warm.

3. In same skillet, heat remaining 1 tablespoon oil until hot. Add zucchini and mushrooms; cook and stir until zucchini is crisp-tender. If desired, add salt and pepper to taste. Arrange vegetables on platter with turkey.

Nutrition Information Per Serving: Serving Size: ¼ of Recipe • Calories 240 • Calories from Fat 100 • % Daily Value: Total Fat 11 g 17% • Saturated Fat 2 g 10% • Cholesterol 75 mg 25% • Sodium 50 mg 2% • Total Carbohydrate 6 g 2% • Dietary Fiber 2 g 8% • Sugars 3 g • Protein 29 g • Vitamin A 10% • Vitamin C 15% • Calcium 4% • Iron 15%
Dietary Exchanges: 1 Vegetable, 4 Very Lean Meat, 1½ Fat

Honey-Dijon Turkey Medallions

Why should Thanksgiving flavors be limited to November? Turkey tenderloin and a simple selection of trimmings take very little effort.

Yield: 4 servings

---

1 ¼ lb. fresh turkey breast tenderloins

2 tablespoons Dijon mustard

2 tablespoons honey

⅛ teaspoon hot pepper sauce

---

1. Line broiler pan and rack with foil; cut slits in foil on rack. Cut turkey tenderloins crosswise into 1½-inch-thick slices; place cut side up on foil-lined rack in pan.

2. In small bowl, combine all remaining ingredients; mix well. Generously brush tops of turkey slices with about half of mustard mixture.

3. Broil 3 to 4 inches from heat for 6 to 8 minutes. Turn turkey slices; generously brush with remaining mustard mixture. Broil an additional 6 to 8 minutes or until turkey is no longer pink in center.

Nutrition Information Per Serving: Serving Size: ¼ of Recipe • Calories 180 • Calories from Fat 10 • % Daily Value: Total Fat 1 g 2% • Saturated Fat 0 g 0% • Cholesterol 95 mg 32% • Sodium 250 mg 10% • Total Carbohydrate 9 g 3% • Dietary Fiber 0 g 0% • Sugars 9 g • Protein 34 g • Vitamin A 0% • Vitamin C 0% • Calcium 2% • Iron 10%
Dietary Exchanges: ½ Fruit, 5 Very Lean Meat OR ½ Carbohydrate, 5 Very Lean Meat

menu

HONEY-DIJON TURKEY MEDALLIONS

Herb stuffing

Mixed vegetables with butter and fresh chives

Pumpkin pie

Snip the chives and set aside to garnish the vegetables. Start the turkey, then put the vegetables on to boil and prepare the stuffing mix.

Country Scrambled Breakfast Burritos

This egg dish performs equally well for breakfast, brunch or a quick evening meal.

Yield: 4 servings

¼ lb. bulk turkey breakfast sausage

¼ cup chopped onion

2 small red potatoes, unpeeled, diced (¾ cup)

1 (8-oz.) carton (1 cup) refrigerated or frozen fat-free egg product, thawed, or 4 eggs, beaten

4 (8-inch) flour tortillas

4 tablespoons reduced-fat smoky Cheddar cold pack cheese food

1. Heat oven to 375°F. Spray cookie sheet with nonstick cooking spray.

2. Spray large nonstick skillet with nonstick cooking spray. Heat over medium-high heat until hot. Add sausage, onion and potatoes; cook 8 to 10 minutes or until sausage is no longer pink and vegetables are tender, stirring frequently. Remove from skillet; cover to keep warm.

3. Add egg product to same skillet; cook 3 to 5 minutes or until firm but moist, stirring frequently.

4. Spread each tortilla with 1 tablespoon cheese; spread to within ½ inch of edge. Place on sprayed cookie sheet. Spoon ¼ of egg product and ¼ of sausage mixture down center of each tortilla. Fold bottom of each tortilla up over filling; fold right side to center. Fold left side over right side. Secure each with wooden toothpick.

5. Bake at 375°F. for 3 to 4 minutes or until cheese is melted. If desired, serve with salsa.

menu

COUNTRY SCRAMBLED BREAKFAST BURRITOS

Grapefruit halves with brown sugar

Coffee cake or fruit muffins

Early in the day, bake a coffee cake or muffins from scratch or a mix, or purchase them from the bakery. Halve the grapefruit, sprinkle it with brown sugar and let it stand while you prepare the burritos or garnish plates with fresh fruit.

Nutrition Information Per Serving: Serving Size: ¼ of Recipe • Calories 310 • Calories from Fat 110 • % Daily Value: Total Fat 12 g 18% • Saturated Fat 4 g 20% • Cholesterol 35 mg 12% • Sodium 570 mg 24% • Total Carbohydrate 34 g 11% • Dietary Fiber 2 g 8% • Sugars 4 g • Protein 17 g • Vitamin A 8% • Vitamin C 8% • Calcium 15% • Iron 15%
Dietary Exchanges: 2½ Starch, 1½ Very Lean Meat, 1½ Fat OR 2½ Carbohydrate, 1½ Very Lean Meat, 1½ Fat

Turkey Scaloppine

This is a restaurant-style dish, but you don't need a large kitchen staff to succeed. Simply brown the turkey and then prepare the delicious white wine-lemon sauce in the skillet. Thin slices of lemon and chopped parsley provide the garnishing touch.

Yield: 4 servings

---

1 lb. fresh turkey breast slices

½ teaspoon salt

½ cup Italian-style dry bread crumbs

4 teaspoons margarine or butter

½ cup dry white wine

2 tablespoons lemon juice

Lemon slices

Chopped fresh Italian parsley

---

1. Sprinkle turkey slices with salt; coat slices on both sides with bread crumbs.

2. Generously spray large nonstick skillet with nonstick cooking spray. Heat over medium-high heat until hot. Add turkey; cook 2 to 4 minutes or until no longer pink in center, turning once. Remove turkey from skillet; place on serving platter. Cover to keep warm.

3. Add margarine, wine and lemon juice to same skillet; bring to a boil. Pour sauce over turkey. Top with lemon slices and parsley.

Nutrition Information Per Serving: Serving Size: ¼ of Recipe • Calories 220 • Calories from Fat 45 • % Daily Value: Total Fat 5 g 8% • Saturated Fat 1 g 5% • Cholesterol 75 mg 25% • Sodium 580 mg 24% • Total Carbohydrate 11 g 4% • Dietary Fiber 1 g 4% • Sugars 1 g • Protein 29 g • Vitamin A 4% • Vitamin C 6% • Calcium 4% • Iron 15%
Dietary Exchanges: ½ Starch, 4 Very Lean Meat, 1 Fat OR ½ Carbohydrate, 4 Very Lean Meat, 1 Fat

Turkey Broccoli Roll-Ups

Honey-roasted turkey breast encases broccoli in a dill sauce; melted cheese finishes the job.

Yield: 2 servings

2 cups frozen cut broccoli

1 tablespoon light sour cream

1 teaspoon Dijon mustard

⅛ teaspoon dried dill weed

4 (⅛-inch-thick) slices honey-roasted turkey breast
(from deli)

2 (¾-oz.) slices colby-Monterey Jack cheese blend
(from deli)

---

1. Cook broccoli in microwave as directed on package just until crisp-tender.

2. Meanwhile, in small bowl, combine sour cream, mustard and dill; mix well.

3. Drain broccoli well; cut into smaller pieces, if necessary. Spread thin layer of sour cream mixture over each slice of turkey. Place ⅓ cup cooked broccoli on each. Roll turkey around broccoli; secure with toothpick. Place rolls in ungreased 8-inch square (2-quart) glass baking dish. Cover with microwave-safe waxed paper.

4. Microwave on HIGH for 2 to 3 minutes or until thoroughly heated, turning dish once halfway through cooking. Cut each cheese slice crosswise in half; place half slice on each roll-up. Microwave on HIGH for an additional 30 to 60 seconds or until cheese is melted. Remove toothpicks before serving.

TURKEY BROCCOLI ROLL-UPS

Mixed green salad with Italian dressing

Cherry crisp with vanilla ice cream

Assemble the roll-ups in advance and refrigerate them, tightly covered, until dinnertime. Because the dish heats in less than 5 minutes in the microwave, you'll have a nearly instant supper. In that time, assemble the salad. For a quick cherry crisp, heat cherry pie filling at dessert time and top with granola.

Nutrition Information Per Serving: Serving Size: ½ of Recipe • Calories 230 • Calories from Fat 90 • % Daily Value: Total Fat 10 g 15% • Saturated Fat 5 g 25% • Cholesterol 70 mg 23% • Sodium 1,030 mg 43% • Total Carbohydrate 9 g 3% • Dietary Fiber 2 g 8% • Sugars 2 g • Protein 26 g • Vitamin A 15% • Vitamin C 45% • Calcium 20% • Iron 4%
Dietary Exchanges: 2 Vegetable, 3 Lean Meat

HONEY-MUSTARD TURKEY TENDERLOINS

menu

HONEY-MUSTARD TURKEY TENDERLOINS

Cheese stuffed potato halves

Glazed baby carrots

Cranberry apple pie

Cheese-stuffed potato halves are available frozen; heat them while the turkey is on the grill. Meanwhile, microwave or boil baby carrots until tender. Drain most of the cooking water; then stir in a pat of butter and a spoonful of brown sugar. Stir to coat thoroughly.

tip

To broil turkey tenderloins, place on broiler pan; broil 4 to 6 inches from heat using times in recipe as a guide, turning and brushing with salad dressing mixture 2 or 3 times.

Honey-Mustard Turkey Tenderloins

Honey mustard, a "secret ingredient" for spicing up deli sandwiches, is the key component of a basting sauce for grilled turkey tenderloin.

Yield: 6 servings

2 (¾-lb.) fresh turkey breast tenderloins

1 tablespoon olive oil

½ teaspoon salt

¼ teaspoon pepper

1 cup purchased honey-mustard salad dressing

¼ cup chopped fresh basil

1. Heat grill. Brush turkey tenderloins with oil; sprinkle with salt and pepper. In small saucepan, combine salad dressing and basil; mix well.

2. When ready to grill, place turkey on gas grill over medium heat or on charcoal grill 4 to 6 inches from medium coals. Cook 15 to 20 minutes or until turkey is fork-tender and juices run clear, turning and brushing with salad dressing mixture 2 or 3 times.

3. To serve, bring any remaining salad dressing mixture to a boil. Serve with turkey.

Nutrition Information Per Serving: Serving Size: ⅙ of Recipe • Calories 360 • Calories from Fat 210 • % Daily Value: Total Fat 23 g 35% • Saturated Fat 3 g 15% • Cholesterol 110 mg 37% • Sodium 360 mg 15% • Total Carbohydrate 6 g 2% • Dietary Fiber 0 g 0% • Sugars 5 g • Protein 33 g • Vitamin A 0% • Vitamin C 0% • Calcium 2% • Iron 10%
Dietary Exchanges: ½ Fruit, 4½ Very Lean Meat, 4 Fat OR ½ Carbohydrate, 4½ Very Lean Meat, 4 Fat

White Bean-Turkey Chili

Tomato paste gives a bit of color to this stew, but it's still lighter than chili prepared with chunks of beef and kidney beans. Chopped green chiles and cumin provide pleasant seasoning.

Yield: 8 (1¼-cup) servings

1 teaspoon oil

1½ lb. fresh turkey breast tenderloins, cut into bite-sized pieces

1 cup chopped onions

2 (15.5-oz.) cans great northern beans, drained

2 (14½-oz.) cans ready-to-serve chicken broth

2 (4.5-oz.) cans chopped green chiles, undrained

1 (6-oz.) can tomato paste

1 teaspoon cumin

1. Heat oil in Dutch oven over medium-high heat until hot. Add turkey and onions; cook and stir until turkey is no longer pink.

2. Stir in all remaining ingredients. Bring to a boil. Reduce heat to low; simmer 10 to 15 minutes, stirring occasionally.

Nutrition Information Per Serving: Serving Size: 1¼ Cups • Calories 220 • Calories from Fat 20 • % Daily Value: Total Fat 2 g 3% • Saturated Fat 0 g 0% • Cholesterol 55 mg 18% • Sodium 810 mg 34% • Total Carbohydrate 22 g 7% • Dietary Fiber 7 g 28% • Sugars 2 g • Protein 29 g • Vitamin A 15% • Vitamin C 20% • Calcium 15% • Iron 20%
Dietary Exchanges: 1½ Starch, 3½ Very Lean Meat OR 1½ Carbohydrate, 3½ Very Lean Meat

WHITE BEAN-TURKEY CHILI

Warmed tortilla roll-ups with cheese filling

Chocolate chip ice cream

This dish reheats well; in fact, making it a day or two ahead gives the flavors a chance to mingle. At serving time, sprinkle cheese onto flour tortillas, roll up, and microwave for about 25 seconds each; cut into serving pieces.

menu

SAUSAGE TORTELLINI SOUP

Whole-grain Italian rolls

Hot fudge sundaes

Chop the onion and slice the carrots for the soup. Warm the rolls in the oven while the soup simmers. Just as you're about to sit down for the meal, take the lid off the jar of hot fudge sauce and set the jar into a saucepan of water over very low heat—the sauce can heat gently while you eat—or microwave it just before serving.

Sausage Tortellini Soup

Traditional Italian cooks make tortellini by hand, but the refrigerated version used here is also delicious, and a whole lot faster. Sprinkle Parmesan cheese and minced fresh parsley on top before serving.

Yield: 6 (1½-cup) servings

½ lb. bulk Italian turkey sausage

½ cup chopped onion

1 cup sliced carrots

1 (28-oz.) can tomato puree

1 (14½-oz.) can ready-to-serve chicken broth

2 cups water

1 teaspoon dried basil leaves

1 (9-oz.) pkg. refrigerated cheese-filled tortellini

3 cups frozen cut broccoli

1. In Dutch oven, combine sausage and onion; cook over medium heat for 8 minutes or until sausage is no longer pink, stirring frequently. Drain.

2. Add carrots; cook and stir 1 minute. Add tomato puree, broth, water and basil. Bring to a boil. Add tortellini; return to a boil. Add broccoli; cook 6 to 8 minutes or until tortellini is tender, stirring occasionally.

Nutrition Information Per Serving: Serving Size: 1½ Cups • Calories 280 • Calories from Fat 60 • % Daily Value: Total Fat 7 g 11% • Saturated Fat 3 g 15% • Cholesterol 45 mg 15% • Sodium 650 mg 27% • Total Carbohydrate 37 g 12% • Dietary Fiber 5 g 20% • Sugars 10 g • Protein 17 g • Vitamin A 150% • Vitamin C 45% • Calcium 8% • Iron 20%
Dietary Exchanges: 2 Starch, 1½ Vegetable, 1 Medium-Fat Meat OR 2 Carbohydrate, 1½ Vegetable, 1 Medium-Fat Meat

Turkey and Broccoli Nugget Soup

This chunky soup starts with canned broth and adds fresh ingredients for homemade flavor without all-day simmering.

Yield: 4 (1¾-cup) servings

2 teaspoons margarine or butter

½ cup chopped onion

1 garlic clove, minced

2 (14½-oz.) cans ready-to-serve chicken broth

2 cups water

½ teaspoon dried rosemary leaves, crushed

3 oz. (1 cup) uncooked pasta nuggets (radiatore)

2 cups fresh or frozen small broccoli florets

2 cups cubed cooked turkey breast

1. Melt margarine in large saucepan or Dutch oven medium heat. Add onion and garlic; cook and stir 2 to 3 minutes or just until garlic begins to brown.

2. Add broth, water and rosemary; mix well. Bring to a boil. Add pasta; return to a boil. Cook over medium-high heat for 8 to 10 minutes or until pasta nuggets are of desired doneness.

3. Add broccoli and turkey; mix well. Return to a boil. Cook an additional 3 to 5 minutes or until broccoli is tender and soup is thoroughly heated, stirring occasionally.

Nutrition Information Per Serving: Serving Size: 1¾ Cups • Calories 240 • Calories from Fat 35 • % Daily Value: Total Fat 4 g 6% • Saturated Fat 1 g 5% • Cholesterol 60 mg 20% • Sodium 730 mg 30% • Total Carbohydrate 21 g 7% • Dietary Fiber 2 g 8% • Sugars 2 g • Protein 29 g • Vitamin A 25% • Vitamin C 50% • Calcium 4% • Iron 15%
Dietary Exchanges: 1 Starch, 1 Vegetable, 3½ Very Lean Meat OR 1 Carbohydrate, 1 Vegetable, 3½ Very Lean Meat

TURKEY AND BROCCOLI NUGGET SOUP

Assorted crackers

Peppermint ice cream with chocolate syrup

As with most soup recipes, you can vary ingredients somewhat to use what you have on hand. Leftover cooked macaroni can substitute for the radiatore, for example (they will need a very short cooking time, just to heat through), and chopped green beans or zucchini can stand in for the broccoli.

menu

Old World Sausage and Beer Soup

Coleslaw blend, sold in the grocery store produce section, is a versatile mix of shredded cabbage and carrots. Try it in this piping hot onion- and beer-flavored soup.

Yield: 5 (1½-cup) servings

1 lb. Italian turkey sausage links, cut into ¼-inch slices

3 cups water

1 (12-oz.) can beer

1 (1-oz.) pkg. dry onion soup mix

2 cups purchased coleslaw blend (from 16-oz. pkg.)

½ cup uncooked instant brown rice

1. Cook sausage in large saucepan over medium-high heat for 5 minutes or until browned, stirring occasionally. Drain.

2. Add water, beer and soup mix; mix well. Bring to a boil. Add coleslaw blend and rice. Reduce heat to low; cover and simmer 5 to 7 minutes or until sausage is thoroughly cooked and rice is tender.

Nutrition Information Per Serving: Serving Size: 1½ Cups • Calories 220 • Calories from Fat 90 • % Daily Value: Total Fat 10 g 15% • Saturated Fat 3 g 15% • Cholesterol 50 mg 17% • Sodium 1,110 mg 46% • Total Carbohydrate 14 g 5% • Dietary Fiber 1 g 4% • Sugars 3 g • Protein 17 g • Vitamin A 15% • Vitamin C 10% • Calcium 4% • Iron 15%
Dietary Exchanges: 1 Starch, 2 Medium-Fat Meat OR 1 Carbohydrate, 2 Medium-Fat Meat

---

menu

OLD WORLD SAUSAGE AND BEER SOUP

Rye-topped with Swiss cheese

Red grapes

Ginger cookies

As the soup finishes simmering, slice the bread and cheese. Top-brown the cheese bread under the broiler or in the toaster oven.

menu

**TURKEY-VEGETABLE-
CHEDDAR SOUP**

Pumpernickel bagel sandwiches with
cream cheese and sliced tomatoes

Applesauce

Make the sandwiches while the
soup heats. Try one of the variety
of flavored cream cheeses available, such as chive, scallion or
vegetable.

Turkey-Vegetable-Cheddar Soup

With the addition of chicken broth, a casserole-type dish becomes a hearty soup. The recipe specifies smoked turkey breast, but the soup responds just as well to leftover roast turkey or chicken.

Yield: 4 (1½-cup) servings

1 (1-lb.) pkg. frozen pasta, broccoli and carrots in creamy
       Cheddar sauce

1 cup (5 oz.) cubed smoked turkey breast (from deli)

⅛ teaspoon pepper

1¾ cups water

1 (14½-oz.) can ready-to-serve chicken broth

1. In large saucepan, combine all ingredients; stir to blend. Bring to a boil.

2. Reduce heat; simmer 5 minutes or until vegetables are tender, stirring occasionally.

Nutrition Information Per Serving: Serving Size: 1½ Cups • Calories 200 • Calories from Fat 50 • % Daily Value: Total Fat 6 g 9% • Saturated Fat 2 g 10% • Cholesterol 20 mg 7% • Sodium 1,070 mg 45% • Total Carbohydrate 22 g 7% • Dietary Fiber 3 g 12% • Sugars 3 g • Protein 14 g • Vitamin A 45% • Vitamin C 6% • Calcium 10% • Iron 8%
Dietary Exchanges: 1½ Starch, 1 Very Lean Meat, 1 Fat OR 1½ Carbohydrate, 1 Very Lean Meat, 1 Fat

Hot Turkey and Gravy Open-Faced Sandwiches

Although this is an open-faced sandwich, you'd better serve it with a fork and knife, thanks to the generous amount of rich gravy.

Yield: 4 sandwiches

2 tablespoons margarine or butter

1 large onion, thinly sliced

¾ lb. cooked turkey breast, cut into ⅛-inch-thick slices

1 (12-oz.) jar turkey gravy

4 slices bread

1. Melt margarine in large nonstick skillet over medium-high heat. Add onion; cover and cook 4 to 6 minutes or until onion is tender and lightly browned, stirring occasionally.

2. Add turkey and gravy; cook until thoroughly heated, stirring occasionally.

3. To serve, place 1 slice of bread on each individual plate. Top bread with turkey and onion mixture.

Nutrition Information Per Serving: Serving Size: 1 Sandwich • Calories 290 • Calories from Fat 80 • % Daily Value: Total Fat 9 g 14% • Saturated Fat 2 g 10% • Cholesterol 75 mg 25% • Sodium 740 mg 31% • Total Carbohydrate 21 g 7% • Dietary Fiber 2 g 8% • Sugars 3 g • Protein 30 g • Vitamin A 6% • Vitamin C 4% • Calcium 6% • Iron 15%
Dietary Exchanges: 1½ Starch, 3½ Very Lean Meat, 1 Fat OR 1½ Carbohydrate, 3½ Very Lean Meat, 1 Fat

HOT TURKEY AND GRAVY OPEN-FACED SANDWICHES

Mashed potatoes

Buttered corn

Cranberry relish

Banana cream pie

Slice the turkey and the onion and begin the sandwich recipe. While the turkey cooks, prepare instant mashed potatoes and heat the corn. The pie can be purchased or simply assembled in advance from vanilla pudding with added banana slices poured into a purchased, prebaked pie shell. Top with whipped cream before serving.

QUICK TURKEY PIZZA

Deli Italian broccoli and cauliflower salad

Bakery cupcakes

Chop all the pizza ingredients while the oven preheats.

Quick Turkey Pizza

An unusual trio of cheeses makes this turkey-topped pizza far more intriguing than the average combo. Salty feta and smooth cream cheese complement the classic mozzarella. Deli turkey works fine, but the recipe also presents a great opportunity for using leftover roast turkey.

Yield: 6 servings

---

1 (16-oz.) prebaked Italian pizza crust

⅓ cup cream cheese with roasted garlic (from 8-oz. container)

1½ cups cubed or sliced cooked turkey

1 (14-oz.) can quartered artichoke hearts, drained, coarsely chopped

1 medium tomato, chopped (½ cup)

¼ cup chopped green bell pepper

2 oz. (½ cup) crumbled feta cheese

4 oz. (1 cup) shredded mozzarella cheese

---

1. Heat oven to 450° F. Place pizza crust on ungreased cookie sheet or pizza pan. Spread cream cheese evenly over crust to within ½ inch of edge. Top with all remaining ingredients.

2. Bake at 450° F. for 10 to 13 minutes or until thoroughly heated and mozzarella cheese is melted.

Nutrition Information Per Serving: Serving Size: ⅙ of Recipe • Calories 430 • Calories from Fat 150 • % Daily Value: Total Fat 17 g 26% • Saturated Fat 9 g 45% • Cholesterol 70 mg 23% • Sodium 630 mg 26% • Total Carbohydrate 41 g 14% • Dietary Fiber 3 g 12% • Sugars 4 g • Protein 28 g • Vitamin A 15% • Vitamin C 15% • Calcium 25% • Iron 20%
Dietary Exchanges: 2½ Starch, 1 Vegetable, 2½ Lean Meat, 1½ Fat OR 2½ Carbohydrate, 1 Vegetable, 2½ Lean Meat, 1½ Fat

Smoked Turkey and Salsa Pizzas

The inspiration is Italian, the flavors are Southwestern, and the combination is fantastic. This innovative pizza will be ready before you can call for takeout.

Yield: 8 pizzas

1 (1 lb. 0.3-oz.) can large refrigerated buttermilk biscuits

1 cup salsa

½ lb. smoked turkey breast (from deli), cut into 2x1-inch strips (2 cups)

6 oz. (1½ cups) shredded 4-cheese Mexican cheese blend

1. Heat oven to 350°F. Lightly grease cookie sheets. Separate dough into 8 biscuits. Press or roll each biscuit to form 5½-inch round. Place on greased cookie sheets. Bake at 350°F. for 10 minutes. Cool.

2. Spread each biscuit with 2 tablespoons salsa. Top each with ¼ cup turkey strips and 3 tablespoons cheese.

3. Return to oven; bake an additional 5 to 7 minutes or until thoroughly heated and cheese is melted.

Nutrition Information Per Serving: Serving Size: 1 Pizza • Calories 310 • Calories from Fat 140 • % Daily Value: Total Fat 16 g 25% • Saturated Fat 7 g 35% • Cholesterol 30 mg 10% • Sodium 1,240 mg 52% • Total Carbohydrate 27 g 9% • Dietary Fiber 1 g 4% • Sugars 5 g • Protein 14 g • Vitamin A 8% • Vitamin C 0% • Calcium 20% • Iron 8%
Dietary Exchanges: 2 Starch, 1 Very Lean Meat, 2½ Fat OR 2 Carbohydrate, 1 Very Lean Meat, 2½ Fat

SMOKED TURKEY AND SALSA PIZZAS

Tossed green salad with French dressing

Strawberry ice cream with sliced strawberries and bananas

Once the pizza is in the oven, wash and drain the greens; wait until serving time to toss with the dressing. You can slice the strawberries in advance, too, but add the bananas at the last minute for best color and texture.

menu

DILLED TURKEY BURGERS

Potato salad

Corn on the cob

Strawberry and blueberry shortcakes

Heat the grill. Place the husked corn in a large pot of boiling water on the stove top. Cover; cook 5 to 8 minutes. Place the burgers on the grill. While the burgers and corn cook, rinse the berries and slice the strawberries.

tip

To broil patties, place on broiler pan; broil 4 to 6 inches from heat using times in recipe as a guide, turning once.

Dilled Turkey Burgers

To ensure zesty flavor in every bite, the condiments—ketchup and pickle relish—are mixed right into the ground turkey before grilling.

Yield: 4 sandwiches

---

1 lb. lean ground turkey

¼ cup unseasoned dry bread crumbs

1 teaspoon dried dill weed

2 tablespoons hot dog pickle relish

2 tablespoons ketchup

1 egg

4 (1-oz.) slices Muenster cheese

4 burger buns, split

4 tablespoons purchased dill dip

---

1. Heat grill. In large bowl, combine ground turkey, bread crumbs, dill, relish, ketchup and egg; mix well. Shape mixture into four 4-inch patties.

2. When ready to grill, carefully oil grill rack. Place patties on gas grill over medium heat or on charcoal grill 4 to 6 inches from medium coals. Cook 13 to 15 minutes or until no longer pink in center, turning once. Place cheese slice on each patty during last minute of cooking time. If desired, to toast buns, place cut side down on grill during last 1 to 2 minutes of cooking time.

3. Spread dip on both cut sides of each bun. Place patties in buns.

Nutrition Information Per Serving: Serving Size: 1 Sandwich • Calories 550 • Calories from Fat 270 • % Daily Value: Total Fat 30 g 46% • Saturated Fat 11 g 55% • Cholesterol 175 mg 58% • Sodium 820 mg 34% • Total Carbohydrate 33 g 11% • Dietary Fiber 2 g 8% • Sugars 10 g • Protein 36 g • Vitamin A 10% • Vitamin C 2% • Calcium 30% • Iron 20%
Dietary Exchanges: 1½ Starch, ½ Fruit, 4½ Medium-Fat Meat, 1½ Fat OR 2 Carbohydrate, 4½ Medium-Fat Meat, 1½ Fat

Turkey Burgers with Avocado Mayonnaise

Seasoned ground turkey patties on the grill make a nice change of pace from beef burgers, and have the bonus of less fat and calories.

Yield: 4 sandwiches

1 lb. lean ground turkey

¼ cup unseasoned dry bread crumbs

1 teaspoon chili powder

½ teaspoon garlic salt

¼ cup mayonnaise

1 avocado, peeled, pitted and cut up

2 teaspoons lemon juice

¼ teaspoon garlic powder

4 whole grain burger buns, split

4 slices tomato

1. Heat grill. In medium bowl, combine ground turkey, bread crumbs, chili powder and garlic salt; mix well. Shape mixture into four 4-inch patties.

2. When ready to grill, oil grill rack. Place patties on gas grill over medium-high heat or on charcoal grill 4 to 6 inches from medium-high coals. Cook 10 to 15 minutes or until no longer pink in center, turning once.

3. Meanwhile, in blender container, combine mayonnaise, avocado, lemon juice and garlic powder. Cover; blend until smooth.

4. Spread bottom halves of buns with mayonnaise mixture. Top with turkey patties and tomato slices. Cover with top halves of buns.

Nutrition Information Per Serving: Serving Size: 1 Sandwich • Calories 530 • Calories from Fat 290 • % Daily Value: Total Fat 32 g 49% • Saturated Fat 6 g 30% • Cholesterol 90 mg 30% • Sodium 670 mg 28% • Total Carbohydrate 31 g 10% • Dietary Fiber 6 g 24% • Sugars 4 g • Protein 29 g • Vitamin A 15% • Vitamin C 8% • Calcium 8% • Iron 20%
Dietary Exchanges: 2 Starch, 3½ Medium-Fat Meat, 2½ Fat OR 2 Carbohydrate, 3½ Medium-Fat Meat, 2½ Fat

To broil patties, place on broiler pan; broil 4 to 6 inches from heat using times in recipe as a guide, turning once.

Southwest Turkey Burgers

The spicy intensity of both canned green chiles and salsa can vary quite a bit, so tailor the heat of the dish to your taste.

Yield: 4 sandwiches

---

1 lb. lean ground turkey

1 (4.5-oz.) can chopped green chiles

1 cup salsa

4 (1-oz.) slices Monterey Jack cheese

4 onion burger buns, split

---

1. In medium bowl, combine turkey, chiles and ½ cup of the salsa; mix well. Shape into four ½-inch-thick patties. Place on broiler pan.

2. Broil 4 to 6 inches from heat for 12 to 15 minutes or until no longer pink in center, turning once.

3. Top each burger with cheese slice; broil an additional 30 seconds or until cheese is melted. Place burgers in buns. Serve with remaining ½ cup salsa.

Nutrition Information Per Serving: Serving Size: 1 Sandwich • Calories 460 • Calories from Fat 200 • % Daily Value: Total Fat 22 g 34% • Saturated Fat 9 g 45% • Cholesterol 110 mg 37% • Sodium 1,110 mg 46% • Total Carbohydrate 32 g 11% • Dietary Fiber 2 g 8% • Sugars 8 g • Protein 34 g • Vitamin A 10% • Vitamin C 10% • Calcium 35% • Iron 20%
Dietary Exchanges: 2 Starch, 4 Medium-Fat Meat OR 2 Carbohydrate, 4 Medium-Fat Meat

SOUTHWEST TURKEY BURGERS

Refried beans

Tortilla chips

Chopped tomato, yellow bell pepper and avocado salad

Brownies

While the burgers cook, heat the refried beans in the microwave or in a small saucepan on the stove. Make the salad early in the day, if you wish, as long as you toss the mixture with something acidic (such as lemon or lime juice or vinaigrette) to keep the avocado vibrant green.

menu

SMOKED TURKEY REUBEN SANDWICHES

Home-style French fries

Waldorf salad

Neapolitan ice cream with banana slices

Preheat the oven and cook the French fries in a single layer on a baking sheet. Set out Waldorf salad or prepare your own by tossing together chopped fresh apples, chopped celery and walnuts in a dressing made of mayonnaise thinned with orange juice.

Smoked Turkey Reuben Sandwiches

A classic deli sandwich, the Reuben, gets a lighter touch with smoked turkey instead of corned beef, making it a Rachel.

Yield: 4 sandwiches

8 slices marble rye bread

¼ cup purchased Thousand Island salad dressing

½ lb. thinly sliced smoked turkey breast (from deli)

1 (8-oz.) can sauerkraut, drained, rinsed

2 (1½-oz.) slices Swiss cheese, halved

¼ cup margarine or butter, softened

1. Spread one side of each bread slice with salad dressing. Layer 4 slices with turkey, sauerkraut and Swiss cheese. Top each with remaining bread slice, salad dressing side down. Spread outside of sandwiches with margarine.

2. Heat medium skillet over medium heat until hot. Cook 2 sandwiches at a time for 4 minutes, turning after 2 minutes.

Nutrition Information Per Serving: Serving Size: 1 Sandwich • Calories 440 • Calories from Fat 230 • % Daily Value: Total Fat 25 g 38% • Saturated Fat 8 g 40% • Cholesterol 45 mg 15% • Sodium 1,560 mg 65% • Total Carbohydrate 29 g 10% • Dietary Fiber 4 g 16% • Sugars 4 g • Protein 24 g • Vitamin A 15% • Vitamin C 6% • Calcium 25% • Iron 15%
Dietary Exchanges: 2 Starch, 2½ Very Lean Meat, 4½ Fat OR 2 Carbohydrate, 2½ Very Lean Meat, 4½ Fat

Turkey Hoagies

The hoagie, also known as the grinder, hero or submarine sandwich, fills the bill when you need a quick, hearty meal.

Yield: 4 sandwiches

¼ cup butter, softened

1 tablespoon Dijon mustard

4 French-style rolls, split

Lettuce

4 (1-oz.) slices turkey pastrami

4 (1-oz.) slices Swiss cheese

4 (1-oz.) slices cooked turkey

2 Italian plum tomatoes, thinly sliced

1. In small bowl, combine butter and mustard; blend well. Spread on both cut sides of each roll.

2. Arrange lettuce on bottom half of each roll. Top each with pastrami, cheese, turkey and tomato slices. Cover with top halves of rolls.

Nutrition Information Per Serving: Serving Size: 1 Sandwich • Calories 670 • Calories from Fat 330 • % Daily Value: Total Fat 37 g 57% • Saturated Fat 21 g 105% • Cholesterol 125 mg 42% • Sodium 1,320 mg 55% • Total Carbohydrate 53 g 18% • Dietary Fiber 4 g 16% • Sugars 3 g • Protein 31 g • Vitamin A 25% • Vitamin C 8% • Calcium 40% • Iron 20%
Dietary Exchanges: 3½ Starch, 3 Medium-Fat Meat, 4 Fat OR 3½ Carbohydrate, 3 Medium-Fat Meat, 4 Fat

TURKEY HOAGIES

Deli Italian vegetable pasta salad

Potato chips

Chocolate sandwich cookies

Assemble the sandwiches and serve them on plates alongside a scoop of pasta salad and some chips. Choose any flavor potato chips—plain, barbecue, sour cream and onion—or for a crowd, put out bowls of several different kinds.

fish & shellfish

OPPOSITE PAGE:
Grilled Dill-Mustard Salmon, page 224

☺ **Kid-Pleasing Recipe**
◕ **20-Minutes-or-Less Recipe**

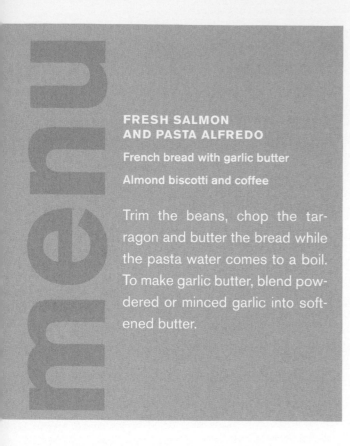
Fresh Salmon and Pasta Alfredo

At the supermarket, choose salmon fillets that are displayed in a pan set on ice and that look glossy, not dried out.

Yield: 4 (1½-cup) servings

8 oz. (3½ cups) uncooked bow tie pasta (farfalle)

8 oz. fresh green beans, trimmed, halved crosswise

¼ cup water

1 (1-lb.) salmon fillet

1 (10-oz.) container refrigerated Alfredo sauce

¼ cup milk

1 tablespoon chopped fresh tarragon

1. Cook pasta to desired doneness as directed on package. Drain; cover to keep warm.

2. Meanwhile, in large skillet, combine green beans and water. Push beans to sides of skillet. Place salmon fillet, skin side down, in center of skillet. Bring to a boil. Reduce heat to medium-low; cover and cook 7 to 10 minutes or until fish flakes easily with fork.

3. Remove salmon from skillet; cover to keep warm. Add Alfredo sauce, milk and tarragon to green beans in skillet; cook and stir 2 to 3 minutes or until sauce is bubbly.

4. Remove and discard skin from salmon. Break salmon into pieces; add to skillet. Add cooked pasta; stir gently to coat with sauce.

Nutrition Information Per Serving: Serving Size: 1½ Cups • Calories 670 • Calories from Fat 310 • % Daily Value: Total Fat 34 g 52% • Saturated Fat 15 g 75% • Cholesterol 130 mg 43% • Sodium 380 mg 16% • Total Carbohydrate 51 g 17% • Dietary Fiber 3 g 12% • Sugars 6 g • Protein 39 g • Vitamin A 10% • Vitamin C 10% • Calcium 15% • Iron 20%
Dietary Exchanges: 3½ Starch, 4 Lean Meat, 4 Fat OR 3½ Carbohydrate, 4 Lean Meat, 4 Fat

Basil Salmon and Vegetables

Salmon has a full, yet not "fishy," flavor and a substantial texture closer to that of meat than sole, flounder or another more delicate fish.

Yield: 4 (1¼-cup) servings

1 (9-oz.) pkg. frozen mixed vegetables in a pouch

2 tablespoons margarine or butter

4 to 6 (about ½ lb.) small red potatoes, thinly sliced (about 2 cups)

½ cup sliced green onions

½ cup half-and-half or milk

½ teaspoon dried basil leaves

¼ teaspoon salt

⅛ teaspoon pepper

1 (14¾-oz.) can salmon, drained, skin and large bones removed, salmon broken into chunks

1. Microwave mixed vegetables in pouch on HIGH for 2 to 3 minutes or until thawed.

2. Meanwhile, melt margarine in large skillet over medium-high heat. Add potatoes; toss to coat with margarine. Cover; cook 5 minutes, stirring once.

3. Add onions and thawed mixed vegetables; cover and cook 5 to 7 minutes or until crisp-tender, stirring once.

4. Reduce heat to medium-low. Add half-and-half, basil, salt and pepper; mix well. Gently stir in salmon chunks. Cook 2 to 3 minutes or until thoroughly heated, stirring occasionally. DO NOT BOIL.

BASIL SALMON AND VEGETABLES

Refrigerated buttermilk biscuits

Vanilla ice cream with pecan-stuffed dates

Prepare the dates in advance by tucking a pecan half into each date and rolling the tops in granulated sugar. To start the meal preparation, preheat the oven for the biscuits and slice the potatoes while the vegetable pouch heats.

Nutrition Information Per Serving: Serving Size: 1¼ Cups • Calories 280 • Calories from Fat 110 • % Daily Value: Total Fat 12 g 18% • Saturated Fat 5 g 25% • Cholesterol 40 mg 13% • Sodium 720 mg 30% • Total Carbohydrate 24 g 8% • Dietary Fiber 4 g 16% • Sugars 4 g • Protein 19 g • Vitamin A 30% • Vitamin C 15% • Calcium 6% • Iron 10%
Dietary Exchanges: 1½ Starch, 2 Lean Meat, 1 Fat OR 1½ Carbohydrate, 2 Lean Meat, 1 Fat

menu

SALMON CAKES

Boiled new potatoes

Asparagus with lemon garnish

Chocolate chip ice cream

Scrub the potatoes and set them to boil. Chop up the ingredients you need for the salmon cakes, plus parsley for the vegetables, and start cooking. While the salmon cakes are cooking, cook the asparagus.

Salmon Cakes

Canned salmon is shelf-stable and easy to use, and it provides a rich source of calcium and beneficial fish oils.

Yield: 4 servings

¾ cup unseasoned dry bread crumbs

¼ cup finely chopped celery

¼ cup finely chopped onion

¼ cup nonfat sour cream

1 tablespoon Dijon mustard

1 egg white, beaten

1 (14¾-oz.) can salmon, drained, skin and large bones removed, flaked

1 (4.5-oz.) can chopped green chiles, drained

1. In large bowl, combine all ingredients; mix well. Cover; refrigerate 10 minutes or until slightly firm.

2. Shape mixture into 4 patties, about ¾ inch thick.

3. Spray 12-inch nonstick skillet with nonstick cooking spray. Heat over medium-high heat until hot. Add patties; cook 6 to 8 minutes or until golden brown, turning once. If desired, serve with additional nonfat sour cream.

Nutrition Information Per Serving: Serving Size: ¼ of Recipe • Calories 240 • Calories from Fat 70 • % Daily Value: Total Fat 8 g 12% • Saturated Fat 2 g 10% • Cholesterol 35 mg 12% • Sodium 870 mg 36% • Total Carbohydrate 18 g 6% • Dietary Fiber 2 g 8% • Sugars 2 g • Protein 23 g • Vitamin A 6% • Vitamin C 10% • Calcium 30% • Iron 15%
Dietary Exchanges: 1 Starch, 3 Very Lean Meat, 1 Fat OR 1 Carbohydrate, 3 Very Lean Meat, 1 Fat

Olive Linguine with Tuna and Tomato Sauce

In hot weather, substitute chilled radiatore or macaroni for the linguine and toss it with the other ingredients without heating; chill until mealtime.

Yield: 4 servings

---

8 oz. uncooked linguine

1 (4¼-oz.) can chopped ripe olives, drained

2 tablespoons olive oil

2 tablespoons balsamic vinegar

2 (14½-oz.) cans diced tomatoes with garlic, oregano and basil, drained, reserving ½ cup liquid

1 (12-oz.) can water-packed solid white tuna, drained, flaked

---

1. Cook linguine in large saucepan or Dutch oven to desired doneness as directed on package. Drain; return to saucepan. Cover to keep warm.

2. Meanwhile, in small bowl, combine olives, oil and vinegar; mix well. Set aside. In medium saucepan, combine tomatoes, reserved ½ cup tomato liquid and tuna; mix well. Cook over medium-high heat until thoroughly heated, stirring occasionally.

3. Add olive mixture to cooked linguine in saucepan; toss to coat. Arrange linguine mixture on serving platter. Top with tuna mixture.

Nutrition Information Per Serving: Serving Size: ¼ of Recipe • Calories 450 • Calories from Fat 110 • % Daily Value: Total Fat 12 g 18% • Saturated Fat 2 g 10% • Cholesterol 20 mg 7% • Sodium 950 mg 40% • Total Carbohydrate 59 g 20% • Dietary Fiber 4 g 16% • Sugars 7 g • Protein 27 g • Vitamin A 25% • Vitamin C 30% • Calcium 10% • Iron 30%
Dietary Exchanges: 3½ Starch, 1 Vegetable, 2 Very Lean Meat, 2 Fat OR 3½ Carbohydrate, 1 Vegetable, 2 Very Lean Meat, 2 Fat

OLIVE LINGUINE WITH TUNA AND TOMATO SAUCE

Whole green beans tossed with butter and sunflower seeds

Crusty whole-grain Italian rolls

While the pasta water comes to a boil, drain the olives and open the cans of tuna and tomatoes. Cook the beans and warm the rolls while the tuna mixture heats up. Sprinkle the sunflower seeds over the beans at serving time to keep them crunchy.

TUNA NOODLE SKILLET

Buttered peas

Gelatin fruit salad

Carrot cake with cream cheese frosting

Make the gelatin fruit salad and carrot cake ahead of time or purchase them ready to serve. While the pasta water comes to a boil, chop the celery and peppers for the tuna dish. Start the peas cooking about 6 or 7 minutes before the tuna is done.

Tuna Noodle Skillet

Made on the stove top, this variation on the Casserole Hall of Fame recipe is quicker than the oven method. Made with roasted bell peppers and fat-free dressing, it's also a bit more sophisticated than the familiar formula.

Yield: 4 (1½-cup) servings

8 oz. (3½ cups) mini lasagna noodles (mafalda)

1 cup chopped celery

2 tablespoons water

½ cup nonfat sour cream

½ cup purchased fat-free ranch salad dressing

1 (12-oz.) can water-packed solid white tuna, drained, flaked

1 (7.25-oz.) jar roasted red bell peppers, drained, chopped

1. Cook noodles to desired doneness as directed on package. Drain.

2. Meanwhile, in 12-inch nonstick skillet, combine celery and water. Cover; cook over medium heat for 2 to 3 minutes or until celery is crisp-tender.

3. Add cooked noodles, sour cream, salad dressing, tuna and roasted peppers; mix well. Cook about 5 minutes or until thoroughly heated, stirring frequently.

Nutrition Information Per Serving: Serving Size: 1½ Cups • Calories 370 • Calories from Fat 20 • % Daily Value: Total Fat 2 g 3% • Saturated Fat 0 g 0% • Cholesterol 20 mg 7% • Sodium 630 mg 26% • Total Carbohydrate 60 g 20% • Dietary Fiber 3 g 12% • Sugars 10 g • Protein 28 g • Vitamin A 35% • Vitamin C 80% • Calcium 8% • Iron 20%
Dietary Exchanges: 4 Starch, 2 Very Lean Meat OR 4 Carbohydrate, 2 Very Lean Meat

Tuna Tortellini Gratin

A brief pass under the broiler gives this no-bake casserole an appealing golden-brown crust and oven-simmered taste.

Yield: 3 (1⅓-cup) servings

1 (9-oz.) pkg. refrigerated cheese-filled tortellini

1½ cups frozen broccoli florets, large pieces cut up

1 (10-oz.) container refrigerated light Alfredo sauce

1 (6-oz.) can water-packed solid white tuna, drained, flaked

1 tablespoon butter, melted

¼ cup Italian-style dry bread crumbs

1. Cook tortellini to desired doneness as directed on package, adding broccoli during last 4 minutes of cooking time. Drain; return to saucepan.

2. Add Alfredo sauce and tuna; mix well. Cook and stir over medium heat until thoroughly heated. Spoon into ungreased shallow 1-quart casserole or gratin dish. In small bowl, combine butter and crumbs; mix well. Sprinkle over top.

3. Broil 4 to 6 inches from heat for 1 to 2 minutes or until topping is golden brown.

Nutrition Information Per Serving: Serving Size: 1⅓ Cups • Calories 540 • Calories from Fat 190 • % Daily Value: Total Fat 21 g 32% • Saturated Fat 11 g 55% • Cholesterol 100 mg 33% • Sodium 1,060 mg 44% • Total Carbohydrate 57 g 19% • Dietary Fiber 3 g 12% • Sugars 7 g • Protein 31 g • Vitamin A 8% • Vitamin C 15% • Calcium 30% • Iron 15%
Dietary Exchanges: 3½ Starch, 1 Vegetable, 2½ Very Lean Meat, 3½ Fat OR 3½ Carbohydrate, 1 Vegetable, 2½ Very Lean Meat, 3½ Fat

TUNA TORTELLINI GRATIN

Green salad

Garlic bread

Italian olives and marinated mushrooms

Peach frozen yogurt

Prepare the salad, but wait to toss with dressing until just before serving time. Heat the garlic bread in the oven while you're making the gratin. To make garlic bread, butter slices of Italian bread, sprinkle them with garlic powder, wrap in foil and warm in a 350°F. oven for 10 minutes or so.

Peppery Pan-Roasted Halibut

This simple technique does quick wonders with any type of fish fillet. Increase the cooking time for thicker pieces.

Yield: 2 servings

2 (4-oz.) halibut fillets (½ to ¾ inch thick), skin removed

½ teaspoon seasoned salt

¼ teaspoon coarse ground black pepper

1. Sprinkle both sides of halibut with salt and pepper.

2. Spray medium nonstick skillet with nonstick cooking spray. Heat over high heat until very hot. Immediately place fish in skillet; cook 1 minute or until golden brown.

3. Turn fish; reduce heat to medium. Add 3 tablespoons water; cover and cook 5 to 8 minutes or until fish flakes easily with fork.

Nutrition Information Per Serving: Serving Size: ½ of Recipe • Calories 120 • Calories from Fat 25 • % Daily Value: Total Fat 3 g 5% • Saturated Fat 0 g 0% • Cholesterol 35 mg 12% • Sodium 440 mg 18% • Total Carbohydrate 0 g 0% • Dietary Fiber 0 g 0% • Sugars 0 g • Protein 24 g • Vitamin A 4% • Vitamin C 0% • Calcium 6% • Iron 6%
Dietary Exchanges: 3½ Very Lean Meat

PEPPERY PAN-ROASTED HALIBUT

Home-fried potatoes

Steamed yellow summer squash, zucchini and onions

Chocolate pudding with whipped topping

Prepare instant pudding if you haven't purchased it ready to serve. To prepare the meal, start the potatoes first, then the vegetables, followed by the fish.

menu

Cod Español

Cod is a mild, meaty white fish that's popular on both sides of the Atlantic. We've paired it with the most important flavors of Spain—garlic, salt and olive oil—along with bell pepper and tomato.

Yield: 4 servings

1 tablespoon olive oil

1 lb. cod fillets

¼ teaspoon salt

¾ teaspoon garlic-pepper blend

½ teaspoon dried oregano leaves

1 tomato, sliced

1 small green bell pepper, cut into rings

½ lemon, sliced

1. Heat oil in large nonstick skillet over medium-high heat until hot. If necessary, cut cod to fit in skillet. Sprinkle cod with salt; place in skillet. Cook 2 to 3 minutes or until browned, turning once.

2. Sprinkle cod with garlic-pepper blend and oregano. Top with tomato and bell pepper. Arrange lemon slices around inside edge of skillet. Reduce heat to medium-low; cover and cook 10 to 12 minutes or until fish flakes easily with fork and vegetables are tender. If skillet becomes dry, add 1 to 2 tablespoons water.

Nutrition Information Per Serving: Serving Size: ¼ of Recipe • Calories 140 • Calories from Fat 35 • % Daily Value: Total Fat 4 g 6% • Saturated Fat 1 g 5% • Cholesterol 50 mg 17% • Sodium 260 mg 11% • Total Carbohydrate 4 g 1% • Dietary Fiber 1 g 4% • Sugars 1 g • Protein 21 g • Vitamin A 6% • Vitamin C 30% • Calcium 2% • Iron 4%
Dietary Exchanges: 3 Very Lean Meat, ½ Fat

Poached Sole with Tomato-Mushroom Sauce

Poaching, a technique for gently simmering food in water or flavored liquid, keeps the sole moist and tender, and requires no added fat for cooking.

Yield: 4 servings

Sole

1 cup water

¼ teaspoon salt

1 tablespoon lemon juice

1 lb. sole or flounder fillets

Sauce

2 tablespoons margarine or butter

¼ cup chopped onion

2 tomatoes, peeled, coarsely chopped

¼ cup sliced green olives

1 (4.5-oz.) jar sliced mushrooms, drained

1 teaspoon sugar

¼ teaspoon salt

Dash ground red pepper (cayenne)

1. In large skillet, combine water, ¼ teaspoon salt and lemon juice. Bring to a boil. Add sole fillets. Reduce heat; cover and simmer 5 to 10 minutes or until fish flakes easily with fork.

2. Meanwhile, melt margarine in medium saucepan over medium heat. Add onion; cook and stir until tender. Stir in all remaining sauce ingredients. Cook 5 minutes, stirring occasionally.

3. To serve, carefully lift fish from liquid; place on serving platter. Serve sauce over fish.

menu

POACHED SOLE WITH TOMATO-MUSHROOM SAUCE

Mashed potatoes

Mixed salad greens with Italian salad dressing

Sugar cookies

Assemble the salad, but wait until the last minute to dress it. Cut up the tomatoes and olives for the sauce while the poaching liquid heats. While the fish cooks, prepare the mashed potatoes (using an instant mix) and make the sauce for the fish.

Nutrition Information Per Serving: Serving Size: ¼ of Recipe • Calories 190 • Calories from Fat 7 • % Daily Value: Total Fat 8 g 12% • Saturated Fat 2 g 10% • Cholesterol 60 mg 20% • Sodium 730 mg 30% • Total Carbohydrate 7 g 2% • Dietary Fiber 2 g 8% • Sugars 3 g • Protein 23 g • Vitamin A 15% • Vitamin C 15% • Calcium 4% • Iron 6%
Dietary Exchanges: 1 Vegetable, 3 Very Lean Meat, 1 Fat

SWEET-AND-SOUR FILLETS

Herb-seasoned rice mix

Frozen miniature egg rolls

Mango slices drizzled with lime or lemon juice

Slice the mango and drizzle with lime or lemon juice; chill until dessert. Start the rice, and heat the egg rolls. Chop the ingredients for the sauce before starting to cook the fish.

Sweet-and-Sour Fillets

The counterpoint of sweet and sour never fails to please, as with this saucy dish of orange roughy, snow peas and red bell pepper.

Yield: 4 servings

1 tablespoon oil

8 oz. (2 cups) fresh snow pea pods, trimmed

1 cup coarsely chopped red bell pepper

1 cup purchased sweet-and-sour or duck sauce

1 1/2 teaspoons grated lemon peel

1 lb. orange roughy, sole or flounder fillets

1. Heat oil in large skillet over medium-high heat until hot. Add pea pods and bell pepper; cook and stir 4 to 6 minutes or until vegetables are crisp-tender. Arrange vegetables on serving platter; cover to keep warm.

2. In same skillet, combine sweet-and-sour sauce and 1 teaspoon of the lemon peel. Reduce heat to medium; cook and stir 1 to 2 minutes or until sauce is bubbly.

3. Arrange orange roughy fillets in sauce, spooning sauce over each fillet. Cover; cook 5 to 7 minutes or until fish flakes easily with fork.

4. To serve, carefully arrange fillets over warm vegetables on platter. Spoon sauce from skillet over fillets and vegetables. Sprinkle with remaining 1/2 teaspoon lemon peel.

Nutrition Information Per Serving: Serving Size: 1/4 of Recipe • Calories 210 • Calories from Fat 35 • % Daily Value: Total Fat 4 g 6% • Saturated Fat 0 g 0% • Cholesterol 25 mg 8% • Sodium 450 mg 19% • Total Carbohydrate 24 g 8% • Dietary Fiber 2 g 8% • Sugars 18 g • Protein 19 g • Vitamin A 30% • Vitamin C 100% • Calcium 6% • Iron 8%
Dietary Exchanges: 1 1/2 Fruit, 1 Vegetable, 2 1/2 Very Lean Meat, 1/2 Fat OR 1 1/2 Carbohydrate, 1 Vegetable, 2 1/2 Very Lean Meat, 1/2 Fat

**LEMON BUTTER
FLOUNDER FILLETS**

Garlic mashed potatoes

Asparagus spears with marjoram

Sliced fresh strawberries with cream

Slice the strawberries and chill until dessert. Trim the asparagus and place it in a skillet of water, vegetable steamer or microwave-safe pan. The flounder cooks quickly and is best served immediately, so get the asparagus cooking and the instant mashed potatoes underway before broiling the fish.

Lemon Butter Flounder Fillets

Flounder has an excellent sea-sweet flavor. It's ideal for quick meals, cooking in less than 10 minutes, yet still rendering an elegant dish.

Yield: 4 servings

1 lb. flounder fillets

1 cup water

2 teaspoons cornstarch

1/2 teaspoon chicken-flavor instant bouillon

Dash pepper

2 tablespoons all-natural butter-flavor granules

1 teaspoon grated lemon peel

1 tablespoon chopped fresh chives

1. Line 15x10x1-inch baking pan with foil; spray foil with nonstick cooking spray. Pat flounder fillets dry with paper towels; place in sprayed foil-lined pan.

2. Broil 4 to 6 inches from heat for 6 to 8 minutes or until fish flakes easily with fork, turning once.

3. Meanwhile, in small saucepan, combine water, cornstarch, bouillon and pepper; blend well. Cook and stir over medium heat until bubbly and thickened. Reduce heat to low; stir in butter-flavor granules and lemon peel. Remove from heat; stir in chives. Serve sauce over fish.

Nutrition Information Per Serving: Serving Size: 1/4 of Recipe • Calories 120 • Calories from Fat 20 • % Daily Value: Total Fat 2 g 3% • Saturated Fat 0 g 0% • Cholesterol 60 mg 20% • Sodium 490 mg 20% • Total Carbohydrate 3 g 1% • Dietary Fiber 0 g 0% • Sugars 0 g • Protein 22 g • Vitamin A 0% • Vitamin C 0% • Calcium 2% • Iron 0%
Dietary Exchanges: 3 Very Lean Meat

Easy Breaded Fish Fillets

A final spritz of cooking spray before baking helps to brown the fillets.

Yield: 4 servings

Nonstick cooking spray

¾ cup crushed seasoned croutons

¼ cup grated Parmesan cheese

2 teaspoons dried parsley flakes

¼ teaspoon paprika

1 egg

1 tablespoon water

1 tablespoon lemon juice

1 lb. fish fillets (¼ to ½ inch thick)*

1. Heat oven to 350°F. Spray 15x10x1-inch baking pan with nonstick cooking spray. In shallow bowl, combine croutons, Parmesan cheese, parsley flakes and paprika; blend well. In another shallow bowl, combine egg, water and lemon juice; beat well.

2. Cut fish fillets into serving-sized pieces. Dip in egg mixture; coat with crouton mixture. (Tuck thin ends of fish under to form pieces of uniform thickness.) Place fish in sprayed pan. Spray fish with cooking spray for about 5 seconds.

3. Bake at 350°F. for 10 to 15 minutes or until fish flakes easily with fork.

Nutrition Information Per Serving: Serving Size: ¼ of Recipe • Calories 250 • Calories from Fat 80 • % Daily Value: Total Fat 9 g 14% • Saturated Fat 3 g 15% • Cholesterol 110 mg 37% • Sodium 460 mg 19% • Total Carbohydrate 14 g 5% • Dietary Fiber 1 g 4% • Sugars 1 g • Protein 27 g • Vitamin A 8% • Vitamin C 4% • Calcium 15% • Iron 10%
Dietary Exchanges: 1 Starch, 3½ Very Lean Meat, 1 Fat OR 1 Carbohydrate, 3½ Very Lean Meat, 1 Fat

menu

EASY BREADED FISH FILLETS

Tartar sauce

Deli pasta and vegetable salad

Bakery banana bread

Chocolate ice cream

If you have time earlier in the day, prepare the banana bread from scratch or a mix if you haven't purchased it ready to serve. To prepare the meal, put the salad into a serving bowl while the fish is in the oven. Cut a lemon into wedges to garnish each plate.

tip

*Any mild white fish fillets can be used. Sole, turbot or flounder (usually thinner fillets) or cod or halibut (thicker) are all good choices. Adjust cook time if needed–thinner fillets cook faster.

Fish Fillets Primavera

An assortment of vegetables brightens a lemony, oven-baked fish dish.

Yield: 4 servings

3 tablespoons margarine or butter

4 (4- to 5-oz.) orange roughy fillets

1 tablespoon lemon juice

Dash salt and pepper

1 garlic clove, minced

1½ cups fresh broccoli florets

1 cup fresh cauliflower florets

1 cup julienne-cut (2 × ⅛ × ⅛-inch) carrots

1 cup sliced fresh mushrooms or 1 (2.5-oz.) jar sliced
    mushrooms, drained

½ cup diagonally sliced celery

¼ teaspoon salt

¼ teaspoon dried basil leaves

¼ cup grated Parmesan cheese

1. Heat oven to 450° F. In oven, melt 2 tablespoons of the margarine in 13x9-inch (3-quart) glass baking dish. Place fish in melted margarine; turn to coat. Sprinkle with lemon juice, salt and pepper. Bake at 450° F. for 5 minutes. Remove from oven.

2. While fish is baking, in large skillet, melt remaining 1 tablespoon margarine over medium-high heat. Add garlic; cook until lightly browned. Add all remaining ingredients except Parmesan cheese; cook and stir 5 to 6 minutes or until vegetables are crisp-tender.

3. Spoon hot vegetables in center of baking dish, moving fish to ends of dish. Sprinkle with Parmesan cheese. Return to oven; bake an additional 3 to 5 minutes or until fish flakes easily with fork.

FISH FILLETS PRIMAVERA

Caesar salad

Crisp garlic toast

While the fish bakes, prepare the garlic toast and the salad. To make a Caesar salad without the classic raw-egg dressing, toss chilled romaine lettuce with an anchovy fillet or two, sprinkle in some Parmesan cheese and top with croutons. Toss with bottled Caesar dressing.

Nutrition Information Per Serving: Serving Size: ¼ of Recipe • Calories 240 • Calories from Fat 110 • % Daily Value: Total Fat 12 g 18% • Saturated Fat 3 g 15% • Cholesterol 35 mg 12% • Sodium 510 mg 21% • Total Carbohydrate 8 g 3% • Dietary Fiber 3 g 12% • Sugars 3 g • Protein 26 g • Vitamin A 200% • Vitamin C 50% • Calcium 15% • Iron 6%
Dietary Exchanges: 1 Vegetable, 3½ Very Lean Meat, 2 Fat

**BROILED SNAPPER
WITH CILANTRO SAUCE**

Frozen twice-baked potatoes

Steamed fresh spinach with butter
and lemon

Coconut layer cake

menu

Make the sour cream sauce ahead of time if you wish. To begin preparing the meal, start the twice-baked potatoes in the microwave. Rinse and drain the spinach several times to remove grit; rinse it only once if you purchased the packaged variety. Place the spinach into the pot without any extra water. Cook it at the last minute; it only takes 3 to 4 minutes.

Broiled Snapper with Cilantro Sauce

Cilantro is a good partner for fish. Also known as Chinese parsley and fresh coriander, cilantro is an important herb in the cuisines of Asia, India and Latin America.

Yield: 4 servings

Sauce

1/2 cup sour cream

1/4 cup chopped fresh cilantro

1/4 cup mayonnaise or salad dressing

2 tablespoons chopped fresh parsley

1 teaspoon chopped shallots

Snapper

2 tablespoons margarine or butter, melted

1 tablespoon chopped fresh parsley

1 tablespoon lemon juice

4 (6- to 8-oz.) red snapper fillets (3/4 to 1 inch thick)

1. In blender container, combine all sauce ingredients; blend on high speed until well mixed. Set aside.

2. In small bowl, combine margarine, 1 tablespoon parsley and lemon juice; mix well. Brush margarine mixture over snapper fillets. If desired, sprinkle with salt and pepper. Place fillets, skin side down, on broiler pan.

3. Broil 4 to 6 inches from heat for 8 to 10 minutes or until fish flakes easily with fork. Serve sauce with fillets.

Nutrition Information Per Serving: Serving Size: 1/4 of Recipe • Calories 290 • Calories from Fat 150 • % Daily Value: Total Fat 17 g 26% • Saturated Fat 5 g 25% • Cholesterol 70 mg 23% • Sodium 210 mg 9% • Total Carbohydrate 2 g 1% • Dietary Fiber 0 g 0% • Sugars 1 g • Protein 32 g • Vitamin A 15% • Vitamin C 6% • Calcium 8% • Iron 2%
Dietary Exchanges: 4 1/2 Very Lean Meat, 3 Fat

Baked Breaded Walleye

Quickly baked in a very hot oven, breaded fish fillets emerge moist and tender with a crisp exterior.

Yield: 4 servings

1 lb. walleye fillets or other lean white fish

2 egg whites

¼ cup skim milk

¼ cup all-purpose flour

½ cup unseasoned dry bread crumbs

¼ teaspoon pepper

¼ teaspoon paprika

1. Place 1 oven rack in center rack position; heat oven to 500° F. Line cookie sheet with foil; spray with nonstick cooking spray. Remove skin from walleye fillets; cut into 8 equal pieces, cutting diagonally if necessary for uniform size.

2. In shallow bowl, combine egg whites and milk; beat well. Place flour and bread crumbs on separate dinner-sized plates. Add pepper to flour; mix well. Add paprika to bread crumbs; mix well.

3. Dip fish in flour mixture, coating thoroughly. Dip floured fish in egg white mixture; dip in bread crumbs mixture, coating thoroughly. Place on sprayed foil-lined cookie sheet.

4. Place cookie sheet on center oven rack; bake at 500° F. for 10 minutes.

5. Reduce oven temperature to 450° F. Remove cookie sheet from oven; carefully turn fish over. Return to oven; bake an additional 5 minutes or until fish flakes easily with fork. If desired, sprinkle with salt and pepper before serving.

BAKED BREADED WALLEYE

Mixed white and wild rice

Deli coleslaw

Strawberry ice cream with wafer cookies

While the fillets cook, cook the rice and put the coleslaw into a serving dish.

Nutrition Information Per Serving: Serving Size: ¼ of Recipe • Calories 190 • Calories from Fat 20 • % Daily Value: Total Fat 2 g 3% • Saturated Fat 0 g 0% • Cholesterol 100 mg 33% • Sodium 190 mg 8% • Total Carbohydrate 16 g 5% • Dietary Fiber 1 g 4% • Sugars 1 g • Protein 27 g • Vitamin A 4% • Vitamin C 0% • Calcium 15% • Iron 15%
Dietary Exchanges: 1 Starch, 3 Very Lean Meat OR 1 Carbohydrate, 3 Very Lean Meat

GRILLED TUNA WITH AVOCADO MAYONNAISE

menu

GRILLED TUNA WITH AVOCADO MAYONNAISE

Green salad

Asparagus and yellow summer squash

Blueberry pie with vanilla ice cream

Prepare the avocado mayonnaise ahead of time and refrigerate it until dinner. Get the salad and the vegetables ready while the grill heats; cook the asparagus and summer squash while the fish cooks on the grill.

Grilled Tuna with Avocado Mayonnaise

This zesty avocado mayonnaise is also excellent with grilled shrimp. For an appetizer, spread it on cocktail bread and top with chilled salad shrimp.

Yield: 4 steaks

Avocado Mayonnaise

¼ cup mayonnaise

1 ripe avocado, pitted, peeled and cut up

2 teaspoons lime juice

¼ to ½ teaspoon hot pepper sauce

2 tablespoons chopped fresh cilantro

Fish

4 (6- to 8-oz.) tuna steaks

1 to 2 tablespoons olive oil

1½ teaspoons peppered seasoned salt

1 teaspoon cumin

1. Heat grill. In food processor bowl with metal blade, combine all mayonnaise ingredients. Cover; blend until smooth. Place mixture in small bowl. Refrigerate while preparing tuna.

2. When ready to grill, brush both sides of tuna steaks with olive oil; sprinkle with peppered seasoned salt and cumin. Place on gas grill over medium-high heat or on charcoal grill 4 to 6 inches from medium-high coals. Cook 8 to 12 minutes or until fish flakes easily with fork, turning once. Serve with avocado mayonnaise.

Nutrition Information Per Serving: Serving Size: ¼ of Recipe • Calories 570 • Calories from Fat 330 • % Daily Value: Total Fat 37 g 57% • Saturated Fat 7 g 35% • Cholesterol 95 mg 32% • Sodium 340 mg 14% • Total Carbohydrate 5 g 2% • Dietary Fiber 3 g 12% • Sugars 1 g • Protein 54 g • Vitamin A 100% • Vitamin C 4% • Calcium 4% • Iron 20%
Dietary Exchanges: ½ Fruit, 7½ Very Lean Meat, 6 Fat OR ½ Carbohydrate, 7½ Very Lean Meat, 6 Fat

Pesto Sea Bass

Pesto is a green sauce made of pine nuts, olive oil, Parmesan cheese, garlic and lots of fresh basil. Traditional cooks pound the mixture in a mortar and pestle until it forms a paste. Purchasing the sauce is much easier, while still giving incomparable fragrance and flavor.

Yield: 2 servings

¼ cup purchased pesto

1 tablespoon butter, softened

1 tablespoon chopped drained roasted red bell peppers

1 (¾-lb.) sea bass fillet, cut into 2 serving-sized pieces

⅛ teaspoon coarse ground black pepper

---

1. Heat grill. In small bowl, combine 2 tablespoons of the pesto, butter and roasted peppers; mix well. Refrigerate while preparing sea bass.

2. When ready to grill, sprinkle sea bass with pepper; brush with remaining 2 tablespoons pesto. Place fish, skin side down, on gas grill over medium-high heat or on charcoal grill 4 to 6 inches from medium-high coals. Cook 12 to 15 minutes or until fish flakes easily with fork. Serve sea bass with pesto-butter mixture.

Nutrition Information Per Serving: Serving Size: ½ of Recipe • Calories 310 • Calories from Fat 170 • % Daily Value: Total Fat 19 g 29% • Saturated Fat 6 g 30% • Cholesterol 90 mg 30% • Sodium 310 mg 13% • Total Carbohydrate 2 g 1% • Dietary Fiber 0 g 0% • Sugars 1 g • Protein 33 g • Vitamin A 15% • Vitamin C 8% • Calcium 6% • Iron 4%
Dietary Exchanges: 5 Very Lean Meat, 3 Fat

PESTO SEA BASS

Capellini pasta tossed with olive oil and garlic-pepper blend

Sliced fresh tomatoes and mozzarella cheese slices

Chocolate cake

Make the cake in advance or purchase one. While waiting for the pasta water to boil and the grill to heat, chop the bell peppers for the fish and arrange the tomatoes and cheese in overlapping slices on a plate.

PACIFIC HALIBUT

Parmesan-flavored couscous

Green salad

Sliced fresh peaches with vanilla yogurt

If you wish to slice the peaches in advance, toss them with a little orange or lemon juice to keep their color bright. While the oven preheats, wash and drain the salad ingredients. Just after the halibut goes into the oven, prepare the couscous according to package directions. Toss the salad with dressing at serving time.

Pacific Halibut

Fresh gingerroot lends its unmistakable spicy-hot flavor to halibut, which is one of the meatier varieties of fish.

Yield: 4 servings

4 (4-oz.) halibut fillets ($\frac{1}{2}$ to $\frac{3}{4}$ inch thick), skin removed

1 tablespoon finely chopped onion

1 teaspoon grated gingerroot

$\frac{1}{4}$ teaspoon coarse ground black pepper

2 tablespoons frozen orange juice concentrate

1. Heat oven to 450° F. Place halibut on foil-lined cookie sheet.

2. In small bowl, combine onion, gingerroot, pepper and orange juice concentrate; mix well. Spread mixture over fish.

3. Bake at 450° F. for 7 to 11 minutes or until fish flakes easily with fork.

Nutrition Information Per Serving: Serving Size: $\frac{1}{4}$ of Recipe • Calories 140 • Calories from Fat 25 • % Daily Value: Total Fat 3 g 5% • Saturated Fat 0 g 0% • Cholesterol 35 mg 12% • Sodium 60 mg 3% • Total Carbohydrate 4 g 1% • Dietary Fiber 0 g 0% • Sugars 3 g • Protein 24 g • Vitamin A 4% • Vitamin C 15% • Calcium 6% • Iron 6%
Dietary Exchanges: $\frac{1}{2}$ Fruit, $3\frac{1}{2}$ Very Lean Meat OR $\frac{1}{2}$ Carbohydrate, $3\frac{1}{2}$ Very Lean Meat

Italian Barbecued Swordfish Steaks with Tomato Relish

This recipe is lower in fat than most, with only 7 grams of fat and 180 calories per serving.

Yield: 4 servings

Fish

½ cup purchased fat-free Italian salad dressing

1 teaspoon paprika

¼ teaspoon coarse ground black pepper

4 (4- to 6-oz.) swordfish steaks (1 inch thick)

Relish

1 large tomato, seeded, chopped

1 (2¼-oz.) can sliced ripe olives, drained

1 to 2 tablespoons chopped fresh basil or parsley

1. In small bowl, combine dressing, paprika and pepper; mix well. Place swordfish steaks in resealable food storage plastic bag. Pour dressing mixture over fish; seal bag. Turn bag to coat both sides of fish. Refrigerate 15 minutes to marinate.

2. Meanwhile, heat grill. In medium bowl, combine relish ingredients; mix well.

3. When ready to grill, carefully oil grill rack. Remove fish from marinade; reserve marinade. Place fish on gas grill over medium heat or on charcoal grill 4 to 6 inches from medium coals. Cook 10 to 13 minutes or until fish flakes easily with fork, turning once and brushing occasionally with marinade. Discard any remaining marinade. Serve relish with fish.

ITALIAN BARBECUED SWORDFISH STEAKS WITH TOMATO RELISH

Romaine and leaf lettuce with creamy Italian salad dressing

Soft breadsticks with butter

Bakery cannoli

If you wish to make the relish for the fish in advance, omit the basil until the last minute so it doesn't discolor. While the grill heats, preheat the oven for the breadsticks. Warm the breadsticks in the oven while the fish grills; meanwhile, prepare the salad but wait until serving time to toss it with the dressing.

Nutrition Information Per Serving: Serving Size: ¼ of Recipe • Calories 180 • Calories from Fat 60 • % Daily Value: Total Fat 7 g 11% • Saturated Fat 2 g 10% • Cholesterol 45 mg 15% • Sodium 330 mg 14% • Total Carbohydrate 4 g 1% • Dietary Fiber 1 g 4% • Sugars 2 g • Protein 24 g • Vitamin A 15% • Vitamin C 15% • Calcium 2% • Iron 10%
Dietary Exchanges: ½ Starch, 3 Very Lean Meat, 1 Fat OR ½ Carbohydrate, 3 Very Lean Meat, 1 Fat

To broil swordfish, place on sprayed broiler pan; broil 4 to 6 inches from heat using times in recipe as a guide, turning once and brushing occasionally with marinade.

menu

GRILLED DILL-MUSTARD SALMON

Grilled potato wedges and red onion

Deli broccoli salad

Fresh raspberries and cream

Partially cook the potato wedges in the microwave; then thread the potatoes and peeled, quartered red onions onto skewers. Spritz them with nonstick cooking spray, and sprinkle with salt and pepper. Grill skewered vegetables alongside the fish, turning as needed to brown them evenly.

tip

To broil salmon, place, skin side up, on broiler pan; do not spread with mustard mixture. Broil 4 to 6 inches from heat using times in recipe as a guide, turning once halfway through broiling and spreading with mustard mixture.

Grilled Dill-Mustard Salmon

Fresh dill, with its feathery leaves and garden flavor, naturally complements salmon. The grilled vegetables make a sweet, smoky and tender accompaniment to the fish.

Yield: 4 servings

1 tablespoon chopped fresh dill

1 tablespoon Dijon mustard

1 tablespoon honey

¼ cup mayonnaise

1 (1½-lb.) salmon fillet, cut into 4 pieces

Nonstick cooking spray

1. Heat grill. In small bowl, combine dill, mustard and honey; mix well. Place 2 tablespoons mustard mixture in small bowl; stir in mayonnaise until well blended. Refrigerate sauce until serving time. Reserve remaining mustard mixture for brushing on salmon.

2. When ready to grill, spray skin side of salmon with nonstick cooking spray. Place salmon, skin side down, on gas grill over medium heat or on charcoal grill 4 to 6 inches from medium coals. Spoon reserved mustard mixture onto salmon, spreading evenly. Cook 10 to 15 minutes or until fish flakes easily with fork. Serve mayonnaise-mustard sauce mixture with salmon.

Nutrition Information Per Serving: Serving Size: ¼ of Recipe • Calories 430 • Calories from Fat 250 • % Daily Value: Total Fat 28 g 43% • Saturated Fat 4 g 20% • Cholesterol 135 mg 45% • Sodium 270 mg 11% • Total Carbohydrate 5 g 2% • Dietary Fiber 0 g 0% • Sugars 5 g • Protein 40 g • Vitamin A 8% • Vitamin C 0% • Calcium 0% • Iron 6%
Dietary Exchanges: ½ Fruit, 5½ Lean Meat, 2 Fat OR ½ Carbohydrate, 5½ Lean Meat, 2 Fat

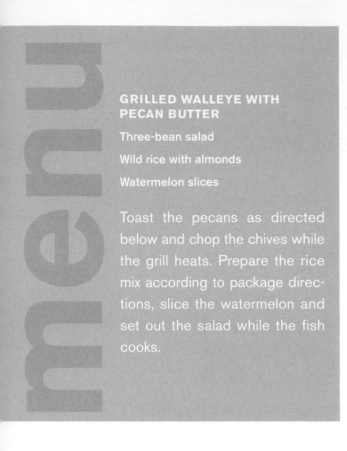

menu

GRILLED WALLEYE WITH PECAN BUTTER

Three-bean salad

Wild rice with almonds

Watermelon slices

Toast the pecans as directed below and chop the chives while the grill heats. Prepare the rice mix according to package directions, slice the watermelon and set out the salad while the fish cooks.

tips

*To toast pecans, spread on cookie sheet; bake at 350°F. for 5 to 7 minutes or until golden brown, stirring occasionally. Or spread pecans in thin layer in microwave-safe pie pan; microwave on HIGH for 4 to 7 minutes or until golden brown, stirring frequently.

To broil walleye, place on broiler pan; broil 4 to 6 inches from heat using times in recipe as a guide, turning once and topping with pecan butter as directed.

Grilled Walleye with Pecan Butter

Grilled fish is delicious, but it needs gentle handling to keep it from falling apart. Here, the fish grills on oiled foil, making it easier to flip.

Yield: 4 servings

¼ cup butter, softened

2 teaspoons chopped fresh chives

2 teaspoons orange juice

½ cup chopped pecans, toasted*

4 (6-oz.) walleye fillets

¼ teaspoon salt

Dash coarse ground black pepper

1. Heat grill. Cut two 12-inch-square pieces of heavy-duty foil. With tip of sharp knife, cut 2-inch slits every 2 inches across foil. Spray foil with nonstick cooking spray.

2. In small bowl, combine butter, chives, orange juice and ¼ cup of the pecans; mix well.

3. When ready to grill, place foil pieces on gas grill over medium heat or on charcoal grill 4 to 6 inches from medium coals. Sprinkle walleye fillets with salt and pepper; place on foil. Cook 8 to 12 minutes or until fish flakes easily with fork, turning once. During last minute, top fillets with pecan butter. Place fillets on serving platter. Sprinkle with remaining ¼ cup pecans.

Nutrition Information Per Serving: Serving Size: ¼ of Recipe • Calories 360 • Calories from Fat 210 • % Daily Value: Total Fat 23 g 35% • Saturated Fat 8 g 40% • Cholesterol 175 mg 58% • Sodium 340 mg 14% • Total Carbohydrate 4 g 1% • Dietary Fiber 1 g 4% • Sugars 1 g • Protein 34 g • Vitamin A 10% • Vitamin C 0% • Calcium 20% • Iron 15%
Dietary Exchanges: 5 Very Lean Meat, 4 Fat

Halibut Kabobs

Timing is everything when grilling. Parboiling the potatoes gives them a head start so they are done at the same time as the zucchini and fish.

Yield: 4 servings

6 small red potatoes, unpeeled, halved

1 lb. halibut, cut into 1¼- to 1½-inch pieces

2 small zucchini, cut into 12 pieces

2 tablespoons chopped fresh chives

2 tablespoons lemon juice

2 tablespoons Dijon mustard

1 tablespoon honey

Dash ground red pepper (cayenne)

1. In medium saucepan, combine potatoes and enough water to cover. Bring to a boil. Reduce heat to medium; cook 5 to 6 minutes or until almost tender. Drain; cool slightly.

2. Meanwhile, heat grill. Alternately thread halibut, partially cooked potatoes and zucchini onto four 12- to 14-inch metal skewers. In small bowl, combine all remaining ingredients; mix well.

3. When ready to grill, oil grill rack. Place kabobs on gas grill over medium heat or on charcoal grill 4 to 6 inches from medium coals. Brush kabobs with chive mixture. Cook 10 to 15 minutes or until fish flakes easily with fork and potatoes are tender, turning and brushing frequently with chive mixture. Discard any remaining chive mixture.

Nutrition Information Per Serving: Serving Size: ¼ of Recipe • Calories 280 • Calories from Fat 25 • % Daily Value: Total Fat 3 g 5% • Saturated Fat 0 g 0% • Cholesterol 35 mg 12% • Sodium 120 mg 5% • Total Carbohydrate 36 g 12% • Dietary Fiber 4 g 16% • Sugars 4 g • Protein 27 g • Vitamin A 8% • Vitamin C 25% • Calcium 8% • Iron 15%
Dietary Exchanges: 2 Starch, ½ Vegetable, 3 Very Lean Meat OR 2 Carbohydrate, ½ Vegetable, 3 Very Lean Meat

menu

HALIBUT KABOBS

Grilled fresh corn on the cob

Refrigerated crescent dinner rolls

Brownies drizzled with caramel sauce

While the grill heats, prepare the potatoes, halibut, zucchini and chives. Place the corn in a pot filled with 1 or 2 inches of boiling water on the stove top. Bake the rolls while the fish cooks.

tip

To broil kabobs, place on sprayed broiler pan; broil 4 to 6 inches from heat using times in recipe as a guide, turning and brushing frequently with chive mixture.

Mixed Seafood Grill

A grill basket resembles two hinged cake racks with long handles, and holds the fish securely for easy grilling and turning. For best results, oil the basket before adding the seafood.

Yield: 6 servings

2 tablespoons butter, melted

1 teaspoon lemon-pepper seasoning

½ teaspoon fennel seed, crushed

¼ teaspoon salt

1 lb. halibut, cut into 1¼- to 1½-inch pieces

12 shelled deveined uncooked large shrimp, tails left on
(about 1 lb.)

1. Heat grill. In large bowl, combine butter, lemon-pepper seasoning, fennel seed and salt; mix well. Add halibut and shrimp; toss to coat. Place in grill basket.

2. When ready to grill, place basket on gas grill over medium-high heat or on charcoal grill 4 to 6 inches from medium-high coals. Cook 5 to 10 minutes or until fish flakes easily with fork and shrimp turn pink, turning once or twice.

Nutrition Information Per Serving: Serving Size: ⅙ of Recipe • Calories 160 • Calories from Fat 50 • % Daily Value: Total Fat 6 g 9% • Saturated Fat 3 g 15% • Cholesterol 140 mg 47% • Sodium 380 mg 16% • Total Carbohydrate 0 g 0% • Dietary Fiber 0 g 0% • Sugars 0 g • Protein 27 g • Vitamin A 8% • Vitamin C 0% • Calcium 6% • Iron 15%
Dietary Exchanges: 4 Very Lean Meat, ½ Fat

MIXED SEAFOOD GRILL

Broccoli spears with Parmesan cheese

Bran muffins

Blueberries and cream

If you have time earlier in the day, bake the muffins from scratch or a mix, or purchase them. While the grill heats, cut up the fish and crush the fennel. When the fish goes on the grill, start the broccoli spears on the stove top. Toss hot, cooked broccoli with shredded fresh Parmesan cheese.

FISH FILLET SANDWICHES

Lettuce leaves, sliced tomatoes and red onion

Chocolate chip cookies

Rinse and pat dry the lettuce leaves. Slice the tomatoes and onion while the fish bakes. Eat the vegetables as a side dish, or top the sandwiches with them.

Fish Fillet Sandwiches

This easy fish and cheese sandwich has all the flavor but less fat than its fast food cousin, because you bake the fish instead of deep-frying it.

Yield: 4 sandwiches

8 frozen 97% fat-free baked breaded fish fillets or patties

2/3 cup fat-free mayonnaise or salad dressing

2 tablespoons pickle relish

4 whole wheat sandwich buns, split, toasted

4 (3/4-oz.) slices light American cheese

1. Prepare fish fillets as directed on package.

2. Meanwhile, in small bowl, combine mayonnaise and relish; mix well. Spread cut sides of buns with mayonnaise mixture. Place 2 fish fillets on bottom half of each bun. Top each with cheese. Cover with top halves of buns.

Nutrition Information Per Serving: Serving Size: 1 Sandwich • Calories 370 • Calories from Fat 80 • % Daily Value: Total Fat 9 g 14% • Saturated Fat 3 g 15% • Cholesterol 40 mg 13% • Sodium 1,480 mg 62% • Total Carbohydrate 51 g 17% • Dietary Fiber 5 g 20% • Sugars 12 g • Protein 20 g • Vitamin A 6% • Vitamin C 0% • Calcium 20% • Iron 15%
Dietary Exchanges: 3 Starch, 1/2 Fruit, 1 1/2 Lean Meat, 1/2 Fat OR 3 1/2 Carbohydrate, 1 1/2 Lean Meat, 1/2 Fat

Tuna Melt Biscuits

Our version, spiked with pineapple, adds a twist to the lunch-counter favorite.

Yield: 10 sandwiches; 5 servings

1 (10.2-oz.) can (5 biscuits) large refrigerated buttermilk biscuits

2 (6-oz.) cans water-packed chunk light tuna, well drained

1/3 cup chopped celery

1/3 cup well-drained crushed pineapple

2 tablespoons finely chopped onion

1/4 cup purchased honey mustard salad dressing

5 (3/4-oz.) slices American cheese

1. Heat oven to 375°F. Bake biscuits as directed on can. Cool slightly.

2. Meanwhile, in medium bowl, combine tuna, celery, pineapple, onion and salad dressing; mix well.

3. Split biscuits; arrange, cut side up, on same cookie sheet. Spoon mixture evenly onto biscuit halves. Cut cheese slices in half diagonally; place 1 piece on each topped biscuit half.

4. Bake at 375°F. for 5 to 7 minutes or until filling is hot and cheese is melted.

Nutrition Information Per Serving: Serving Size: 1/5 of Recipe • Calories 370 • Calories from Fat 160 • % Daily Value: Total Fat 18 g 28% • Saturated Fat 7 g 35% • Cholesterol 40 mg 13% • Sodium 1,190 mg 50% • Total Carbohydrate 30 g 10% • Dietary Fiber 1 g 4% • Sugars 10 g • Protein 23 g • Vitamin A 6% • Vitamin C 2% • Calcium 15% • Iron 15%
Dietary Exchanges: 1 1/2 Starch, 1/2 Fruit, 2 1/2 Very Lean Meat, 3 Fat OR 2 Carbohydrate, 2 1/2 Very Lean Meat, 3 Fat

menu

TUNA MELT BISCUITS

Tomato slices on lettuce with cottage cheese

Dill pickle spears

Ice cream sandwiches

While the biscuits are baking, arrange tomato slices, lettuce and cottage cheese on individual plates.

menu

CREAMY SHRIMP AND BROCCOLI ROTINI

Crusty French bread

Sliced fresh peaches or nectarines

Start the water for the pasta, and slice the bread. Slice the peaches or nectarines at the last minute or, if slicing them in advance, toss them with lemon or orange juice to prevent browning.

Creamy Shrimp and Broccoli Rotini

An updated shrimp "wiggle," made with rotini and broccoli, gets garlicky flavor from the cheese spread used in the sauce.

Yield: 4 (1⅓-cup) servings

6 oz. (2 cups) uncooked rotini (spiral pasta)

2 cups small broccoli florets

½ lb. shelled deveined uncooked medium shrimp, tails removed

1 (6.5-oz.) container (about 1 cup) light garlic and herbs soft spreadable cheese

2 tablespoons milk

½ teaspoon salt

1. In large saucepan, cook rotini to desired doneness as directed on package, adding broccoli and shrimp during last 2 to 4 minutes of cooking time. Cook until broccoli is tender and shrimp turn pink. Drain; return to saucepan.

2. Add cheese, milk and salt to cooked rotini, broccoli and shrimp; toss gently to coat.

Nutrition Information Per Serving: Serving Size: 1⅓ Cups • Calories 320 • Calories from Fat 80 • % Daily Value: Total Fat 9 g 14% • Saturated Fat 5 g 25% • Cholesterol 100 mg 33% • Sodium 710 mg 30% • Total Carbohydrate 37 g 12% • Dietary Fiber 2 g 8% • Sugars 4 g • Protein 22 g • Vitamin A 20% • Vitamin C 15% • Calcium 10% • Iron 15%
Dietary Exchanges: 2 Starch, 1 Vegetable, 2 Very Lean Meat, 1½ Fat OR 2 Carbohydrate, 1 Vegetable, 2 Very Lean Meat, 1½ Fat

Garlic and Herb Shrimp and Pasta Supper

Cooked shrimp sets the stage for fast preparation of this recipe. Once the pasta has been cooked and drained, the other ingredients need only be heated together.

Yield: 2 (1¾-cup) servings

4 oz. (1 cup) uncooked small shell pasta

1 cup frozen sweet peas

4 to 5 oz. shelled deveined cooked shrimp

1 (5-oz.) container light garlic and herbs soft spreadable cheese

1 (2.5-oz.) jar sliced mushrooms, drained

2 tablespoons milk

---

1. In large saucepan, cook pasta to desired doneness as directed on package, adding peas during last 2 minutes of cooking time. Drain; return to saucepan.

2. Add shrimp, cheese, mushrooms and milk; cook over low heat for 1 to 2 minutes or until cheese is melted and mixture is hot, stirring constantly.

Nutrition Information Per Serving: Serving Size: 1¾ Cups • Calories 510 • Calories from Fat 120 • % Daily Value: Total Fat 13 g 20% • Saturated Fat 7 g 35% • Cholesterol 165 mg 55% • Sodium 900 mg 38% • Total Carbohydrate 60 g 20% • Dietary Fiber 5 g 20% • Sugars 7 g • Protein 38 g • Vitamin A 30% • Vitamin C 15% • Calcium 20% • Iron 30%
Dietary Exchanges: 4 Starch, 4 Very Lean Meat, 1 Fat OR 4 Carbohydrate, 4 Very Lean Meat, 1 Fat

menu

GARLIC AND HERB SHRIMP AND PASTA SUPPER

Cantaloupe and honeydew melon wedges

Dinner rolls

Chocolate cookies

If necessary, peel and devein the shrimp. While waiting for the pasta water to boil, slice and chill the melon, and heat the oven for the dinner rolls. This recipe needs only 4 ounces of pasta, but you can cook extra for a pasta salad the next day.

SHRIMP PRIMAVERA ALFREDO

Crusty Italian rolls with garlic butter

Jelly roll

If you have time earlier in the day, make the jelly roll from scratch or purchase one. While waiting for the pasta water to come to a boil, cut up the vegetables and blend garlic into softened butter to spread on the rolls before heating.

Shrimp Primavera Alfredo

Packed with vegetables, this pasta dish hides considerable nutrients·in its creamy sauce.

Yield: 4 (1½-cup) servings

---

6 oz. uncooked linguine or spaghetti

8 oz. fresh asparagus spears, trimmed, cut into 1½-inch pieces

4 oz. (1 cup) fresh baby carrots, quartered lengthwise

1 cup sliced fresh mushrooms

1 (9-oz.) pkg. frozen sugar snap peas in a pouch

1 (12-oz.) pkg. frozen shelled deveined uncooked medium shrimp, thawed, tails removed

1 (10-oz.) container refrigerated light Alfredo sauce

2 tablespoons chopped fresh chives

1 teaspoon grated lemon peel

---

1. Cook linguine to desired doneness as directed on package. Drain; cover to keep warm.

2. Meanwhile, in large skillet, combine asparagus, carrots, mushrooms and sugar snap peas. Add ½ cup water. Bring to a boil. Reduce heat; cover and simmer 4 to 6 minutes or until vegetables are crisp-tender.

3. Add shrimp; cook and stir 2 to 3 minutes or until shrimp turn pink. Drain; return mixture to skillet.

4. Stir in Alfredo sauce, chives and lemon peel. Simmer 2 to 4 minutes or until mixture is thoroughly heated. Serve over linguine. If desired, garnish with additional chives.

Nutrition Information Per Serving: Serving Size: 1½ Cups • Calories 390 • Calories from Fat 80 • % Daily Value: Total Fat 9 g 14% • Saturated Fat 4 g 20% • Cholesterol 145 mg 48% • Sodium 550 mg 23% • Total Carbohydrate 51 g 17% • Dietary Fiber 5 g 20% • Sugars 11 g • Protein 27 g • Vitamin A 170% • Vitamin C 20% • Calcium 25% • Iron 25%
Dietary Exchanges: 3 Starch, 1 Vegetable, 2 Very Lean Meat, 1 Fat OR 3 Carbohydrate, 1 Vegetable, 2 Very Lean Meat, 1 Fat

Cayenne Shrimp with Lemon

Zero tolerance for hot peppers? Omit the cayenne from the recipe and remake it into "Paprika Shrimp with Lemon." It will still be delicious.

Yield: 4 servings

1 cup uncooked instant rice

1 cup water

1 lb. shelled deveined uncooked medium shrimp, tails removed

2 tablespoons margarine or butter

1 teaspoon paprika

1/2 teaspoon salt

1/4 teaspoon ground red pepper (cayenne)

2 tablespoons lemon juice

Lemon wedges

1. Cook rice in water, omitting margarine and salt, as directed on package.

2. Meanwhile, spray large nonstick skillet with nonstick cooking spray. Heat over medium-high heat until hot. Add shrimp; cook 2 to 5 minutes or until shrimp turn pink, stirring frequently.

3. Reduce heat to medium-low. Add margarine, paprika, salt and ground red pepper; cook and stir to melt margarine and coat shrimp completely. Add lemon juice; stir to blend thoroughly.

4. Arrange cooked rice on serving platter. Spoon shrimp mixture over rice. Serve with lemon wedges.

CAYENNE SHRIMP WITH LEMON

Mixed fruit kabobs

Sourdough bread with butter

Date bars

Prepare the bars from scratch or a mix ahead of time, or purchase them ready to serve. Prepare the fruit kabobs by threading onto small skewers a variety of fruit chunks, such as strawberry, cantaloupe, pineapple and whole grapes. If you're shelling and deveining the shrimp yourself, do that before starting the rice and proceeding with the recipe.

Nutrition Information Per Serving: Serving Size: 1/4 of Recipe • Calories 220 • Calories from Fat 60 • % Daily Value: Total Fat 7 g 11% • Saturated Fat 1 g 5% • Cholesterol 160 mg 53% • Sodium 520 mg 22% • Total Carbohydrate 20 g 7% • Dietary Fiber 1 g 4% • Sugars 1 g • Protein 19 g • Vitamin A 15% • Vitamin C 15% • Calcium 4% • Iron 20%
Dietary Exchanges: 1 1/2 Starch, 2 Very Lean Meat, 1/2 Fat OR 1 1/2 Carbohydrate, 2 Very Lean Meat, 1/2 Fat

menu

SHRIMP MARINARA WITH ANGEL HAIR PASTA

Buttered broccoli, cauliflower and carrot mixture

Chocolate cheesecake

While waiting for the pasta water to boil, peel and devein the shrimp, if necessary, and mince the garlic. Start the vegetables cooking when you add the shrimp to the skillet.

Shrimp Marinara with Angel Hair Pasta

Lime juice and vodka spike this marinara sauce served atop fine-textured angel hair pasta.

Yield: 4 servings

1 (9-oz.) pkg. refrigerated angel hair pasta (capellini)

1 tablespoon olive or vegetable oil

1 lb. shelled deveined uncooked medium shrimp

2 garlic cloves, minced

1 (15-oz.) container refrigerated marinara sauce

1 tablespoon lime juice

1 tablespoon vodka, if desired

1/8 teaspoon crushed red pepper flakes

1. Cook pasta to desired doneness as directed on package. Drain; cover to keep warm.

2. Meanwhile, heat oil in large skillet over medium-high heat until hot. Add shrimp and garlic; cook and stir 2 to 3 minutes or until shrimp just begin to turn pink.

3. Stir in all remaining ingredients. Simmer 3 to 5 minutes or until mixture is thoroughly heated. Serve over pasta.

Nutrition Information Per Serving: Serving Size: ¼ of Recipe • Calories 370 • Calories from Fat 80 • % Daily Value: Total Fat 9 g 14% • Saturated Fat 1 g 5% • Cholesterol 210 mg 70% • Sodium 610 mg 25% • Total Carbohydrate 43 g 14% • Dietary Fiber 4 g 16% • Sugars 7 g • Protein 26 g • Vitamin A 20% • Vitamin C 4% • Calcium 8% • Iron 35%
Dietary Exchanges: 3 Starch, 2½ Very Lean Meat, 1 Fat OR 3 Carbohydrate, 2½ Very Lean Meat, 1 Fat

SHRIMP SCAMPI

Broccoli spears with shredded Asiago cheese

Hazelnut biscotti with vanilla ice cream

Start the pasta water; then peel and devein the shrimp, if necessary; mince the garlic and grate the lemon peel. Start cooking the broccoli a few minutes before you start the shrimp skillet, and toss it with the cheese while it's still hot.

Shrimp Scampi

This restaurant classic is easy enough for a weeknight supper and elegant enough for company.

Yield: 4 servings

8 oz. uncooked fettuccine

2 tablespoons margarine or butter

1 tablespoon olive or vegetable oil

4 garlic cloves, minced

1 lb. shelled deveined uncooked medium shrimp

¼ cup chopped fresh parsley

2 teaspoons grated lemon peel

¼ teaspoon salt

¼ teaspoon pepper

⅓ cup dry white wine or chicken broth

1. Cook fettuccine to desired doneness as directed on package. Drain; cover to keep warm.

2. Meanwhile, melt margarine with oil in medium skillet over medium heat. Add garlic; cook and stir 1 minute. Add shrimp; cook and stir 1 minute.

3. Add all remaining ingredients; cook and stir 1 to 2 minutes or until shrimp turn pink. Serve over fettuccine.

Nutrition Information Per Serving: Serving Size: ¼ of Recipe • Calories 390 • Calories from Fat 110 • % Daily Value: Total Fat 12 g 18% • Saturated Fat 2 g 10% • Cholesterol 215 mg 72% • Sodium 400 mg 17% • Total Carbohydrate 42 g 14% • Dietary Fiber 2 g 8% • Sugars 2 g • Protein 26 g • Vitamin A 15% • Vitamin C 10% • Calcium 6% • Iron 30%
Dietary Exchanges: 3 Starch, 2½ Very Lean Meat, 1½ Fat OR 3 Carbohydrate, 2½ Very Lean Meat, 1½ Fat

Linguine with Seafood Sauce

If you have fresh basil and oregano, use a table-spoon of each in place of the teaspoon of dried herb specified in the recipe.

Yield: 8 servings

12 oz. uncooked linguine

4 tablespoons margarine or butter

4 green onions, sliced

1 garlic clove, minced

1 (12-oz.) pkg. frozen shelled deveined uncooked medium shrimp, thawed, drained and tails removed

1 (6½-oz.) can minced clams, undrained

1 cup chicken broth

½ cup dry white wine

2 tablespoons lemon juice

¼ cup chopped fresh parsley

1 teaspoon dried basil leaves

1 teaspoon dried oregano leaves

¼ teaspoon pepper

2 tablespoons cold water

2 tablespoons cornstarch

¼ cup sour cream

1. Cook linguine to desired doneness as directed on package. Drain; cover to keep warm.

2. Meanwhile, melt 2 tablespoons of the margarine in large skillet over medium heat. Add onions and garlic; cook and stir until onions are tender. Stir in shrimp, clams, broth, wine, lemon juice, parsley, basil, oregano and pepper. Bring to a boil. Reduce heat to low; simmer 5 minutes or until shrimp turn pink.

LINGUINE WITH SEAFOOD SAUCE

Tomato salad with balsamic vinaigrette

Crusty whole-grain rolls

Filled chocolate candies and sliced oranges

Cut up the tomatoes for the salad. Add the vinaigrette immediately to marinate the tomatoes, or wait until the last minute if you prefer firmer tomatoes. While waiting for the pasta water to boil, assemble all the recipe ingredients. If you'd like to heat the rolls, put them in the oven just before you begin making the seafood sauce.

3. In small bowl, combine water and cornstarch; blend well. Gradually stir into seafood mixture. Cook until mixture boils and thickens, stirring constantly.

4. In large bowl, combine cooked linguine, sour cream and remaining 2 tablespoons margarine; toss to coat. Serve seafood sauce over linguine.

Nutrition Information Per Serving: Serving Size: ⅛ of Recipe • Calories 280 • Calories from Fat 90 • % Daily Value: Total Fat 10 g 15% • Saturated Fat 3 g 15% • Cholesterol 105 mg 35% • Sodium 300 mg 13% • Total Carbohydrate 34 g 11% • Dietary Fiber 2 g 8% • Sugars 2 g • Protein 14 g • Vitamin A 10% • Vitamin C 8% • Calcium 6% • Iron 20%
Dietary Exchanges: 2½ Starch, 1 Very Lean Meat, 1½ Fat OR 2½ Carbohydrate, 1 Very Lean Meat, 1½ Fat

SHRIMP AND SCALLOP KABOBS

Herb seasoned white and wild rice

Buttered broccoli

Bakery lemon-filled pastries

Prepare the rice mix according to package directions. While the grill heats, cook the broccoli on the stove top; drain broccoli and toss with a pat of butter just before the kabobs come off the grill.

Shrimp and Scallop Kabobs

At the fish market or counter, scallops should look glossy and moist. Buy them the same day you plan to use them.

Yield: 6 servings

---

2 tablespoons butter, melted

½ teaspoon grated lemon peel

2 tablespoons fresh lemon juice

½ teaspoon dried marjoram leaves

¼ teaspoon salt

2 garlic cloves, minced

¾ lb. shelled deveined uncooked large shrimp, tails left on

1 lb. uncooked fresh sea scallops

---

1. Heat grill. In medium bowl, combine butter, lemon peel, lemon juice, marjoram, salt and garlic; mix well. Add shrimp and scallops; toss to coat. Alternately thread shrimp and scallops onto six 12- to 14-inch metal skewers. Reserve butter mixture.

2. When ready to grill, place kabobs on gas grill over medium heat or on charcoal grill 4 to 6 inches from medium coals; brush shrimp and scallops with butter mixture. Cook 6 to 8 minutes or until shrimp turn pink and scallops turn opaque, turning and brushing frequently with butter mixture. Discard any remaining butter mixture.

Nutrition Information Per Serving: Serving Size: ⅙ of Recipe • Calories 110 • Calories from Fat 20 • % Daily Value: Total Fat 2 g 3% • Saturated Fat 1 g 5% • Cholesterol 110 mg 37% • Sodium 250 mg 10% • Total Carbohydrate 2 g 1% • Dietary Fiber 0 g 0% • Sugars 0 g • Protein 21 g • Vitamin A 4% • Vitamin C 4% • Calcium 4% • Iron 8%
Dietary Exchanges: 3 Very Lean Meat

Scallop and Broccoli Linguine with Pesto Cream

Bay scallops are tiny and sweet. If using larger sea scallops, cut them into quarters.

Yield: 4 (1½-cup) servings

8 oz. uncooked linguine

1 (14-oz.) pkg. frozen broccoli florets

1 tablespoon margarine or butter

¾ lb. fresh uncooked bay scallops, rinsed

1 (2.5-oz.) jar sliced mushrooms, drained

½ cup nonfat half-and-half or milk

1 tablespoon all-purpose flour

⅓ cup purchased pesto

1. In Dutch oven, cook linguine as directed on package, adding broccoli during last 3 to 5 minutes. Cook until tender. Drain; return to Dutch oven. Cover.

2. Meanwhile, melt margarine in large skillet over medium-high heat. Add scallops and mushrooms; cook 3 minutes.

3. In small bowl, blend half-and-half and flour. Add flour mixture to scallop mixture; cook and stir over medium heat until mixture is bubbly and thickened and scallops are opaque.

4. Add scallop mixture and pesto to cooked linguine and broccoli; toss gently to coat.

Nutrition Information Per Serving: Serving Size: 1½ Cups • Calories 470 • Calories from Fat 140 • % Daily Value: Total Fat 15 g 23% • Saturated Fat 3 g 15% • Cholesterol 30 mg 10% • Sodium 430 mg 18% • Total Carbohydrate 56 g 19% • Dietary Fiber 4 g 16% • Sugars 6 g • Protein 28 g • Vitamin A 20% • Vitamin C 50% • Calcium 15% • Iron 20%
Dietary Exchanges: 3½ Starch, 1 Vegetable, 2 Very Lean Meat, 2 Fat OR 3½ Carbohydrate, 1 Vegetable, 2 Very Lean Meat, 2 Fat

SCALLOP AND BROCCOLI LINGUINE WITH PESTO CREAM

Mixed baby green salad with sliced baby summer squash and lemon vinaigrette

French bread

Pound cake topped with fresh or frozen raspberries

Rinse, drain and chill the raspberries if using fresh. Assemble the salad while waiting for the pasta water to boil, but wait until serving time to add the dressing.

Monterey Shrimp Pitas

Blended with lemon and dill, and sweetened almost imperceptibly with a teaspoon of sugar, yogurt makes a creamy, nonfat dressing for a cool shrimp-artichoke sandwich filler.

Yield: 6 sandwiches

2/3 cup nonfat plain yogurt

1 tablespoon chopped fresh dill or 1 teaspoon dried dill weed

1 teaspoon sugar

1/4 teaspoon salt

1 tablespoon lemon juice

1 lb. shelled deveined cooked shrimp

1 (14-oz.) can artichoke hearts, drained, chopped

1 medium tomato, seeded, chopped

3 (6- to 8-inch) whole wheat pita (pocket) breads, halved

1. In medium bowl, combine yogurt, dill, sugar, salt and lemon juice; blend well. Add shrimp, artichoke hearts and tomato; stir just until combined.

2. Spoon shrimp mixture into pita bread halves.

Nutrition Information Per Serving: Serving Size: 1 Sandwich • Calories 210 • Calories from Fat 20 • % Daily Value: Total Fat 2 g 3% • Saturated Fat 0 g 0% • Cholesterol 150 mg 50% • Sodium 490 mg 20% • Total Carbohydrate 26 g 9% • Dietary Fiber 5 g 20% • Sugars 4 g • Protein 22 g • Vitamin A 8% • Vitamin C 15% • Calcium 10% • Iron 20%
Dietary Exchanges: 1½ Starch, 1 Vegetable, 2 Very Lean Meat OR 1½ Carbohydrate, 1 Vegetable, 2 Very Lean Meat

Fiesta Shrimp Tacos with Cucumber Salsa

The word "salsa" literally means "sauce" in Spanish. In the recipe below, cucumber-sour cream salsa adds both spiciness and coolness to the sautéed shrimp.

Yield: 12 tacos; 6 servings

---

12 taco shells

1½ cups nonfat sour cream

½ cup chopped seeded peeled cucumber

1 (1.25-oz.) pkg. taco seasoning mix

2 avocados, pitted, peeled and coarsely chopped

1 tablespoon lime juice

1 lb. shelled deveined uncooked medium shrimp, tails removed

1 tablespoon olive oil

1 cup salsa

½ cup chopped fresh cilantro

---

1. Heat taco shells as directed on package. Meanwhile, in medium bowl, combine sour cream, cucumber and 2 tablespoons of the taco seasoning mix; mix well. In small bowl, combine avocados and lime juice; toss to coat. Set aside.

2. In another medium bowl, combine shrimp and remaining taco seasoning mix; toss to coat.

3. Heat oil in large skillet over medium-high heat until hot. Add shrimp; cook 3 to 5 minutes or until shrimp turn pink, stirring frequently.

4. Spoon shrimp into warm taco shells. Top each with sour cream mixture, avocado, salsa and cilantro.

FIESTA SHRIMP TACOS WITH CUCUMBER SALSA

Lettuce and tomato salad with French dressing

Cantaloupe chunks

Chocolate pudding with whipped cream

Get everything else ready before you begin making the tacos: Prepare instant pudding if you haven't purchased it ready to serve. Prepare the salad, but wait to add the dressing until serving time. Then heat the taco shells and proceed with the filling and salsa recipe.

Nutrition Information Per Serving: Serving Size: ⅙ of Recipe • Calories 360 • Calories from Fat 160 • % Daily Value: Total Fat 18 g 28% • Saturated Fat 3 g 15% • Cholesterol 110 mg 37% • Sodium 1,190 mg 50% • Total Carbohydrate 31 g 10% • Dietary Fiber 5 g 20% • Sugars 7 g • Protein 19 g • Vitamin A 25% • Vitamin C 10% • Calcium 15% • Iron 20%
Dietary Exchanges: 2 Starch, 2 Very Lean Meat, 3 Fat OR 2 Carbohydrate, 2 Very Lean Meat, 3 Fat

Seaside Shortcakes

The dessert shortcake is reinvented as a savory entree, with shrimp and crab over biscuits.

Yield: 5 servings

1 (10.2-oz.) can (5 biscuits) large refrigerated buttermilk
    biscuits

½ cup dry white wine*

1 (16-oz.) jar Alfredo sauce

1 (8-oz.) container cream cheese with chives and onion

1 cup frozen small sweet peas

½ lb. shelled deveined cooked medium shrimp

1 (6-oz.) can crabmeat, drained

2 oz. (½ cup) shredded Cheddar cheese

¼ cup chopped fresh chives

1. Heat oven to 375° F. Bake biscuits as directed on can.

2. Meanwhile, cook wine in large skillet over high heat for 3 to 5 minutes or until slightly reduced. Reduce heat to medium. Add Alfredo sauce, cream cheese, peas, shrimp and crabmeat; mix well. Cook 8 to 10 minutes or until sauce is smooth and peas are tender, stirring occasionally.

3. Split warm biscuits; place bottom halves on serving plates. Spoon half of seafood mixture over biscuits. Cover with top halves of biscuits. Top with remaining seafood mixture. Sprinkle with cheese and chives.

Nutrition Information Per Serving: Serving Size: ⅕ of Recipe • Calories 650 • Calories from Fat 400 • % Daily Value: Total Fat 44 g 68% • Saturated Fat 22 g 110% • Cholesterol 225 mg 75% • Sodium 1,660 mg 69% • Total Carbohydrate 33 g 11% • Dietary Fiber 2 g 8% • Sugars 8 g • Protein 29 g • Vitamin A 30% • Vitamin C 6% • Calcium 25% • Iron 20%
Dietary Exchanges: 2 Starch, 3½ Lean Meat, 6½ Fat OR 2 Carbohydrate, 3½ Lean Meat, 6½ Fat

menu

SEASIDE SHORTCAKES

Sliced fresh plums

Chocolate frozen yogurt

While the biscuits are in the oven, shred the cheese, chop the chives, and prepare the shrimp and crab mixture. Slice the plums just before serving. For dessert, garnish the frozen yogurt with a few fresh berries, a twirl of whipped cream or a sprig of fresh mint.

tip

*To substitute for wine, omit reducing step and add ⅓ cup milk with Alfredo sauce. Continue as directed.

DELAWARE CRAB CAKES

Tartar sauce

Roasted russet potato wedges

Deli creamy coleslaw

Pecan pie with vanilla ice cream

Preheat the oven to 450° F. and arrange potato wedges in a single layer on a lightly oiled baking tray. Spritz the potatoes with nonstick cooking spray and sprinkle with salt. Cook potatoes for about 20 minutes or until browned. Chop the green onions and fresh dill, and prepare the crab cakes.

Delaware Crab Cakes

Delaware is home to some magnificent beaches. Enjoy a taste of the mid-Atlantic shore with these golden sautéed crab cakes.

Yield: 16 crab cakes; 4 servings

½ cup unseasoned dry bread crumbs

¼ cup chopped green onions

¼ cup nonfat plain yogurt

1 tablespoon chopped fresh dill

1 teaspoon dry mustard

¼ to ½ teaspoon pepper

1 tablespoon lemon juice

1 egg, beaten

1 (8-oz.) pkg. frozen imitation crabmeat (surimi), thawed, finely chopped, or 1 (6-oz.) can crabmeat, drained, flaked

1 teaspoon oil

---

1. In large bowl, combine all ingredients except oil; mix well. Shape mixture into 16 patties, about ½ inch thick.

2. Heat oil in large nonstick skillet over medium heat until hot. Add patties; cook 6 to 8 minutes or until golden brown, turning once. If desired, serve with seafood cocktail sauce.

Nutrition Information Per Serving: Serving Size: ¼ of Recipe • Calories 150 • Calories from Fat 35 • % Daily Value: Total Fat 4 g 6% • Saturated Fat 1 g 5% • Cholesterol 65 mg 22% • Sodium 620 mg 26% • Total Carbohydrate 18 g 6% • Dietary Fiber 1 g 4% • Sugars 6 g • Protein 11 g • Vitamin A 4% • Vitamin C 4% • Calcium 8% • Iron 8%
Dietary Exchanges: 1 Starch, 1 Very Lean Meat, ½ Fat OR 1 Carbohydrate, 1 Very Lean Meat, ½ Fat

Crabmeat and Avocado Wraps

The richness of avocado is an excellent foil for premium crabmeat; shredded lettuce adds a bit of crunch. For variety, try flavored tortillas.

Yield: 4 wraps

4 (10-inch) flour tortillas

²/₃ cup purchased Alfredo sauce

2 (6-oz.) cans crabmeat, well drained, flaked

1 ripe avocado, pitted, peeled and cubed

2 cups shredded lettuce

¼ cup sliced green onions

1. Heat tortillas as directed on package.

2. Meanwhile, in medium saucepan, combine Alfredo sauce and crabmeat; cook over medium heat just until thoroughly heated, stirring occasionally. Fold in avocado.

3. Spoon half of mixture across center of each tortilla; top with lettuce and onions. Fold sides over filling. Fold bottom up over filling and continue rolling to enclose filling.

Nutrition Information Per Serving: Serving Size: 1 Wrap • Calories 470 • Calories from Fat 230 • % Daily Value: Total Fat 25 g 38% • Saturated Fat 9 g 45% • Cholesterol 85 mg 28% • Sodium 660 mg 28% • Total Carbohydrate 38 g 13% • Dietary Fiber 5 g 20% • Sugars 3 g • Protein 22 g • Vitamin A 8% • Vitamin C 10% • Calcium 20% • Iron 15%
Dietary Exchanges: 2½ Starch, 2 Very Lean Meat, 4½ Fat OR 2½ Carbohydrate, 2 Very Lean Meat, 4½ Fat

CRABMEAT AND AVOCADO WRAPS

Mixed fresh fruit salad

Rum cake

Cut up assorted fresh fruit if you haven't purchased a packaged salad. Before assembling the crab mixture, examine the crabmeat carefully; even canned crabmeat sometimes has bits of shell or cartilage in it.

menu

menu

MIXED VEGETABLE CLAM CHOWDER

Oyster crackers

Citrus fruit sections

Chocolate chip cookies

Thaw the frozen vegetables by soaking the bag briefly in a bowl of hot water. Or, spread the vegetables in a single layer in a microwave-safe dish and cook on HIGH for 2 minutes or until the iciness has melted. Section the fruit while the soup simmers.

Mixed Vegetable Clam Chowder

Creamy clam soup becomes more substantial with the addition of mixed vegetables; shredded Cheddar cheese crowns each serving.

Yield: 2 (1¼-cup) servings

1 (18.5-oz.) can ready-to-serve New England clam chowder

1 cup frozen mixed vegetables, thawed

⅛ teaspoon dried thyme leaves

2 tablespoons shredded Cheddar cheese

In medium saucepan, combine all ingredients except cheese; stir to blend. Cook over medium heat until thoroughly heated, stirring frequently. Sprinkle individual servings with cheese.

Nutrition Information Per Serving: Serving Size: 1¼ Cups • Calories 270 • Calories from Fat 120 • % Daily Value: Total Fat 13 g 20% • Saturated Fat 4 g 20% • Cholesterol 25 mg 8% • Sodium 1,070 mg 45% • Total Carbohydrate 29 g 10% • Dietary Fiber 3 g 12% • Sugars 4 g • Protein 10 g • Vitamin A 25% • Vitamin C 10% • Calcium 10% • Iron 10%
Dietary Exchanges: 1½ Starch, 1 Vegetable, ½ High-Fat Meat, 1½ Fat OR 1½ Carbohydrate, 1 Vegetable, ½ High-Fat Meat, 1½ Fat

Clam Sauce
with Linguine

Canned clams make easy work of this herbed sauce for linguine.

Yield: 3 servings

6 oz. uncooked linguine

2 tablespoons olive or vegetable oil

¼ cup finely chopped onion

1 garlic clove, minced

2 tablespoons chopped fresh parsley

½ teaspoon dried oregano leaves

½ teaspoon dried basil leaves

⅛ teaspoon pepper

¼ cup dry white wine

1 (6½-oz.) can minced clams, drained, reserving liquid

2 tablespoons grated Parmesan cheese, if desired

1. Cook linguine to desired doneness as directed on package. Drain; cover to keep warm.

2. Meanwhile, heat oil in medium skillet over medium-high heat until hot. Add onion and garlic; cook 1 to 2 minutes or until onion is tender, stirring constantly. Stir in parsley, oregano, basil, pepper, wine and reserved clam liquid. Cook 5 minutes, stirring constantly.

3. Add clams; cook until thoroughly heated. Serve sauce over linguine. Sprinkle individual servings with Parmesan cheese.

Nutrition Information Per Serving: Serving Size: ⅓ of Recipe • Calories 370 • Calories from Fat 110 • % Daily Value: Total Fat 12 g 18% • Saturated Fat 2 g 10% • Cholesterol 25 mg 8% • Sodium 190 mg 8% • Total Carbohydrate 46 g 15% • Dietary Fiber 2 g 8% • Sugars 3 g • Protein 17 g • Vitamin A 8% • Vitamin C 15% • Calcium 10% • Iron 60%
Dietary Exchanges: 3 Starch, 1 Very Lean Meat, 2 Fat OR 3 Carbohydrate, 1 Very Lean Meat, 2 Fat

**CLAM SAUCE
WITH LINGUINE**

Steamed asparagus spears

Sliced pears sprinkled with walnuts

Butterscotch pudding with whipped topping

Put the pasta water on to boil; then prepare instant pudding if you haven't purchased it ready to serve. Cut up the onion, garlic and parsley for the clam sauce; trim the asparagus and place it in a skillet or microwave-safe casserole with a small amount of water. Cook the asparagus while you make the clam sauce.

MENU

MUSSELS IN WINE SAUCE

Herb-seasoned white and wild rice

Glazed baby carrots with basil

Layer cake

Begin cooking the rice mix and the carrots so they are ready when the mussels are done. When the carrots are tender, drain off most of the liquid and stir in a pat of butter and a sprinkling of sugar, honey or brown sugar; stir to glaze, and sprinkle with fresh or dried basil.

Mussels in Wine Sauce

The thyme- and garlic-scented wine sauce could also be used for small, hard-shell clams.

Yield: 4 servings

4 lb. fresh mussels

1 teaspoon oil

2 garlic cloves, minced

2 cups dry white wine

1 teaspoon dried thyme leaves

1 teaspoon cracked black pepper

2 lemons, cut into wedges

1. Place mussels in large bowl; cover with cold water. Let stand 10 minutes.

2. Meanwhile, heat oil in large saucepan over medium heat until hot. Add garlic; cook about 1 minute. Stir in wine, thyme and pepper. Bring to a boil.

3. Remove beards from mussels; scrub well under cold running water. Discard any mussels that do not close. Add cleaned mussels to boiling wine mixture. Cover; cook about 5 minutes or until mussels are open. Discard any mussels that do not open. Serve mussels with lemon wedges.

Nutrition Information Per Serving: Serving Size: ¼ of Recipe • Calories 150 • Calories from Fat 35 • % Daily Value: Total Fat 4 g 6% • Saturated Fat 1 g 5% • Cholesterol 35 mg 12% • Sodium 380 mg 16% • Total Carbohydrate 9 g 3% • Dietary Fiber 1 g 4% • Sugars 1 g • Protein 16 g • Vitamin A 4% • Vitamin C 40% • Calcium 6% • Iron 30%
Dietary Exchanges: ½ Fruit, 2½ Very Lean Meat, ½ Fat OR ½ Carbohydrate, 2½ Very Lean Meat, ½ Fat

Fried Oysters

Fresh oysters are a real treat. Like clams, which can substitute for oysters in this recipe, deep-frying brings out their sweetness. It's like a trip to the beach.

Yield: 4 servings

1/3 cup all-purpose flour

1 teaspoon salt

1/8 teaspoon pepper

1 egg

1 tablespoon water

2/3 cup cracker crumbs or unseasoned dry bread crumbs

1/4 cup oil or butter

1 pint (2 cups) fresh oysters, drained

---

1. In shallow dish, combine flour, salt and pepper. In another shallow dish, combine egg and water; beat well. Place crumbs in medium bowl.

2. Heat oil in medium skillet over medium-high heat until hot. Coat oysters with flour mixture; dip in egg mixture. Coat with crumbs. Add oysters to skillet; cook 8 to 10 minutes or until golden brown, turning once. If desired, serve with lemon wedges or tartar sauce.

Nutrition Information Per Serving: Serving Size: 1/4 of Recipe • Calories 350 • Calories from Fat 200 • % Daily Value: Total Fat 22 g 34% • Saturated Fat 4 g 20% • Cholesterol 145 mg 48% • Sodium 1,020 mg 43% • Total Carbohydrate 22 g 7% • Dietary Fiber 0 g 0% • Sugars 0 g • Protein 16 g • Vitamin A 4% • Vitamin C 6% • Calcium 10% • Iron 70%
Dietary Exchanges: 1 1/2 Starch, 1 1/2 Lean Meat, 3 1/2 Fat OR 1 1/2 Carbohydrate, 1 1/2 Lean Meat, 3 1/2 Fat

menu

FRIED OYSTERS

Baked potatoes with sour cream and chives

Fresh asparagus spears with butter

Green salad with purchased lemon-poppy seed dressing

Cheesecake topped with raspberries or blueberries

Like most fried foods, these oysters are best hot from the pan, so make sure the rest of the dinner is ready before you begin frying. Wash and dry the salad greens in advance, but toss with the dressing at the last minute. Trim the asparagus and start cooking it just before the oysters go into the skillet.

Variations

Fried Clams: Substitute shucked fresh clams for oysters.

Fried Frog Legs: Substitute 3 lb. frog legs for oysters. Cook about 10 minutes on each side or until golden brown. If legs are large, add a little water. Cover; simmer 10 minutes. Remove cover; continue frying until crisp.

Oysters can be cooked in deep fryer at 375° F. for 2 to 3 minutes.

vegetarian

☺ Kid-Pleasing Recipe
◔ 20-Minutes-or-Less Recipe

OPPOSITE PAGE:
Chili-Stuffed Potatoes, page 274

**CAJUN BEANS AND
RICE SUPPER**

Mixed fresh fruit salad

Pecan pralines

Before you start the beans and rice, chop the fruit. If you include peaches, bananas, apples or another fruit that will discolor, toss with orange or lemon juice to keep the colors bright. Pralines are available in some supermarkets and bakeries or at specialty stores.

Cajun Beans and Rice Supper

Rice and beans is a pairing that has stood the test of time. It's affordable, it appeals to the "small planet" movement to eat lower on the food chain and it's a high-protein, low-fat health food—*and* it's quick and simple to prepare.

Yield: 3 (1½-cup) servings

1 tablespoon olive or vegetable oil

1 medium zucchini, chopped

½ cup chopped green bell pepper

1 (7.4- to 8-oz.) pkg. red beans and rice mix

Water

1 medium tomato, chopped

1. Heat oil in large skillet over medium heat until hot. Add zucchini and bell pepper; cook and stir 2 to 3 minutes or until crisp-tender. Remove vegetables from skillet; cover to keep warm.

2. In same skillet, combine rice mix with any seasonings and amount of water called for on package. Bring to a boil. Reduce heat to low; cover and simmer 15 minutes.

3. Add zucchini mixture and tomato; stir gently to mix. Cover; cook 3 to 5 minutes or until thoroughly heated.

Nutrition Information Per Serving: Serving Size: 1½ Cups • Calories 220 • Calories from Fat 45 • % Daily Value: Total Fat 5 g 8% • Saturated Fat 1 g 5% • Cholesterol 0 mg 0% • Sodium 730 mg 30% • Total Carbohydrate 34 g 11% • Dietary Fiber 14 g 56% • Sugars 6 g • Protein 10 g • Vitamin A 10% • Vitamin C 35% • Calcium 4% • Iron 6%
Dietary Exchanges: 2 Starch, 1 Vegetable, 1 Fat OR 2 Carbohydrate, 1 Vegetable, 1 Fat

Coconut Curried Vegetables with Rice

In less than half an hour, bring the exotic flavors of curry, lime and coconut to the dinner table and travel to a faraway land.

Yield: 4 servings

1 cup uncooked regular long-grain white rice

2 cups water

2 tablespoons all-purpose flour

1 ½ teaspoons curry powder

½ teaspoon salt

⅛ teaspoon pepper

1 (14-oz.) can light coconut milk

1 teaspoon lime juice

1 (1-lb.) pkg. frozen broccoli florets, carrots and cauliflower

1 cup frozen sweet peas

1. Cook rice in water as directed on package.

2. Meanwhile, in small bowl, combine flour, curry powder, salt, pepper and ¼ cup of the coconut milk; beat with wire whisk until smooth. Stir in remaining coconut milk and lime juice. Set aside.

3. In large saucepan, combine frozen vegetables, peas and ½ cup water. Bring to a boil. Reduce heat to low; cover and simmer 6 to 8 minutes or until vegetables are crisp-tender. Drain; set aside.

4. Pour coconut milk mixture into same saucepan. Bring to a boil, stirring constantly. Boil and stir 1 minute. Stir in vegetables. Cook over medium heat until thoroughly heated, stirring frequently. Serve over rice.

COCONUT CURRIED VEGETABLES WITH RICE

Warmed pita bread

Purchased mango chutney

Butter pecan ice cream

Warm the pita bread in the oven or toaster oven shortly before the rice is done.

menu

Nutrition Information Per Serving: Serving Size: ¼ of Recipe • Calories 310 • Calories from Fat 50 • % Daily Value: Total Fat 6 g 9% • Saturated Fat 5 g 25% • Cholesterol 0 mg 0% • Sodium 420 mg 18% • Total Carbohydrate 55 g 18% • Dietary Fiber 5 g 20% • Sugars 9 g • Protein 8 g • Vitamin A 60% • Vitamin C 35% • Calcium 6% • Iron 35%
Dietary Exchanges: 2 Starch, 1 Fruit, 2 Vegetable, 1 Fat OR 3 Carbohydrate, 2 Vegetable, 1 Fat

Vegetable Chili
Skillet Supper

Vary this recipe according to what's in your pantry. Use black beans or kidney beans in place of the pintos; substitute a pound of whatever single or mixed frozen vegetable you have on hand.

Yield: 3 (1⅓-cup) servings

1 tablespoon olive or vegetable oil

½ cup chopped onion

1 (1-lb.) pkg. frozen broccoli florets, carrots and cauliflower

1 (8-oz.) can tomato sauce

1 teaspoon chili powder

½ teaspoon sugar

¼ teaspoon salt

⅛ to ¼ teaspoon ground red pepper (cayenne)

1 (15.5-oz.) can pinto beans, drained

4 oz. (1 cup) shredded Cheddar cheese

1. Heat oil in large skillet over medium-high heat until hot. Add onion and frozen vegetables; cook and stir 7 to 10 minutes or until vegetables are crisp-tender.

2. Add tomato sauce, chili powder, sugar, salt and ground red pepper; mix well. Bring to a boil. Reduce heat to low; simmer 5 minutes.

3. Add beans; simmer an additional 5 minutes or until thoroughly heated. Sprinkle with cheese.

Nutrition Information Per Serving: Serving Size: 1⅓ Cups • Calories 390 • Calories from Fat 160 • % Daily Value: Total Fat 18 g 28% • Saturated Fat 9 g 45% • Cholesterol 40 mg 13% • Sodium 1,120 mg 47% • Total Carbohydrate 37 g 12% • Dietary Fiber 10 g 40% • Sugars 11 g • Protein 19 g • Vitamin A 100% • Vitamin C 60% • Calcium 40% • Iron 15%
Dietary Exchanges: 2 Starch, 2 Vegetable, 1½ Very Lean Meat, 3 Fat OR 2 Carbohydrate, 2 Vegetable, 1½ Very Lean Meat, 3 Fat

VEGETABLE CHILI SKILLET SUPPER

Carrot and celery sticks with flavored sour cream dip

Cornbread

Apple pie with vanilla ice cream

Prepare the carrot and celery sticks in advance, or clean and cut them while the frozen vegetables cook in the skillet for the chili. Make the cornbread from scratch or a mix, or purchase cornbread muffins from the bakery. Heat the pie while you're eating dinner.

**GREEK RICE AND
VEGETABLE DINNER**

Sliced cheeses and rye crackers with
Greek olives

Mixed melon salad with honey Dijon
salad dressing

Baklava

Set out the cheeses, crackers
and olives. Cut one or more
types of melon into cubes and
chill; drizzle with the dressing at
the last minute. Chop the eggplant and onion, and start them
cooking; chop the remaining
ingredients while the eggplant
and onion cook.

Greek Rice and Vegetable Dinner

Quick-cooking brown rice brings nutty flavor to this gardenful of vegetables.

Yield: 4 (1¼-cup) servings

2 tablespoons olive or vegetable oil

2 cups diced eggplant

¼ cup chopped onion

2 cups uncooked instant brown rice

½ cup chopped green bell pepper

1 medium zucchini, sliced

½ teaspoon salt

⅛ teaspoon pepper

1¾ cups water

1 medium tomato, chopped

1 tablespoon chopped fresh basil

1 tablespoon chopped fresh oregano

4 oz. (1 cup) crumbled feta cheese

1. Heat oil in large skillet over medium heat until hot. Add eggplant and onion; cover and cook 6 to 8 minutes or until vegetables are crisp-tender, stirring occasionally.

2. Add rice, bell pepper, zucchini, salt, pepper and water; mix well. Bring to a boil. Stir. Reduce heat to medium-low; cover and cook 5 minutes.

3. Add tomato, basil, oregano and cheese; stir gently to mix. Remove from heat. Cover; let stand 5 minutes.

Nutrition Information Per Serving: Serving Size: 1¼ Cups • Calories 340 • Calories from Fat 140 • % Daily Value: Total Fat 15 g 23% • Saturated Fat 5 g 25% • Cholesterol 25 mg 8% • Sodium 600 mg 25% • Total Carbohydrate 42 g 14% • Dietary Fiber 4 g 16% • Sugars 5 g • Protein 10 g • Vitamin A 15% • Vitamin C 25% • Calcium 15% • Iron 6%
Dietary Exchanges: 2½ Starch, 1 Vegetable, 3 Fat OR 2½ Carbohydrate, 1 Vegetable, 3 Fat

Middle Eastern Pasta Skillet

Hummus, a spread made with ground chickpeas, spikes a sauce that is chunky with eggplant, pepper and onion. It is a zesty change of pace from smoother Italian-style sauces.

Yield: 4 (1¾-cup) servings

8 oz. (2¼ cups) uncooked ziti (long tubular pasta) or penne (tube-shaped pasta)

3 tablespoons olive or vegetable oil

3 cups cubed eggplant

1 small green bell pepper, cut into bite-sized strips

1 small onion, cut into thin wedges

½ cup water

½ teaspoon salt

4 Italian plum tomatoes, diced

1 (6-oz.) container (⅔ cup) purchased garlic or roasted pepper hummus

1. Cook ziti to desired doneness as directed on package. Drain.

2. Meanwhile, heat 1 tablespoon of the oil in 12-inch skillet over medium-high heat until hot. Add eggplant, bell pepper and onion; cover and cook 3 minutes, stirring once. Add water and salt; cook 4 minutes or until eggplant is tender.

3. Stir in tomatoes, hummus and remaining 2 tablespoons oil; cook 2 to 3 minutes or until heated. Add cooked ziti; toss gently to coat.

Nutrition Information Per Serving: Serving Size: 1¾ Cups • Calories 410 • Calories from Fat 140 • % Daily Value: Total Fat 15 g 23% • Saturated Fat 2 g 10% • Cholesterol 0 mg 0% • Sodium 430 mg 18% • Total Carbohydrate 56 g 19% • Dietary Fiber 6 g 24% • Sugars 6 g • Protein 12 g • Vitamin A 8% • Vitamin C 25% • Calcium 4% • Iron 20%
Dietary Exchanges: 3½ Starch, 1 Vegetable, 2½ Fat OR 3½ Carbohydrate, 1 Vegetable, 2½ Fat

MIDDLE EASTERN PASTA SKILLET

Ripe olives

Celery sticks

Orange sherbet

While waiting for the pasta water to boil, cut up the eggplant, bell pepper, onion and tomato; scrub and trim the celery.

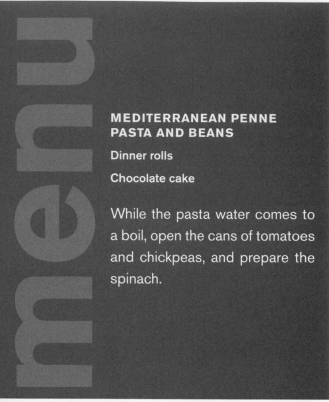

menu

MEDITERRANEAN PENNE PASTA AND BEANS

Dinner rolls

Chocolate cake

While the pasta water comes to a boil, open the cans of tomatoes and chickpeas, and prepare the spinach.

Mediterranean Penne Pasta and Beans

Spinach, feta cheese and olives dress up noodles and chickpeas. If you wish, substitute cannellini or kidney beans for the chickpeas.

Yield: 4 servings

---

6 oz. (1¾ cups) uncooked penne (tube-shaped pasta)

1 tablespoon olive or vegetable oil

2 garlic cloves, minced

2 (14.5-oz.) cans no-salt-added tomatoes, undrained, cut up

1 (15-oz.) can garbanzo beans or chickpeas, drained, rinsed

1½ teaspoons dried Italian seasoning

1 teaspoon sugar

1 (10-oz.) pkg. prewashed fresh spinach, stems removed, chopped (about 8 cups)

2 oz. (½ cup) crumbled feta cheese

¼ cup sliced ripe olives

---

1. Cook penne to desired doneness as directed on package. Drain; cover to keep warm.

2. Meanwhile, heat oil in large skillet or Dutch oven over medium-high heat until hot. Add garlic; cook and stir 30 seconds. Add tomatoes, beans, Italian seasoning and sugar; mix well. Bring to a boil. Reduce heat; simmer 10 minutes.

3. Add spinach; cook 3 minutes or until spinach wilts, stirring frequently.

4. Arrange cooked penne on large serving platter. Top with tomato mixture. Sprinkle with cheese and olives.

Nutrition Information Per Serving: Serving Size: ¼ of Recipe • Calories 400 • Calories from Fat 90 • % Daily Value: Total Fat 10 g 15% • Saturated Fat 3 g 15% • Cholesterol 15 mg 5% • Sodium 470 mg 20% • Total Carbohydrate 61 g 20% • Dietary Fiber 10 g 40% • Sugars 8 g • Protein 16 g • Vitamin A 110% • Vitamin C 60% • Calcium 25% • Iron 35%
Dietary Exchanges: 3 Starch, 3 Vegetable, 2 Fat OR 3 Carbohydrate, 3 Vegetable, 2 Fat

Easy Italian Skillet

Beans and tomatoes stretch a frozen pasta-vegetable mix into a hearty supper, aromatic with herbs and enriched with mozzarella cheese.

Yield: 4 servings

---

1 (1-lb.) pkg. frozen pasta, broccoli, corn and carrots in a garlic seasoned sauce

1 (15.5- or 15-oz.) can pinto or kidney beans, drained

1 (14.5-oz.) can diced tomatoes, undrained

1 teaspoon dried Italian seasoning

2 oz. (½ cup) shredded mozzarella cheese

---

1. In large skillet, combine all ingredients except cheese. Bring to a boil. Reduce heat; simmer 8 to 10 minutes or until vegetables and pasta are tender, stirring occasionally.

2. Remove skillet from heat. Sprinkle with cheese. Cover; let stand until cheese is melted.

Nutrition Information Per Serving: Serving Size: ¼ of Recipe • Calories 310 • Calories from Fat 80 • % Daily Value: Total Fat 9 g 14% • Saturated Fat 4 g 20% • Cholesterol 15 mg 5% • Sodium 830 mg 35% • Total Carbohydrate 43 g 14% • Dietary Fiber 7 g 28% • Sugars 7 g • Protein 13 g • Vitamin A 35% • Vitamin C 30% • Calcium 20% • Iron 15%
Dietary Exchanges: 2½ Starch, 1 Vegetable, ½ Very Lean Meat, 1½ Fat OR 2½ Carbohydrate, 1 Vegetable, ½ Very Lean Meat, 1½ Fat

menu

EASY ITALIAN SKILLET

Escarole salad with creamy Caesar salad dressing

Whole-grain Italian rolls

Fresh Bing cherries

Rinse and drain the cherries and set them in a serving dish. Clean the greens, but wait to toss with the dressing until ready to serve. Warm the rolls while the entree cooks.

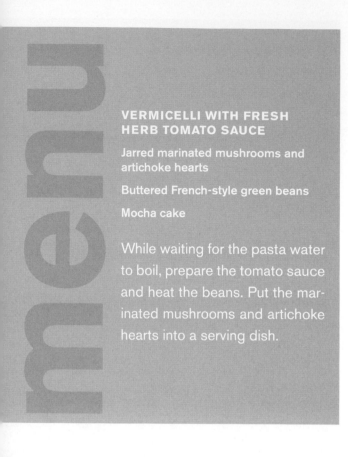

menu

VERMICELLI WITH FRESH HERB TOMATO SAUCE

Jarred marinated mushrooms and artichoke hearts

Buttered French-style green beans

Mocha cake

While waiting for the pasta water to boil, prepare the tomato sauce and heat the beans. Put the marinated mushrooms and artichoke hearts into a serving dish.

Vermicelli with Fresh Herb Tomato Sauce

You can't beat the flavors of fresh herbs and fresh tomatoes. Here's a taste of the old country, with a recipe whose flavors come close to capturing those enjoyed before the invention of canned tomatoes. Ripe tomatoes are a must.

Yield: 5 (1¼-cup) servings

7 oz. uncooked vermicelli

3 medium tomatoes, seeded, chopped

2 oz. (½ cup) shredded fresh Parmesan cheese

2 tablespoons chopped fresh basil

2 tablespoons chopped fresh chives

2 tablespoons olive oil

½ teaspoon salt

½ teaspoon finely grated lemon peel

⅛ teaspoon coarse ground black pepper

1 garlic clove, minced

1. Cook vermicelli to desired doneness as directed on package. Drain.

2. Meanwhile, in large bowl, combine all remaining ingredients.

3. Add cooked vermicelli; toss gently to mix.

Nutrition Information Per Serving: Serving Size: 1¼ Cups • Calories 260 • Calories from Fat 80 • % Daily Value: Total Fat 9 g 14% • Saturated Fat 3 g 15% • Cholesterol 10 mg 3% • Sodium 400 mg 17% • Total Carbohydrate 34 g 11% • Dietary Fiber 2 g 8% • Sugars 3 g • Protein 10 g • Vitamin A 10% • Vitamin C 20% • Calcium 15% • Iron 10%
Dietary Exchanges: 2 Starch, 1 Vegetable, 1½ Fat OR 2 Carbohydrate, 1 Vegetable, 1½ Fat

Linguine Vegetable Toss

Italian plum tomatoes are meatier and less watery than most round tomatoes, making them ideal for cooking with a host of vegetables, as in this dish.

Yield: 4 (1½-cup) servings

8 oz. uncooked linguine

1 tablespoon olive or vegetable oil

3 large garlic cloves, minced

2 cups fresh sugar snap peas

1½ cups cut (1-inch) fresh asparagus spears

4 Italian plum tomatoes, diced

⅓ cup chopped fresh basil or 1 tablespoon dried basil leaves

¼ teaspoon salt

⅛ teaspoon coarse ground black pepper

1 oz. (¼ cup) finely shredded fresh Parmesan cheese

1. In Dutch oven or large saucepan, cook linguine to desired doneness as directed on package. Drain; return to Dutch oven. Cover to keep warm.

2. Meanwhile, heat oil in large nonstick skillet over medium-high heat until hot. Add garlic; cook 30 seconds, stirring constantly. Reduce heat to medium; add sugar snap peas and asparagus. Cover; cook 3 minutes. (If vegetables begin to stick, add 1 to 2 tablespoons water to skillet.)

3. Add tomatoes; cook an additional 2 to 4 minutes or until vegetables are crisp-tender, stirring occasionally. Stir in basil, salt and pepper. Add to cooked linguine in Dutch oven; toss to mix. Sprinkle with cheese.

LINGUINE VEGETABLE TOSS

Refrigerated soft breadsticks

Chocolate cream pie

Purchase the pie, or assemble it in advance from instant pudding and a graham cracker crust. While the pasta water comes to a boil and the oven preheats, cut the vegetables with which the pasta will be mixed. Bake the breadsticks while the pasta is cooking.

Nutrition Information Per Serving: Serving Size: 1½ Cups • Calories 330 • Calories from Fat 60 • % Daily Value: Total Fat 7 g 11% • Saturated Fat 2 g 10% • Cholesterol 5 mg 2% • Sodium 260 mg 11% • Total Carbohydrate 53 g 18% • Dietary Fiber 5 g 20% • Sugars 7 g • Protein 14 g • Vitamin A 15% • Vitamin C 70% • Calcium 15% • Iron 25%
Dietary Exchanges: 3 Starch, 2 Vegetable, 1 Fat OR 3 Carbohydrate, 2 Vegetable, 1 Fat

PENNE WITH ZUCCHINI AND RICOTTA

Sliced tomatoes drizzled with olive oil and sprinkled with fresh green onion and fresh basil

Crisp Italian breadsticks

Frozen yogurt sundaes

While waiting for the pasta water to boil, chop the ingredients for the pasta recipe. To make yogurt sundaes, top frozen yogurt with chocolate or fruit sauce and one or more of the following: granola, roasted sunflower seeds, chopped fresh or dried fruit.

Penne with Zucchini and Ricotta

Ricotta and half-and-half form a creamy sauce laced with the bold flavor of pungent fresh basil.

Yield: 6 (1²/₃-cup) servings

1 (16-oz.) pkg. uncooked penne (tube-shaped pasta)

1 tablespoon olive or vegetable oil

2 garlic cloves, minced

1 lb. small zucchini, sliced (3½ cups)

1 cup ricotta cheese

1 cup half-and-half

½ teaspoon salt

½ cup finely sliced fresh basil

2²/₃ oz. (²/₃ cup) shredded fresh Parmesan cheese

1. Cook penne to desired doneness as directed on package. Drain; cover to keep warm.

2. Meanwhile, heat oil in 12-inch nonstick skillet over medium-high heat until hot. Add garlic and zucchini; cook and stir 3 to 4 minutes or until zucchini is tender.

3. In small bowl, combine ricotta cheese, half-and-half and salt; stir until well blended. Add to zucchini mixture; cook and stir until hot.

4. In large serving bowl, combine cooked penne, zucchini mixture and basil; toss gently to mix. Sprinkle with Parmesan cheese.

Nutrition Information Per Serving: Serving Size: 1²/₃ Cups • Calories 460 • Calories from Fat 130 • % Daily Value: Total Fat 14 g 22% • Saturated Fat 7 g 35% • Cholesterol 35 mg 12% • Sodium 440 mg 18% • Total Carbohydrate 63 g 21% • Dietary Fiber 3 g 12% • Sugars 6 g • Protein 21 g • Vitamin A 15% • Vitamin C 10% • Calcium 30% • Iron 20%
Dietary Exchanges: 4 Starch, 1 Medium-Fat Meat, 1½ Fat OR 4 Carbohydrate, 1 Medium-Fat Meat, 1½ Fat

NEW POTATO, PASTA AND VEGETABLE STIR-FRY

Red and green cabbage salad

Bakery bran muffins

Coffee ice cream with toasted hazelnuts

Purchase the salad or prepare it ahead of time. Chop the vegetables for the entree in advance, if desired, and refrigerate. Cut potatoes, however, will turn an unsightly gray unless you keep them submerged in cold water; pat them dry before cooking. Warm the muffins while the vegetables are cooking.

New Potato, Pasta and Vegetable Stir-Fry

Potatoes and pasta may seem like an unusual combination, but the partnership is delightful.

Yield: 4 (1¾-cup) servings

8 oz. (3½ cups) uncooked bow tie pasta (farfalle)

2 tablespoons olive or vegetable oil

1 medium onion, cut into 8 wedges

4 new red potatoes, unpeeled, sliced

8 oz. fresh asparagus spears, trimmed, cut into 2-inch pieces

1 medium red or yellow bell pepper, cut into strips

2 tablespoons chopped fresh oregano

½ teaspoon salt

⅛ teaspoon pepper

4 oz. (1 cup) shredded Swiss cheese

1. Cook pasta to desired doneness as directed on package. Drain; cover to keep warm.

2. Meanwhile, heat oil in large skillet over medium-high heat until hot. Add onion; cook and stir 2 minutes. Add potatoes; cover and cook 5 to 6 minutes or until partially cooked, stirring occasionally.

3. Stir in asparagus, bell pepper, oregano, salt and pepper. Reduce heat to medium-low; cover and cook 5 to 8 minutes or until vegetables are tender, stirring occasionally.

4. Stir in cooked pasta; cook until thoroughly heated. Remove from heat. Sprinkle with cheese. Cover; let stand until cheese is melted.

Nutrition Information Per Serving: Serving Size: 1¾ Cups • Calories 510 • Calories from Fat 140 • % Daily Value: Total Fat 16 g 25% • Saturated Fat 6 g 30% • Cholesterol 25 mg 8% • Sodium 350 mg 15% • Total Carbohydrate 72 g 24% • Dietary Fiber 6 g 24% • Sugars 7 g • Protein 19 g • Vitamin A 35% • Vitamin C 70% • Calcium 30% • Iron 25%
Dietary Exchanges: 4½ Starch, 1 Vegetable, ½ High-Fat Meat, 2 Fat OR 4½ Carbohydrate, 1 Vegetable, ½ High-Fat Meat, 2 Fat

Ravioli with Salsa-Black Bean Sauce

A lively mix of salsa and black beans tops cheese-filled pasta in this Italy-meets-Mexico feast.

Yield: 3 (1⅓-cup) servings

1 (9-oz.) pkg. refrigerated cheese-filled ravioli

1 (14.5-oz.) can salsa-style tomatoes, undrained

1 (15-oz.) can black beans, drained

2 teaspoons chili powder

½ teaspoon cumin

2 tablespoons chopped fresh cilantro

1. In large saucepan, cook ravioli to desired doneness as directed on package. Drain in colander; cover to keep warm.

2. In same saucepan, combine tomatoes, beans, chili powder and cumin; mix well. Cook over medium heat for 5 minutes or until thoroughly heated, stirring occasionally.

3. Add cooked ravioli; stir gently to mix. Spoon onto serving platter or into serving bowl. Sprinkle with cilantro.

Nutrition Information Per Serving: Serving Size: 1⅓ Cups • Calories 440 • Calories from Fat 100 • % Daily Value: Total Fat 11 g 17% • Saturated Fat 5 g 25% • Cholesterol 75 mg 25% • Sodium 930 mg 39% • Total Carbohydrate 64 g 21% • Dietary Fiber 10 g 40% • Sugars 6 g • Protein 22 g • Vitamin A 30% • Vitamin C 20% • Calcium 30% • Iron 25%
Dietary Exchanges: 4 Starch, 1 Vegetable, 1 Very Lean Meat, 1½ Fat OR 4 Carbohydrate, 1 Vegetable, 1 Very Lean Meat, 1½ Fat

RAVIOLI WITH SALSA-BLACK BEAN SAUCE

Tossed green salad with Italian dressing

Dinner rolls

Sliced fresh peaches

While waiting for the pasta water to boil, assemble the salad, but wait to toss with the dressing until serving time. Warm the rolls in the oven while the ravioli cooks. Wait to slice the peaches until it's time for dessert.

Ravioli in Spinach Alfredo Sauce

Cheese-filled ravioli nestle in a cream sauce richly flavored with spinach. You can use regular or spinach pasta ravioli, or a combination.

Yield: 6 (1-cup) servings

1 (10-oz.) pkg. frozen creamed spinach in a pouch

1 (25-oz.) pkg. frozen cheese-filled ravioli

1 (16-oz.) jar Alfredo sauce

2 oz. (½ cup) shredded fresh Parmesan cheese

1. Fill Dutch oven or large saucepan ¾ full with water. Bring to a boil. Add spinach pouch; cook 3 minutes. Add ravioli; return to a boil. Reduce heat; simmer 5 minutes or until ravioli are tender and begin to float. Remove spinach pouch from water; drain ravioli.

2. Open spinach pouch; pour into same Dutch oven. Add Alfredo sauce; mix well. Cook over medium heat for 5 minutes or until thoroughly heated, stirring occasionally.

3. Add cooked ravioli; stir gently to mix. Sprinkle individual servings with cheese.

Nutrition Information Per Serving: Serving Size: 1 Cup • Calories 600 • Calories from Fat 270 • % Daily Value: Total Fat 30 g 46% • Saturated Fat 15 g 75% • Cholesterol 150 mg 50% • Sodium 1,340 mg 56% • Total Carbohydrate 56 g 19% • Dietary Fiber 4 g 16% • Sugars 6 g • Protein 27 g • Vitamin A 25% • Vitamin C 8% • Calcium 45% • Iron 15%
Dietary Exchanges: 3½ Starch, 1 Vegetable, 2 High-Fat Meat, 2½ Fat OR 3½ Carbohydrate, 1 Vegetable, 2 High-Fat Meat, 2½ Fat

menu

RAVIOLI IN SPINACH ALFREDO SAUCE

Deli Italian vegetable salad

Fresh blueberries with cream and lemon

Put the water on to boil for the spinach and ravioli. Pick over and rinse the blueberries, and chill until dessert. Set out the salad while the Alfredo sauce heats.

menu

COUSCOUS WITH VEGETARIAN SPAGHETTI SAUCE

Steamed fresh spinach

Garlic toast

Watermelon wedges drizzled with lime

Slice the watermelon and drizzle with lime juice; chill. Rinse and drain the spinach and place it in the pot, ready for last-minute steaming. Warm the purchased garlic toast, available at delis and bakeries, while the spaghetti sauce heats.

Couscous with Vegetarian Spaghetti Sauce

In Morocco, couscous is typically steamed in a basket set over a spicy, simmering stew. The supermarket version cooks in a fraction of the time, making it ideal for last-minute meals.

Yield: 4 servings

2 cups water

1 ⅓ cups uncooked couscous

1 (28-oz.) jar chunky vegetable spaghetti sauce

1 (15-oz.) can garbanzo beans or chickpeas, drained, rinsed

⅛ to ¼ teaspoon crushed red pepper flakes

2 tablespoons chopped fresh parsley

1. In medium saucepan, bring water to a boil. Stir in couscous. Cover; remove from heat. Let stand 5 minutes or until liquid is absorbed.

2. Meanwhile, in another medium saucepan, combine spaghetti sauce, beans and red pepper flakes. Cook over medium heat for 5 to 7 minutes or until thoroughly heated, stirring occasionally.

3. Fluff couscous with fork. Serve sauce mixture over couscous. Sprinkle with parsley. If desired, sprinkle with shredded fresh Parmesan cheese.

Nutrition Information Per Serving: Serving Size: ¼ of Recipe • Calories 430 • Calories from Fat 50 • % Daily Value: Total Fat 6 g 9% • Saturated Fat 1 g 5% • Cholesterol 0 mg 0% • Sodium 980 mg 41% • Total Carbohydrate 79 g 26% • Dietary Fiber 11 g 44% • Sugars 2 g • Protein 16 g • Vitamin A 20% • Vitamin C 20% • Calcium 10% • Iron 15%
Dietary Exchanges: 4 Starch, 1 Fruit, 1 Vegetable, ½ Very Lean Meat, ½ Fat OR 5 Carbohydrate, 1 Vegetable, ½ Very Lean Meat, ½ Fat

Garden Tofu Stir-Fry for Two

This stir-fry is chunky with vegetables and strips of marinated tofu, making it perfectly suited to chopsticks.

Yield: 2 servings

1 cup oil

2 oz. uncooked rice sticks (rice noodles)

6½ oz. firm or extra-firm tofu, cut into ½-inch cubes (1 cup)

2 tablespoons purchased Thai ginger marinade

2 teaspoons oil

2 cups frozen broccoli florets, carrots and water chestnuts

¼ red bell pepper, cut into bite-sized strips

2 green onions, sliced

2 tablespoons water

1. Heat 1 cup oil in medium nonstick skillet or wok over medium-high heat to 400° F. Break rice stick bundle into pieces; fry in hot oil until puffed. Remove rice sticks from oil; drain on paper towels. Discard remaining oil.

2. Gently press tofu cubes between layers of paper towels to remove excess moisture. Place tofu in shallow bowl. Drizzle with marinade; stir gently to coat. Let stand at room temperature for at least 5 minutes to marinate.

3. Heat 2 teaspoons oil in same skillet over medium heat until hot. Add frozen vegetables; cook and stir 3 to 4 minutes or until thawed. Add bell pepper, onions, water and tofu with marinade; cook and gently stir 3 to 4 minutes or until vegetables are crisp-tender. Serve over cooked rice sticks.

menu

GARDEN TOFU STIR-FRY FOR TWO

Baby mixed greens with oriental salad dressing

Cheesecake slices with fresh fruit topping

Prepare the greens, but wait to toss with the dressing until the last minute. Assemble all the ingredients for the entree so you can focus on the stir-frying once you start.

Nutrition Information Per Serving: Serving Size: ½ of Recipe • Calories 350 • Calories from Fat 150 • % Daily Value: Total Fat 17 g 26% • Saturated Fat 2 g 10% • Cholesterol 0 mg 0% • Sodium 450 mg 19% • Total Carbohydrate 38 g 13% • Dietary Fiber 3 g 12% • Sugars 6 g • Protein 10 g • Vitamin A 70% • Vitamin C 50% • Calcium 20% • Iron 15%
Dietary Exchanges: 1½ Starch, ½ Fruit, 2 Vegetable, ½ Medium-Fat Meat, 2½ Fat OR 2 Carbohydrate, 2 Vegetable, ½ Medium-Fat Meat, 2½ Fat

menu

SWEET-AND-SOUR TOFU STIR-FRY

Deli Asian lettuce salad

Sliced date-nut bread

Custard pudding

If you have time earlier in the day, prepare the date-nut bread and custard pudding from scratch or a mix, or purchase them ready to serve. Set out the salad while the tofu cooks.

Sweet-and-Sour Tofu Stir-Fry

Tofu, with little flavor of its own, soaks up the tastes of other ingredients—in this case, a sweet-and-sour sauce with vegetables and pineapple.

Yield: 4 servings

---

1 cup uncooked regular long-grain white rice

2 cups water

1 (12.3-oz.) pkg. firm or extra-firm tofu, drained, cut into ¾-inch cubes

1 (1 lb. 5-oz.) pkg. frozen sweet-and-sour stir-fry meal starter

¼ cup slivered almonds

---

1. Cook rice in water as directed on package.

2. Meanwhile, spray large nonstick skillet with nonstick cooking spray. Heat over medium-high heat until hot. Add tofu; cook 5 to 7 minutes or until lightly browned on all sides, turning carefully with pancake turner. Remove tofu from skillet.

3. Add frozen sauce from meal starter to skillet. Cover; cook until sauce is thawed, stirring frequently. Stir in frozen vegetables and pineapple. Cover; cook 7 to 10 minutes or until vegetables are crisp-tender, stirring occasionally.

4. Gently stir in tofu; cook 1 to 2 minutes or until tofu is thoroughly heated. Serve over rice. Sprinkle with almonds.

Nutrition Information Per Serving: Serving Size: ¼ of Recipe • Calories 390 • Calories from Fat 70 • % Daily Value: Total Fat 8 g 12% • Saturated Fat 1 g 5% • Cholesterol 0 mg 0% • Sodium 400 mg 17% • Total Carbohydrate 67 g 22% • Dietary Fiber 4 g 16% • Sugars 23 g • Protein 13 g • Vitamin A 50% • Vitamin C 15% • Calcium 20% • Iron 20%
Dietary Exchanges: 3 Starch, 1 Fruit, 1 Vegetable, ½ Medium-Fat Meat, ½ Fat OR 4 Carbohydrate, 1 Vegetable, ½ Medium-Fat Meat, ½ Fat

Salad Bar Vegetable Stir-Fry

Take advantage of your supermarket salad bar, where the washing, peeling and slicing is already done. Your only job may be chopping larger vegetables into bite-sized pieces.

Yield: 4 servings

²/3 cup uncooked regular long-grain white rice

1 ¹/3 cups water

1 tablespoon sesame oil

8 cups assorted cut-up fresh vegetables from salad bar*

3 tablespoons water

¹/2 cup purchased stir-fry sauce

¹/4 cup nuts or shelled sunflower seeds from salad bar, if desired

1. Cook rice in 1¹/3 cups water as directed on package.

2. Meanwhile, heat oil in large skillet or wok over medium-high heat until hot. Add firm vegetables;* cook and stir 4 minutes.

3. Add medium-firm vegetables;* cook and stir 1 minute. Add 3 tablespoons water. Reduce heat to medium; cover and cook 2 to 3 minutes or until vegetables are crisp-tender, stirring occasionally.

4. Add stir-fry sauce and tender vegetables;* cook and stir until thoroughly heated. Sprinkle with nuts. Serve over rice.

Nutrition Information Per Serving: Serving Size: ¹/4 of Recipe • Calories 410 • Calories from Fat 80 • % Daily Value: Total Fat 9 g 14% • Saturated Fat 1 g 5% • Cholesterol 0 mg 0% • Sodium 1,090 mg 45% • Total Carbohydrate 71 g 24% • Dietary Fiber 7 g 28% • Sugars 11 g • Protein 12 g • Vitamin A 200% • Vitamin C 100% • Calcium 8% • Iron 25%
Dietary Exchanges: 4 Starch, 2 Vegetable, 1 Fat OR 4 Carbohydrate, 2 Vegetable, 1 Fat

menu

SALAD BAR VEGETABLE STIR-FRY

Sliced cheeses and crisp crackers

Fruit yogurt topped with granola

Start the rice, and heat the skillet or wok. Set out the cheeses and crackers so that you can serve the stir-fry immediately when it's ready.

tip

*Vegetables require different cooking times depending on their firmness. Firm vegetables include cauliflower, carrots, celery and onions. Medium-firm vegetables include bean sprouts, bell peppers, broccoli, mushrooms, pea pods and zucchini. Tender vegetables include spinach, precooked sweet peas and tomatoes.

menu

CHILI-STUFFED POTATOES

Buttered broccoli spears

Strawberries and blueberries with whipped cream

Shred the cheese unless you have preshredded, and then prepare the potatoes. While the potatoes cook, heat the broccoli, and rinse and chill the berries for dessert.

Chili-Stuffed Potatoes

Too often reduced to a supporting role, potatoes are stars in their own right in this hearty entree, filled with chili and cheese.

Yield: 4 servings

4 medium russet potatoes

1 (15-oz.) can fat-free vegetarian chili

4 oz. (1 cup) shredded reduced-fat Cheddar or Cheddar-Monterey Jack cheese blend

1. Scrub potatoes. Pierce potatoes with fork; arrange in circle on paper towel in microwave. Microwave on HIGH for 14 to 16 minutes or until tender, rearranging once. Let stand 5 minutes.

2. Meanwhile, heat chili in small saucepan until hot.

3. To serve, cut potatoes in half lengthwise; place on 4 individual plates. Mash potatoes slightly with fork. Top each potato with ⅓ cup chili. Sprinkle with cheese. If desired, garnish with chopped fresh cilantro.

Nutrition Information Per Serving: Serving Size: ¼ of Recipe • Calories 310 • Calories from Fat 60 • % Daily Value: Total Fat 7 g 11% • Saturated Fat 4 g 20% • Cholesterol 20 mg 7% • Sodium 390 mg 16% • Total Carbohydrate 45 g 15% • Dietary Fiber 9 g 36% • Sugars 5 g • Protein 16 g • Vitamin A 100% • Vitamin C 30% • Calcium 20% • Iron 20%
Dietary Exchanges: 3 Starch, 1 Medium-Fat Meat OR 3 Carbohydrate, 1 Medium-Fat Meat

Tofu Piccata

A citrusy trio—lemon peel, lemon juice, lemon-pepper seasoning—lends a perky note to golden-brown tofu slices.

Yield: 8 servings

⅓ cup all-purpose flour

1 teaspoon garlic salt

1 teaspoon lemon-pepper seasoning

1 teaspoon paprika

1 lb. firm tofu

2 tablespoons oil

¼ cup water

1 teaspoon grated lemon peel

3 tablespoons lemon juice

1. In small shallow bowl, combine flour, garlic salt, lemon-pepper seasoning and paprika; mix well.

2. Cut tofu into 8 slices. If necessary, dip slices in water to moisten. Dip each slice in flour mixture, turning to coat both sides.

3. Heat oil in large nonstick skillet over medium-high heat until hot. Add tofu slices; cook 4 to 8 minutes or until golden brown, turning once.

4. Add water, lemon peel and lemon juice. Reduce heat to low; simmer 5 minutes or until thoroughly heated.

Nutrition Information Per Serving: Serving Size: ⅛ of Recipe • Calories 100 • Calories from Fat 50 • % Daily Value: Total Fat 6 g 9% • Saturated Fat 1 g 5% • Cholesterol 0 mg 0% • Sodium 310 mg 13% • Total Carbohydrate 6 g 2% • Dietary Fiber 0 g 0% • Sugars 1 g • Protein 5 g • Vitamin A 4% • Vitamin C 4% • Calcium 10% • Iron 6%
Dietary Exchanges: ½ Starch, ½ Medium-Fat Meat, ½ Fat OR ½ Carbohydrate, ½ Medium-Fat Meat, ½ Fat

menu

TOFU PICCATA

Orzo pasta with herbs and olive oil

Sliced fresh tomatoes and cucumbers with creamy Italian dressing

Coffee ice cream with cookies

While waiting for the pasta water to boil, slice the tomatoes and cucumbers, but wait to add the dressing until just before serving. Chop some fresh herbs such as chives, parsley or thyme to toss with the cooked pasta.

Scrambled Huevos Rancheros Biscuits

Huevos rancheros—ranch-style eggs—are sometimes served as fried eggs. Scrambling them is considerably quicker and just as tasty.

Yield: 4 servings

1 (1 lb. 0.3-oz.) can large refrigerated buttermilk biscuits

8 eggs

½ cup milk

¼ teaspoon salt

⅛ teaspoon pepper

1 (4.5-oz.) can chopped green chiles, drained

4 oz. (1 cup) shredded hot pepper Monterey Jack cheese

½ cup salsa, heated

1. Heat oven to 375°F. Bake biscuits as directed on can.

2. Meanwhile, in large bowl, combine eggs, milk, salt and pepper; beat until well blended. Add chiles; mix well.

3. Spray large nonstick skillet with nonstick cooking spray. Heat over medium heat until hot. Add egg mixture; cook 4 to 5 minutes or until almost set. Add cheese; stir gently. Cover; remove from heat. Let stand 2 minutes or until cheese is melted and eggs are set.

4. Split 4 warm biscuits. (Cool remaining biscuits; place in food storage plastic bag and reserve for a later use.) Place biscuit halves on individual plates. Spoon egg mixture over biscuits. Top with warm salsa.

menu

SCRAMBLED HUEVOS RANCHEROS BISCUITS

Refried beans

Fresh fruit

Bakery cinnamon crumb cake

Cut up a favorite combination of fruit—oranges, kiwi and strawberries, for example—as a garnish. Start the biscuits; then chop the chiles and shred the cheese. Heat the beans and the salsa separately while you scramble the eggs.

Nutrition Information Per Serving: Serving Size: ¼ of Recipe • Calories 660 • Calories from Fat 330 • % Daily Value: Total Fat 37 g 57% • Saturated Fat 14 g 70% • Cholesterol 460 mg 153% • Sodium 2,000 mg 83% • Total Carbohydrate 54 g 18% • Dietary Fiber 3 g 12% • Sugars 13 g • Protein 28 g • Vitamin A 25% • Vitamin C 8% • Calcium 40% • Iron 25%
Dietary Exchanges: 2½ Starch, 1 Fruit, 3 Medium-Fat Meat, 4 Fat OR 3½ Carbohydrate, 3 Medium-Fat Meat, 4 Fat

Nacho Bean Soup

The ingredients of a favorite appetizer, blended with chicken broth, become a robust soup.

Yield: 3 (1½-cup) servings

---

1 (14½-oz.) can ready-to-serve vegetable broth

1 cup milk

2 tablespoons all-purpose flour

1 (15.5- or 15-oz.) can pinto beans, drained, rinsed

1 (4.5-oz.) can chopped green chiles

8 oz. (2 cups) shredded taco-flavored cheese blend

2 tablespoons chopped fresh cilantro

1 cup broken tortilla or corn chips

---

1. In large saucepan, combine broth, milk and flour; blend well. Cook and stir over medium heat until mixture comes to a boil.

2. Stir in beans, chiles, cheese and cilantro. Cook 5 minutes or until thoroughly heated and cheese is melted, stirring constantly. Sprinkle individual servings with tortilla chips.

Nutrition Information Per Serving: Serving Size: 1½ Cups • Calories 590 • Calories from Fat 300 • % Daily Value: Total Fat 33 g 51% • Saturated Fat 19 g 95% • Cholesterol 80 mg 27% • Sodium 1,690 mg 70% • Total Carbohydrate 46 g 15% • Dietary Fiber 8 g 32% • Sugars 8 g • Protein 28 g • Vitamin A 35% • Vitamin C 10% • Calcium 70% • Iron 15%
Dietary Exchanges: 3 Starch, 3 High-Fat Meat, 1 Fat OR 3 Carbohydrate, 3 High-Fat Meat, 1 Fat

NACHO BEAN SOUP

Warm rolled flour tortillas

Sliced peaches and strawberries

Slice the fruit in advance, if you wish, tossing the peaches with lemon or orange juice to preserve the color; or slice the fruit at dessert time. Warm the tortillas while the soup is heating.

menu

Cheesy Spinach Soup

Emerald-green spinach is twirled into a creamy soup flavored with cheese.

Yield: 5 (1¼-cup) servings

1 (9-oz.) pkg. frozen spinach in a pouch

1 (16-oz.) can ready-to-serve fat-free chicken broth with 30% less sodium

1 teaspoon onion powder

1 (12-oz.) can evaporated milk

3 tablespoons all-purpose flour

8 oz. (2 cups) shredded American cheese

1. Remove spinach from pouch; place in medium saucepan. Add broth and onion powder. Bring to a boil. Reduce heat to low; cover and simmer 5 to 7 minutes or until spinach is thoroughly cooked.

2. In small bowl, combine milk and flour; blend until smooth. Add to soup; cook and stir over medium heat until bubbly and thickened.

3. Reduce heat to low; simmer 2 minutes. Add cheese; cook and stir until cheese is melted and soup is thoroughly heated.

Nutrition Information Per Serving: Serving Size: 1¼ Cups • Calories 300 • Calories from Fat 170 • % Daily Value: Total Fat 19 g 29% • Saturated Fat 12 g 60% • Cholesterol 65 mg 22% • Sodium 1,050 mg 44% • Total Carbohydrate 14 g 5% • Dietary Fiber 1 g 4% • Sugars 8 g • Protein 18 g • Vitamin A 50% • Vitamin C 15% • Calcium 50% • Iron 6%
Dietary Exchanges: 1 Starch, 2 High-Fat Meat, ½ Fat OR 1 Carbohydrate, 2 High-Fat Meat, ½ Fat

CHEESY SPINACH SOUP

Egg salad sandwiches

Carrot sticks

Chocolate-covered ice cream sandwiches

Cut the carrots ahead of time, if you wish, and keep them covered in water until dinnertime. Make the egg salad sandwiches with deli salad while the soup is cooking.

menu

BLACK BEAN AND SALSA SOUP

Tortilla chips

Sliced fresh pears

Cream-filled chocolate cookies

Start the soup; then slice the pears.

Black Bean and Salsa Soup

Black beans soak up the earthy flavor of cumin and the zestiness of salsa. For an additional garnish, sprinkle some chopped fresh cilantro over the sour cream and green onions.

Yield: 2 (1-cup) servings

---

1 (15-oz.) can black beans, drained, rinsed

¾ cup vegetable broth

½ cup salsa

½ teaspoon cumin

2 tablespoons sour cream

1 tablespoon sliced green onions

---

1. In food processor bowl with metal blade or blender container, combine beans, broth, salsa and cumin. Process 1 minute or until smooth.

2. Heat bean mixture in medium saucepan over medium heat until thoroughly heated.

3. Top individual servings with 1 tablespoon sour cream; swirl gently. Sprinkle with onions.

Nutrition Information Per Serving: Serving Size: 1 Cup • Calories 220 • Calories from Fat 35 • % Daily Value: Total Fat 4 g 6% • Saturated Fat 2 g 10% • Cholesterol 5 mg 2% • Sodium 1,130 mg 47% • Total Carbohydrate 36 g 12% • Dietary Fiber 9 g 36% • Sugars 5 g • Protein 11 g • Vitamin A 10% • Vitamin C 10% • Calcium 8% • Iron 15%
Dietary Exchanges: 2 Starch, ½ Fruit, ½ Very Lean Meat, ½ Fat OR 2½ Carbohydrate, ½ Very Lean Meat, ½ Fat

Tomato Tortellini Soup

Unlike condensed soups, which must be diluted with water or milk, ready-to-serve soups already contain the right amount of liquid. Tomato-basil soup makes a lovely base for cheese-filled tortellini.

Yield: 4 (1¼-cup) servings

---

2 (19-oz.) cans ready-to-serve tomato basil soup

1 (9-oz.) pkg. refrigerated cheese-filled tortellini

2 tablespoons grated Parmesan cheese

---

1. In large saucepan, combine soup and tortellini. Cook over medium-high heat until mixture comes to a boil, stirring occasionally.

2. Reduce heat; cover and simmer 4 to 5 minutes or until tortellini are of desired doneness. Sprinkle individual servings with Parmesan cheese.

Nutrition Information Per Serving: Serving Size: 1¼ Cups • Calories 310 • Calories from Fat 60 • % Daily Value: Total Fat 7 g 11% • Saturated Fat 3 g 15% • Cholesterol 35 mg 12% • Sodium 1,100 mg 46% • Total Carbohydrate 51 g 17% • Dietary Fiber 3 g 12% • Sugars 12 g • Protein 11 g • Vitamin A 10% • Vitamin C 15% • Calcium 10% • Iron 15%
Dietary Exchanges: 3½ Starch, 1 Fat OR 3½ Carbohydrate, 1 Fat

TOMATO TORTELLINI SOUP

Crisp breadsticks

Caesar salad

Shortbread cookies

Assemble the salad but wait to toss it with the dressing until just before serving. Heat the soup.

menu

**QUICK POTATO AND
CORN CHOWDER**

Mixed green salad with French
dressing

Blueberry crisp or pie

Prepare the salad while the
chowder cooks; dress the greens
at the last minute. Warm the
crisp or pie in the oven while you
eat.

Quick Potato and Corn Chowder

Cream of celery soup, a starting point for many casseroles, lends its lush texture to this chunky, fast chowder.

Yield: 4 (1½-cup) servings

---

4 cups frozen southern-style hash-brown potatoes

1 (11-oz.) can vacuum-packed whole kernel corn with red
  and green peppers

1 teaspoon instant minced onion

2 cups water

1 (10¾-oz.) can condensed cream of celery soup

---

1. In large saucepan or Dutch oven, combine all ingredients; mix well. Bring to a boil over medium-high heat.

2. Reduce heat; cover and simmer 5 to 10 minutes or until potatoes are tender. If desired, add salt and pepper to taste.

Nutrition Information Per Serving: Serving Size: 1½ Cups • Calories 300 •
Calories from Fat 45 • % Daily Value: Total Fat 5 g 8% • Saturated Fat 1 g 5% •
Cholesterol 10 mg 3% • Sodium 1,060 mg 44% • Total Carbohydrate 57 g 19% •
Dietary Fiber 5 g 20% • Sugars 5 g • Protein 7 g • Vitamin A 4% • Vitamin C 20% •
Calcium 6% • Iron 15%
Dietary Exchanges: 3½ Starch, ½ Fat OR 3½ Carbohydrate, ½ Fat

Spicy Black Bean Chili

Cumin, a seed that looks similar to caraway, gives earthy undertones to this wintertime favorite.

Yield: 4 (1-cup) servings

1 cup chopped onions

1 (15-oz.) can southwestern-style black beans with cumin and chili spices, undrained

1 (14.5-oz.) can diced tomatoes with chili or salsa seasonings, undrained

1 (11-oz.) can vacuum-packed whole kernel corn with red and green peppers

4 oz. (1 cup) shredded Cheddar cheese

1. Spray large nonstick skillet with nonstick cooking spray. Heat over medium-high heat until hot. Add onions; cook and stir until tender.

2. Stir in beans, tomatoes and corn. Bring to a boil. Reduce heat to low; simmer 5 to 8 minutes or until thoroughly heated.

3. Sprinkle with cheese; cover and cook an additional 1 to 2 minutes or until cheese is melted.

Nutrition Information Per Serving: Serving Size: 1 Cup • Calories 320 • Calories from Fat 100 • % Daily Value: Total Fat 11 g 17% • Saturated Fat 6 g 30% • Cholesterol 30 mg 10% • Sodium 1,270 mg 53% • Total Carbohydrate 39 g 13% • Dietary Fiber 10 g 40% • Sugars 9 g • Protein 16 g • Vitamin A 25% • Vitamin C 10% • Calcium 30% • Iron 15%
Dietary Exchanges: 2 Starch, 2 Vegetable, 1 Very Lean Meat, 2 Fat OR 2 Carbohydrate, 2 Vegetable, 1 Very Lean Meat, 2 Fat

SPICY BLACK BEAN CHILI
Cornbread
Jelly roll

Prepare the cornbread from scratch or a mix, or purchase corn muffins. Purchase the jelly roll or assemble it early in the day. Make the chili in advance, if you wish, and reheat it; the flavors improve as they mingle. The recipe is a good one to double, too. At serving time, garnish each serving with sour cream, chopped cilantro or minced onion.

White, Pinto and Black Bean Chili

The combination of white, black and spotted beans makes for a colorful bowl of chili.

Yield: 6 (1½-cup) servings

1 (28-oz.) can whole round tomatoes, undrained, cut up

1 (28-oz.) can crushed tomatoes, undrained

1 (15.5- or 15-oz.) can great northern beans, drained

1 (15.5- or 15-oz.) can pinto beans, drained, rinsed

1 (15-oz.) can black beans, drained, rinsed

1 (4.5-oz.) can chopped green chiles, undrained

2 tablespoons chili powder

2 teaspoons brown sugar

In large saucepan or Dutch oven, combine all ingredients; mix well. Bring to a boil. Reduce heat to medium; cover and simmer 10 minutes to blend flavors.

Nutrition Information Per Serving: Serving Size: 1½ Cups • Calories 250 • Calories from Fat 10 • % Daily Value: Total Fat 1 g 2% • Saturated Fat 0 g 0% • Cholesterol 0 mg 0% • Sodium 890 mg 37% • Total Carbohydrate 46 g 15% • Dietary Fiber 13 g 52% • Sugars 11 g • Protein 13 g • Vitamin A 40% • Vitamin C 40% • Calcium 20% • Iron 30%
Dietary Exchanges: 2 Starch, 1 Fruit, 1 Very Lean Meat OR 3 Carbohydrate, 1 Very Lean Meat

WHITE, PINTO AND BLACK BEAN CHILI

Tortilla chips, salsa and guacamole

Bakery chocolate cookies

Make this chili in advance, if you like, and reheat it. Set out assorted garnishes: minced red or green onions, chopped fresh cilantro or parsley, sour cream or plain yogurt, shredded cheese, chopped olives, salsa or hot pepper sauce.

menu

menu

HARVEST VEGETABLE PIZZA

Mixed fresh fruit salad

Peanut butter cookies

While the grill heats, cut up the fruit for the salad and the vegetables for the pizza. Slice the yellow squash thinly to make sure it cooks thoroughly. Zucchini or thin slices of eggplant can substitute for the squash.

tip

To bake pizza, heat oven to 425° F. Prepare dough as directed in recipe to form crust; bake at 425° F. for 6 to 8 minutes or just until crust begins to brown. Top pizza as directed; bake an additional 11 to 15 minutes or until crust is deep golden brown and cheese is melted.

Harvest Vegetable Pizza

If you wish, sprinkle the pizza pan with cornmeal before pressing in the dough.

Yield: 3 servings

1 (10-oz.) can refrigerated pizza crust

½ cup chunky-style tomato sauce

2 Italian plum tomatoes, sliced

1 small yellow summer squash, thinly sliced (1 cup)

1 cup small broccoli florets

6 oz. (1½ cups) shredded mozzarella cheese

1. Heat grill. Lightly grease 12-inch pizza pan or 13x9-inch pan. Unroll dough; place in greased pan. Starting at center, press out with hands.

2. When ready to grill, place pan on gas grill over medium heat or on charcoal grill 4 to 6 inches from medium coals. Cook 5 minutes or just until crust begins to brown.

3. Remove crust from grill; spread tomato sauce evenly over partially baked crust. Arrange vegetables over sauce. Sprinkle with cheese. Return pizza to grill. Cook an additional 10 minutes or until crust is deep golden brown and cheese is melted.

Nutrition Information Per Serving: Serving Size: ⅓ of Recipe • Calories 440 • Calories from Fat 130 • % Daily Value: Total Fat 14 g 22% • Saturated Fat 7 g 35% • Cholesterol 30 mg 10% • Sodium 1,120 mg 47% • Total Carbohydrate 54 g 18% • Dietary Fiber 4 g 16% • Sugars 10 g • Protein 25 g • Vitamin A 35% • Vitamin C 45% • Calcium 50% • Iron 20%
Dietary Exchanges: 3 Starch, 1 Vegetable, 2 Medium-Fat Meat, ½ Fat OR 3 Carbohydrate, 1 Vegetable, 2 Medium-Fat Meat, ½ Fat

Three-Pepper Pizza

Red, green and yellow bell peppers look beautiful together. For greater interest, add sliced Italian plum tomatoes, chopped ripe olives or shredded fresh basil to the pizza.

Yield: 3 servings

1 (10-oz.) can refrigerated pizza crust

6 oz. (1½ cups) shredded mozzarella cheese

½ teaspoon dried Italian seasoning

1 medium green bell pepper, chopped

1 medium red bell pepper, chopped

1 medium yellow bell pepper, chopped

1. Heat oven to 425° F. Lightly grease 12-inch pizza pan or 13x9-inch pan. Unroll dough; place in greased pan. Starting at center, press out with hands. Bake at 425° F. for 4 to 6 minutes or just until crust begins to brown.

2. Remove crust from oven. Top with ½ cup of the cheese. Sprinkle with Italian seasoning. Arrange peppers evenly over top. Sprinkle with remaining 1 cup cheese.

3. Return to oven; bake an additional 8 to 12 minutes or until crust is deep golden brown and cheese is melted.

Nutrition Information Per Serving: Serving Size: ⅓ of Recipe • Calories 420 • Calories from Fat 120 • % Daily Value: Total Fat 13 g 20% • Saturated Fat 7 g 35% • Cholesterol 30 mg 10% • Sodium 910 mg 38% • Total Carbohydrate 51 g 17% • Dietary Fiber 3 g 12% • Sugars 8 g • Protein 24 g • Vitamin A 40% • Vitamin C 130% • Calcium 45% • Iron 15%
Dietary Exchanges: 3 Starch, 1 Vegetable, 2 Medium-Fat Meat OR 3 Carbohydrate, 1 Vegetable, 2 Medium-Fat Meat

THREE-PEPPER PIZZA
Iceberg lettuce wedges with creamy cucumber salad dressing
Strawberry shortcake

While the oven is heating, chop the bell peppers for the pizza. While the pizza bakes, prepare the lettuce and slice the strawberries. Drizzle the dressing over the lettuce wedges just before serving.

Tomato-Olive-Pesto Pizza

Pesto, a fragrant paste of basil, Parmesan cheese, garlic and pine nuts, is a perfect companion for sliced fresh plum tomatoes in this quickly assembled home-baked pizza.

Yield: 4 servings

1 (10-oz.) can refrigerated pizza crust

⅓ cup purchased pesto

4 Italian plum tomatoes, thinly sliced

1 (2¼-oz.) can sliced ripe olives, drained

¼ cup finely chopped red onion

6 oz. (1½ cups) shredded Italian cheese blend

1. Heat oven to 425°F. Spray cookie sheet with nonstick cooking spray. Unroll dough; place on sprayed cookie sheet. Starting at center, press out dough with hands to form 13x9-inch rectangle.

2. Spread pesto evenly over dough. Top with tomatoes, olives, onion and cheese.

3. Bake at 425°F. for 10 to 12 minutes or until crust is deep golden brown and cheese is melted.

Nutrition Information Per Serving: Serving Size: ¼ of Recipe • Calories 460 • Calories from Fat 230 • % Daily Value: Total Fat 25 g 38% • Saturated Fat 10 g 50% • Cholesterol 35 mg 12% • Sodium 1,120 mg 47% • Total Carbohydrate 40 g 13% • Dietary Fiber 2 g 8% • Sugars 7 g • Protein 19 g • Vitamin A 15% • Vitamin C 10% • Calcium 40% • Iron 15%
Dietary Exchanges: 2½ Starch, 1½ High-Fat Meat, 2½ Fat OR 2½ Carbohydrate, 1½ High-Fat Meat, 2½ Fat

menu

FIESTA QUESADILLAS

Tomato soup

Chocolate almond candy

Warm the soup while the quesadillas are on the grill

tip

To broil filled tortillas, place on ungreased cookie sheet; broil 4 to 6 inches from heat using times in recipe as a guide, turning as directed.

Fiesta Quesadillas

These quesadillas are plumped up with chiles and beans for a quick, light meal. For an appetizer, cut them into smaller wedges.

Yield: 4 quesadillas

---

1 (11-oz.) can vacuum-packed whole kernel corn with red and green peppers, drained

1 (4.5-oz.) can chopped green chiles

1 cup fat-free refried beans

8 (8- to 10-inch) fat-free flour tortillas

4 oz. (1 cup) shredded colby-Monterey Jack cheese blend

---

1. Heat grill. In medium bowl, combine corn, chiles and refried beans; mix well. Spread ¼ of mixture onto each of 4 tortillas. Top with remaining tortillas.

2. When ready to grill, place filled tortillas on gas grill over low heat or on charcoal grill 4 to 6 inches from low coals. Cook 5 minutes.

3. With pancake turner, carefully turn tortillas. Sprinkle with cheese. Cook an additional 3 to 5 minutes or until cheese is melted. Cut each quesadilla into wedges.

Nutrition Information Per Serving: Serving Size: 1 Quesadilla • Calories 450 • Calories from Fat 90 • % Daily Value: Total Fat 10 g 15% • Saturated Fat 6 g 30% • Cholesterol 25 mg 8% • Sodium 1,420 mg 59% • Total Carbohydrate 73 g 24% • Dietary Fiber 8 g 32% • Sugars 8 g • Protein 18 g • Vitamin A 10% • Vitamin C 8% • Calcium 25% • Iron 20%
Dietary Exchanges: 4½ Starch, ½ Fruit, ½ High-Fat Meat, ½ Fat OR 5 Carbohydrate, ½ High-Fat Meat, ½ Fat

Spicy Garden Quesadillas

For quesadillas with added appeal, substitute flavored tortillas for the plain ones.

Yield: 8 quesadillas

1 cup chopped yellow or red bell peppers

1 cup chopped tomatoes

2 (4.5-oz.) cans chopped green chiles, undrained

12 oz. (3 cups) shredded colby-Monterey Jack cheese blend

16 (6-inch) flour tortillas

1/2 cup salsa

1/2 cup sour cream

1. In small bowl, combine bell peppers, tomatoes and chiles; mix well. Spoon about 1/3 cup pepper mixture and heaping 1/3 cup cheese onto each of 8 tortillas. Top with remaining tortillas.

2. Spray large nonstick skillet with nonstick cooking spray. Heat over medium heat until hot. Add filled tortillas 2 at a time; cook 1 to 2 minutes on each side or until cheese is melted and tortillas are toasted.

3. Cut each quesadilla into wedges. Serve with salsa and sour cream.

Nutrition Information Per Serving: Serving Size: 1 Quesadilla • Calories 340 • Calories from Fat 170 • % Daily Value: Total Fat 19 g 29% • Saturated Fat 11 g 55% • Cholesterol 45 mg 15% • Sodium 680 mg 28% • Total Carbohydrate 28 g 9% • Dietary Fiber 2 g 8% • Sugars 3 g • Protein 15 g • Vitamin A 15% • Vitamin C 40% • Calcium 40% • Iron 10%
Dietary Exchanges: 2 Starch, 1 1/2 High-Fat Meat, 1 Fat OR 2 Carbohydrate, 1 1/2 High-Fat Meat, 1 Fat

menu

SPICY GARDEN QUESADILLAS

Corn on the cob with cilantro butter

Spanish rice

Maple nut ice cream

Blend chopped cilantro with soft butter to pass at the table. Place the corn in 1 or 2 inches of boiling water on the stove top, and chop the ingredients for the quesadillas. Start the rice from a mix, and cook the corn while the quesadilla mixture cooks.

Vegetarian Fajitas

Fajitas were originally made with skirt steak, but the name has come to mean almost any sizzling ingredients eaten with a flour tortilla.

Yield: 8 fajitas

---

2 tablespoons oil

1 green bell pepper, cut into strips

1 yellow bell pepper, cut into strips

1 medium onion, sliced

1 (11-oz.) can vacuum-packed whole kernel corn, drained

1 large tomato, chopped

¼ teaspoon salt

⅛ teaspoon pepper

8 (8-inch) flour tortillas, heated

Guacamole, sour cream and/or salsa, if desired

---

1. Heat oil in large skillet or wok over medium-high heat until hot. Add bell peppers and onion; cook and stir 2 to 3 minutes or until vegetables are crisp-tender. Add corn, tomato, salt and pepper; cook until thoroughly heated.

2. Place ½ cup vegetable mixture in center of each warm tortilla. Top each with desired toppings; fold or roll up.

Nutrition Information Per Serving: Serving Size: 1 Fajita • Calories 260 • Calories from Fat 100 • % Daily Value: Total Fat 11 g 17% • Saturated Fat 4 g 20% • Cholesterol 5 mg 2% • Sodium 540 mg 23% • Total Carbohydrate 34 g 11% • Dietary Fiber 3 g 12% • Sugars 6 g • Protein 6 g • Vitamin A 8% • Vitamin C 40% • Calcium 8% • Iron 8%
Dietary Exchanges: 2 Starch, 1 Vegetable, 2 Fat OR 2 Carbohydrate, 1 Vegetable, 2 Fat

Asparagus Melts with Horseradish Sauce

Fancier than grilled cheese and easier than asparagus with hollandaise, these open-faced sandwiches borrow a little inspiration from both.

Yield: 4 sandwiches

¾ lb. fresh asparagus spears

2 mini baguettes (French rolls)

4 tablespoons horseradish sauce

2 slices red onion, halved, separated into strips

6 tomato slices, halved

3 (1½-oz.) slices mozzarella cheese

---

1. Cut or snap off tough ends of asparagus; rinse thoroughly. Arrange spears, tips toward center, in 12x8-inch (2-quart) microwave-safe dish. Add ¼ cup water; cover with microwave-safe plastic wrap. Microwave on HIGH for 4 to 8 minutes or until crisp-tender, rearranging once.

2. Meanwhile, cut baguettes in half lengthwise. Spread 1 tablespoon horseradish sauce evenly onto cut side of each baguette half.

3. Top each baguette half with cooked asparagus, onion and tomato. Cut cheese crosswise into 1-inch-wide strips; arrange over tomato. Place sandwiches on broiler pan or cookie sheet.

4. Broil 4 to 6 inches from heat for 1 to 2 minutes or until cheese is melted.

Nutrition Information Per Serving: Serving Size: 1 Sandwich • Calories 190 • Calories from Fat 80 • % Daily Value: Total Fat 9 g 14% • Saturated Fat 5 g 25% • Cholesterol 15 mg 5% • Sodium 350 mg 15% • Total Carbohydrate 15 g 5% • Dietary Fiber 2 g 8% • Sugars 3 g • Protein 12 g • Vitamin A 15% • Vitamin C 15% • Calcium 25% • Iron 8%
Dietary Exchanges: 1 Starch, 1½ Medium-Fat Meat OR 1 Carbohydrate, 1½ Medium-Fat Meat

menu

ASPARAGUS MELTS WITH HORSERADISH SAUCE

Deli German potato salad

Selection of pitted olives

Gingerbread with whipped cream

If you have time earlier in the day, prepare the gingerbread from scratch or a mix, or buy it ready to serve. While the asparagus cooks, set out the olives and potato salad.

menu

GRILLED PROVOLONE AND ROASTED RED PEPPER SANDWICHES

Lentil or bean soup

Red grapes

Ice cream sandwiches

Rinse the grapes. Assemble the sandwiches and heat them at the same time as the soup.

Grilled Provolone and Roasted Red Pepper Sandwiches

Sliced provolone, an Italian deli favorite, pairs with roasted red bell pepper for a more elegant take on the classic grilled cheese sandwich.

Yield: 2 sandwiches

4 slices multi-grain bread

4 (¾-oz.) slices provolone cheese (from deli)

2 roasted red bell peppers (from 7.25-oz. jar), drained, cut into 1-inch strips

1 tablespoon margarine or butter, softened

1. Top each of 2 slices of bread with 1 cheese slice, half of bell pepper strips and another cheese slice. Top with remaining bread slices. Spread margarine on both sides of sandwiches.

2. Heat large skillet or griddle over medium heat until hot, or to 375° F. Add sandwiches; cook 2 to 4 minutes on each side or until bread is golden brown and cheese is melted.

Nutrition Information Per Serving: Serving Size: 1 Sandwich • Calories 360 • Calories from Fat 170 • % Daily Value: Total Fat 19 g 29% • Saturated Fat 9 g 45% • Cholesterol 30 mg 10% • Sodium 730 mg 30% • Total Carbohydrate 30 g 10% • Dietary Fiber 5 g 20% • Sugars 3 g • Protein 17 g • Vitamin A 30% • Vitamin C 50% • Calcium 40% • Iron 15%
Dietary Exchanges: 2 Starch, 2 Medium-Fat Meat, 1½ Fat OR 2 Carbohydrate, 2 Medium-Fat Meat, 1½ Fat

Mediterranean Wraps

Lavosh, a traditional Armenian cracker bread that's practically paper-thin, comes in a crisp version that's good for dipping, and a soft version to roll up with fillings, such as in this hummus and vegetable sandwich.

Yield: 4 wraps

2 soft cracker breads, halved

1 (8-oz.) container hummus

½ cup chopped fresh parsley

¼ cup sliced ripe olives

1 medium cucumber, thinly sliced

1 tomato, seeded, chopped

2 oz. (½ cup) crumbled feta cheese

1. Spread each bread half evenly with hummus to within ½ inch of edges.

2. Arrange parsley, olives, cucumber, tomato and cheese over hummus. Roll up each bread half.

Nutrition Information Per Serving: Serving Size: 1 Wrap • Calories 400 • Calories from Fat 110 • % Daily Value: Total Fat 12 g 18% • Saturated Fat 2 g 10% • Cholesterol 15 mg 5% • Sodium 970 mg 40% • Total Carbohydrate 58 g 19% • Dietary Fiber 5 g 20% • Sugars 8 g • Protein 16 g • Vitamin A 15% • Vitamin C 30% • Calcium 10% • Iron 25%
Dietary Exchanges: 4 Starch, ½ High-Fat Meat, 1 Fat OR 4 Carbohydrate, ½ High-Fat Meat, 1 Fat

menu

MEDITERRANEAN WRAPS

Deli couscous salad

Selection of pickles and olives

Fig-filled cookies

Set out the couscous and pickles and olives. Chop the vegetables and prepare the wraps.

index